Edinburgh Bilingual Library (3)

EDINBURGH BILINGUAL LIBRARY
OF EUROPEAN LITERATURE

General Editor
A. A. Parker, Professor of
Spanish, University of Texas
Editorial Board
W. H. Bruford
C. P. Brand
A. J. Steele

Edinburgh Bilingual Library (3)

Anthology of
Troubadour Lyric Poetry

Edited and Translated by
ALAN R. PRESS
Lecturer in French
University of Belfast

for the University Press
Edinburgh

© Alan R. Press 1971
EDINBURGH UNIVERSITY PRESS
22 George Square, Edinburgh

ISBN 0 85224 180 1

North America
Aldine Publishing Company
529 SouthWabash Avenue, Chicago

Library of Congress
Catalog Card Number 73-115060

Set in 10/11 'Monotype' Barbou
and printed in Great Britain by
W & J Mackay & Co Ltd, Chatham, Kent

Contents

Introduction	1
William IX	9
Jaufré Rudel de Blaye	27
Marcabrun	41
Bernard de Ventadour	63
Peire d'Auvergne	86
Raimbaut d'Orange	103
Giraut de Borneil	125
Bertran de Born	153
Arnaut Daniel	173
Peire Vidal	193
Aimeric de Péguilhan	217
Sordello	237
Guilhem de Montanhagol	257
Peire Cardenal	279
Guiraut Riquier	306

Anthology of
Troubadour Lyric Poetry

INTRODUCTION

It is now generally recognized that the work of the troubadours lies at the origin of a centuries-long tradition of high lyric poetry in western Europe. A large number of the concepts which their work elaborated soon spilled over into other literary genres of the Middle Ages and thence into later, post-mediaeval literature, so providing certain elements of our own, modern, cultural heritage. The result is that more than once the opinion has been formulated that, even today, certain modes of thought, of feeling, and of expression are influenced in some measure by those same concepts.[1] The ideals of courtesy and chivalry, for example, are not yet totally extinct, nor that of a love which, for all its demands of entire self-commitment and for all its grounding in physical attraction and desire, still seeks to lift that desire above the instinctual level and to integrate the lover fully into the society of his peers. Since, then, there is at least a case for affirming that such ideals were first celebrated in the lyric poetry of the troubadours, one obvious way better to understand them is to consider some examples of their original formulation. An obvious way but not an easy one since, for many who might otherwise be interested in the subject, the language of the troubadours, mediaeval Provençal—or Occitan as it should more correctly, if less traditionally, be termed[2]—remains inaccessible. For such considerations as these alone, it has seemed to me not altogether useless to make available to an English-speaking public some translations of the original troubadour texts.

There are of course other considerations too. We know that to translate is to betray, and that, specifically, it is impossible to recreate in a modern, Anglo-Saxon idiom the full aesthetic effect of a troubadour lyric, with its subtle blend of verbal and musical harmonies and rhythms, its abundant tropes and linguistic figures, and its intricate weaving of more or less fixed formulae and clichés into ever-changing, kaleidoscopic patterns. Nevertheless, some betrayals are worse than others, and among the very worst, to my mind, is the widely current but utterly deformed picture of troubadour lyric poetry which, inherited from a low form of early nineteenth-century romanticism, still represents it as the charmingly naïve but entirely immoral outpourings of poor wandering minstrels, hawking from castle to castle their songs of hopeless love for the proud but maybe half-indulgent wife of some great feudal lord. As a first step to correcting the picture, to making good this fundamental betrayal, it appears to me desirable that a representative selection of the works of the troubadours themselves be made available, and accessible. The treachery of translation then imposes itself, unavoidably.

However, several precautions have been taken in the present selection to ensure that the treachery be as relatively innocuous as possible. First of all, the original texts—as far as they can be reconstructed from a varied and widely scattered number of manuscripts—have been reproduced along with their translated versions. My debt to those modern scholars who have established critical editions of the texts is, of course, immense, although it must be admitted also that for the sake of textual coherence—that is, in accordance with the principle of one base manuscript for each single text—I have not hesitated to modify certain of the critically established texts whenever it has appeared to me that a rejected MS reading is in fact to be preferred to the one adopted by my mentors. The reference then, included in the preliminary note on each troubadour selected, to the standard edition of his works is rather more than an acknowledgement; it is an indication of where the reader, if he so wishes, can most easily find the critical material underlying the version of the text which is published here.[3]

As a second precaution, in the translated versions elegance and grace have been—not always without remorse—sacrificed to literal accuracy, even in such respects as word order and the strangely loose but at the same time complex grammatical constructions indulged in by the troubadours. Thus, all other things being equal, whether a translated version reads smoothly or not is intended to reflect the quality of the original text in this respect. It is only too easy to fall into the trap of facile elegance or quaint charm, aided by an abundance of pseudo-mediaeval, pseudo-poetic diction, and thus to distort once more the original image.[4] It has to be recognized that the troubadours themselves, above all in the initial period, were in the process of forging from a primitive Romance tongue, scarcely emerged from its parent Latin form and hardly ever before used for literary composition of any sort, an entirely new literary medium. And this medium, furthermore, was to formulate concepts which were themselves uniquely original and characterized by both subtle complexity and tenuous abstraction. To take a simple example, one notes in the original texts the frequent use of the connecting particle *que* to create a network of inter-related clauses so constructed as to tie down, albeit fleetingly, the myriad facets of the complex emotional and conceptual world which the troubadours were exploring. Yet the precise functional value of this *que* constantly shifts and changes; it moves within a wide area which only in the course of time will be delimited by a number of more specific, less polyvalent forms. The result is that very often *que* can only be interpreted on the indications of its general context. That is to say that the linguistic process in which the troubadours were engaged leads inevitably to some measure of textual incoherence, disconnectedness, and obscurity. I do not conceive it to be the translator's task to reduce it—not, at least, in a work of this kind which seeks merely to present, not to explain. On occasion, of course, the demands of clarity and of simple English grammar have imposed some modifications of an absolutely literal rendering, some resolution of intolerable ambiguities, and even the interpolation of words corresponding to no form in the original text, though such interpolations can at least be—and of course have been—admitted by the use of parentheses.

Thirdly, in addition to the original texts and their English versions, a summary note on the life and works of each troubadour selected has been included, together with an equally summary comment on the selected texts themselves. The former is intended to sketch out the historical, social and literary context of each poet's activity, while the latter has been limited to the indication of certain material and aesthetic features of the original which, although not apparent in the translated version, seem nevertheless conducive to a fuller appreciation of the poem. To have introduced further critical and analytical material would have been to frustrate the basic purpose of this anthology, and it is this same consideration which has led me to renounce any form of detailed justification of the choice of poets and texts. Suffice it to say that from the more than two thousand lyric poems which have been conserved, the work of over four hundred troubadours still known to us by name, I have simply tried to make a selection which might be as varied and as representative as possible, in as many respects as possible. Many restrictions have been unavoidably imposed by the mundane but pressing exigencies of space and time; the one major limitation which has been deliberately adopted, however, is an almost exclusive concentration on the major poetic genres of *canso* and *sirventès*—love-song and poem of political, moral, or personal comment—since the numerous minor genres appeared to me of more limited interest and appeal. But to dwell further on this topic would, I feel, bring too much attention to bear on my own conceptions of what is important and attractive about the poetry of the troubadours; this I would prefer the reader to discover for himself.

Perhaps a few words should nevertheless be added, by way of a final introductory note, concerning the sounds and rhythms of troubadour lyric poetry. On the one hand, while we know that early mediaeval lyric poetry was, by definition, accompanied by a melody, and while the melodies composed by the troubadours for many of their songs have been conserved in manuscript form, certain particularities of early mediaeval musical notation make the task of reconstruction and reproduction in modern form an extremely problematical one. From the findings and solutions of modern musicologists, therefore, one can only hazard a few, tentative, generalizations. Firstly, troubadour melodies seem to correspond to two basic types, in tone and movement; the slow, rather subdued and serious song which is immediately evocative of the Gregorian chant, and the lively, gay and skipping tune which must in some way be associated with mediaeval dance forms of popular, or communal, origin. Secondly, although the melody of the *canso*[5] clearly makes its own specific contribution to the total aesthetic effect, echoing, enhancing and pointing up the mood formulated in the text, it is in no way the dominant feature of the work as a whole; the very complexity and, on occasion, the fine subtlety of the linguistic structure itself, so characteristic of troubadour poetry, make it absolutely vital that the melody should not obscure the text to which it is set. In other words, although one certainly misses something when simply reading the text alone, one does not, in my opinion, miss the essentials.

On the other hand, as regards the sounds and rhythms of the text itself, it needs to be pointed out first of all that in spite of an immense orthographic variety in the written forms, a variety which reflects not only the varied provenance of the manuscripts but also, to a lesser extent, the dialectal peculiarities of the different regions from which the troubadours originated, there is nevertheless a general uniformity of pronunciation which distinguishes the language of the troubadours from that of other texts, literary and non-literary, composed in the same area and in the same historical period. How far this uniformity was contrived and how far, on the other hand, it was a spontaneous manifestation of social and cultural unity—the troubadours, after all, were working in a fairly limited social stratum, that of the feudal nobility—it is impossible to determine precisely. But in all events, given the now generally recognized relatively uniform phonetic structure of this *koinè* or conventional literary language, the pleasure of reading aloud—or aloud in one's mind—the original texts need not be reduced or masked by the otherwise rather disconcerting irregularity of the written forms. With this in mind, I feel that the following general observations on the pronunciation of the language of the troubadours may prove helpful.

In general terms, this pronunciation is characterized by a dominance of vowel sounds over consonants, mediaeval Provençal being in this respect closer to modern Italian or Spanish than to modern French, and the vowel sounds themselves are much closer to their Common Latin, or Proto-Romance, origins than those of the language spoken north of the Loire. The pure closed and open vowels, for example, were conserved in many situations, both stressed and unstressed, where in northern French they were already subject to considerable modification or drastic weakening; there were none of the nasal vowel sounds which northern French developed in such abundance—a following [n] or [m] simply closing an otherwise open vowel—and there were still conserved a whole series of diphthongs and triphthongs which already in northern French, when present at all, were being reduced and simplified. It is important to bear in mind that, in the reading of the verse line, these diphthongs and triphthongs —[au], [ai], [ei], [eu], [oi], etc.,[6] and [iei], [ieu], [uou], [uei] etc.,[7]—count as one single syllable, as do those which result from the many contracted forms used regularly by the troubadours such as, for example, *no.us* (= *non* + *vos*), *ie.us* (= *ieu* + *vos*), *qu'ie.m.* (= *que* + *ieu* + *me*) and *doussa.us* (= *doussa* + *vos*). Other contracted forms which, like the English 'don't', 'shan't', etc., entail the complete fall of the vowel of one of their elements, are also monosyllabic in value; so, for example, *si.ns* (= *si* + *nos*), *no.n* (= *non* + *en*), *e.l* (= *e* + *lo*), *no.m.* (= *non* + *me*), *e.s* (= *e* + *se*), *no.ill* (= *non* + *li*), etc. A minor difficulty in the reading of the verse line is to distinguish, on the one hand, certain monosyllabic diphthongs and the equally monosyllabic groups made up of a semi-consonant and a pure vowel, from, on the other hand, groups of two vowels in hiatus which count as two separate syllables; to distinguish, for example, between the [ia] of *preiar* and the [ïa] of *sïa*, the [ai] of *amaire* from the [aï] of *maïstre*, or the [au] of *auzelh* from the [aü] of *saüc*. It is for this reason that such groups of two vowels in hiatus have been distinguished in the text by the use of the diaeresis. One other problem of the same order is posed by the fact that although the [a] or [e] at the end of a word has often—but not always— to be elided with the vowel at the beginning of the following word in order to conserve the correct syllable count of the line, the manuscripts frequently fail to omit it from the written form; there being no question of tampering with the graphy of the MSS, this source of possible misreading cannot easily be eliminated. With the consonants of mediaeval Provençal, however, the spelling is usually much more indicative of the true pronunciation, although it may be noted that the letters 'j', and 'ch' and 'z' often designate the affricate sounds [dj], [tch], and [ts] respectively, while the sounds of palatal [n] and palatal [l] appear in a wide assortment of guises, 'n', 'gn', 'in', 'nh', or any permutation thereof, and, similarly, 'l', 'il', 'lh', 'll', or any permutation.

But this introductory note threatens fast to become a treatise. It must now come to an end. Not, however, before I fulfil the most pleasant duty of recording my gratitude to the members of the Committee of the Edinburgh University Press, whose acceptance of my original project constituted a great encouragement to proceed further, to the Secretary of the University Press, Mr A. R. Turnbull, whose enthusiasm has more than once come to urge me on, and to my wife, without whose constant and inestimable support the following pages would probably never have seen the light of day.

NOTES
1. See, for example, C.S. Lewis, *The Allegory of Love*, p. 1. 'Neither the form nor the sentiments of this old poetry [of the troubadours] has passed away without leaving indelible traces on our minds.' or H. Davenson, *Les Troubadours*, p. 10, attributing to the troubadours 'une nouvelle conception de l'amour qui a profondément modelé la structure de la psychè occidentale.'
2. Since it was the language not only of Provence, but of the whole of the South of France, which opposed its *langue d'oc* to the *langue d'oïl* of France north of the Loire.
3. Two further, minor, remarks on the constitution of the original texts: (a) the use of square brackets indicates that the base MS itself is defective—having omitted a line, a word, or a single syllable necessary for the regular structure of the stanza, or being materially mutilated; (b) the punctuation, introduced into the original text, has as its sole purpose to indicate more clearly what has appeared to me to be the grammatical articulation of each stanza.
4. The type of distortion which R. Lafont had in mind when he observed that 'On *féminise* aussi les troubadours par la traduction en une langue moderne, qui développe les phrases, explicite les concepts, à la recherche d'une clarté discursive qui ne pouvait être de leur propos'. (in *Cahiers du Sud*, Vol. 55 1963, p. 165; my italics.)
5. With the *sirventès*, the situation is rather different, because each poem of this genre normally borrows its melody from a lyric composition already in existence, usually a *canso*.
6. Approximately, [au] as in Eng. 'now'; [ai] as in Eng. 'my'; [ei] as in Eng. 'day'; [eu] as in Cockney Eng. 'bell'; [oi] as in Eng. 'joy'
7. Approximately, [iei] as in Eng. 'yea'; [ieu] as in Cockney Eng. 'Yale'; [uou] as in Eng. 'woe'; [uei] as in Eng. 'weigh'.

William IX, Count of Poitou, Duke of Aquitaine
1071 – 1127

LIFE. Born in 1071, William IX acceded to the titles and territories of his father in 1086, thereby becoming one of the most powerful feudal overlords of his times, with territories more extensive than those held directly by the French king himself. Having refused to take part in the first crusade of 1098, he nevertheless led his own expedition to Asia Minor in 1101; it was a military disaster. In constant conflict with the Church, he was threatened with excommunication several times for his dissolute way of life and for his lack of regard for the teachings, the property, the personnel and the protégés of the Church. In the latter part of his life, however, he seems to have become less turbulent; he is known to have taken part in the crusade-type expeditions against the Moors in Spain, and the sixth poem reproduced here gives direct and moving evidence of his reconciliation with orthodox christian faith. He died in 1127.

WORKS. He is the earliest troubadour known to us. Was he in fact the first, or at least the most eminent of a first generation of poets, or the first only to emerge from a now lost, anonymous line? Certainly his verse-forms, such fragments of his music as have survived, and his rhetorical style, rich in various tropes and figures, indicate his debt to mediaeval latin poetry. But the ideal of courtly life and courtly love which his poetry elaborates is something new in European literature and forms the basis of the inspiration of all later troubadours. While one can well look for *sources* in various directions—mediaeval Latin court poetry and para-liturgical verse, Hispano-Arabic lyric poetry, etc.—the *origins* of his poetry can best be understood as the reaction of the mind of this man—as far as we can still gain insight into it through his own work and his own life—to the particular set of historical, social, and cultural circumstances in which he lived.

EDITION. A. Jeanroy *Les Chansons de Guillaume IX* (2ᵉ éd. Paris 1927).

SELECTION. Eleven poems are attributed to him. While no chronological order can be established, they can be arranged into three groups, the 'course', the 'courtly', and the 'contrite', reflecting three stages in the development of an attitude to life and to love. The first two poems reproduced (Jeanroy nos. 1 and 2) belong to the 'course' group, relatively unelaborate in style and versification, and characterized by a masculine jocularity of tone and, at times, a masculine crudity of expression. The first expresses a simple pride and delight in mastery and possession—both sexual and material—but yet is raised above the level of a barrack-room ballad by the celebration of that 'love and joy and youthfulness' which, in various forms, infuses all this poet's work. The second piece has the air of a manifesto; didactic, demonstrative, argumentative in tone, it seems, by pointing out the evil results of excluding noblewomen from court life, to plead for a more open, more socially amenable, more civilized form of court life where the Lady should have a more positive role to play, mingling freely with her social peers.

The third piece (Jeanroy no. 4), considered by some scholars to be a vernacular imitation of the mediaeval Latin riddle or conundrum-type poem, is yet surprisingly modern in some aspects—in its 'coolness' for example, in its abrupt changes of emotional key, and in its preoccupation with the objective irreality of the subjectively real inner life. Wavering between indifference to love and total commitment to it, it seems to formulate a particularly critical and complex state of mind, a state preceding that final acceptance of a new, positive ideal of love, of life, of joy, which we find expressed in the next two poems (Jeanroy nos. 7 and 8). These clearly belong to the 'courtly' group where we find the earliest known formulation of that ideal love aspired to by the nobility of southern France and cultivated in the troubadour *canso d'amor* throughout the twelfth and thirteenth centuries.

The last poem reproduced here (Jeanroy no. 11), perhaps unique in the troubadour tradition by virtue of its direct, personal, involvement in historical, real-life facts and events, constitutes a precious indication both of the high seriousness of which William IX is capable, and of the value which this aristocrat attributes to the poetic function. Such a poem is not intended to amuse or to entertain; it reveals the effort of a sensitive though turbulent mind to find inner peace and harmony in the act of poetic creation.

I. Companho, faray un vers [. . .] covinen,
Et aura.i mais de foudaz no.y a de sen,
Et er totz mesclatz d'amor e de joy e de joven.

already speaks
for irony at
expense of a
didactic tradition?

E tenguatz lo per vilan qui no l'enten,
O dins son cor voluntiers [. . .] non l'apren;
Greu partir si fai d'amor qui la trob'a son talen.

Dos cavalhs ai a ma selha, ben e gen;
Bon son e adreg per armas, e valen,
Mas no.ls puesc amdos tener, que l'us l'autre non cossen.

Si.ls pogues adomesjar a mon talen,
Ja no volgr'alhors mudar mon garnimen,
Que miels for'encavalguatz de nuill [. . .] ome viven.

La uns fo dels montanhiers lo plus corren,
Mas tan fera estranhez'a longuamen,
Et es tan fers e salvatges que del bailar si defen.

L'autre fo noyritz sa jus, part Cofolen,
E anc no.n vis bellazor, mon esciēn;
Aquest non er ja camjatz ni per aur ni per argen.

Qu'ie.l doney a son senhor polin payssen,
Pero si.m retinc ieu tan, de covinen,
Que, s'ilh lo teni'un an, qu'ieu lo tengues mais de cen.

again, parody of
'question d'amour
tradition?

Cavallier, datz mi cosselh d'un pessamen!
Anc mais no fuy issaratz de cauzimen:
Res no sai ab qual mi tengua, de N'Agnes o de N'Arsen.

De Gimel ai lo castel e.l mandamen,
E per Niol fauc ergueil a tota gen,
C'ambedui me son jurat, e plevit per sagramen.

II. Compaigno, non puesc mudar qu'eo no m'effrei
De novellas qu'ai auzidas e que vei:
Qu'una domna s'es clamada de sos gardadors a mei.   *over*

I. My friends, I'll make a fitting poem and there'll be in it more folly than there's sense, and it will be all mingled with love and joy and youth.

And consider him a serf who doesn't understand it, or in his heart learns it not willingly; it's hard to part from love for one who finds it to his liking.

I have two horses to my saddle, right and properly; good they are and skilled in war, and valiant. But I cannot keep them both, for one can't abide the other.

If I could break them in to my desire, I would never wish to change my gear elsewhere, for I'd be better mounted than any living man.

One was the swiftest of those from the mountains, but for long it's shown such wild restiveness—it's so wild and shy that it refuses to be groomed.

The other was raised down there, by Confolens, and you never saw one more handsome, to my mind; this one will not be changed for either gold or silver.

And I gave it to its lord, a foal in pasture; yet for myself I retained this much, by covenant, that, if he kept it a year, I should keep it for more than a hundred.

Knights, give me counsel in a problem! Never was I more puzzled by a choice; I don't know at all with which one I should stay, with Lady Agnes or with Lady Arsen.

I have the castle of Gimel and its command, and of Nieul I'm proud before all men, for both are sworn to me and pledged by oath.

II. My friends, I cannot help but be dismayed at news which I have heard and which I see, for a lady has complained to me about her guards.

[E] diz que no volo prendre dreit ni lei,
Ans la teno esserada quada trei,
Tan l'us no.ill largua l'estaca, que l'altre plus no la.ill plei.

[E]t aquill fan entre lor aital agrei—
L'us es compains gens a for mandacarrei,
E meno trop major nauza que la mainada del rei.

[E]t eu dic vos, gardador, e vos castei,
E sera ben grans folïa qui no.m crei,
Greu veirez neguna garda que ad oras non sonei.

[Q]u'eu anc non vi nulla domn'ab tan gran fei,
Qui no vol prendre son plait o sa mercei,
S'om la loigna de pröessa, que ab malvestatz non plaidei.

[E] si.l tenez a cartat lo bon conrei,
Adoba.s d'aquel que troba viron sei;
Si non pot aver caval [. . . . . .] compra palafrei.

[N]on i a negu de vos la.m desautrei:
S'om li vedava vi fort, per malavei,
Non begues enanz de l'aiga que.s laisses morir de sei.

[C]hascus beuri'ans de l'aiga que.s laisses morir de sei.

III. Farai un vers de dreyt nïen:
Non er de mi ni d'autra gen,
Non er d'amor ni de joven,
  Ni de ren au;
Qu'enans fo trobatz en durmen
  Sobre chevau.

No sai en qual guiza.m fuy natz:
No suy alegres ni iratz,
No suy estrayns ni sui privatz,
  Ni no.n puesc au;
Qu'enaissi fuy de nueitz fadatz
  Sobr'un pueg au.

over

And she says that they'll observe nor right nor law, they rather keep her shut away, the three of them; as much as one slackens her bond, the other tightens it for her the more.

And between them they behave in such a way—any one of them is as fine a friend as a carter, and they create far greater uproar than the household of the king.

And I say this to you, guards, and I advise you, and great folly would it be not to believe me: you'll hardly find a keeper who at some time doesn't sleep.

And I never saw a lady of such great faith who, if one refuses her plea or her entreaty, excluded from true valour, does not make her peace with baseness.

If for her you set good company at high price, she provides herself with what she finds at hand; if she cannot have a horse, she'll buy a hack.

There's not one of you who would deny me this: if for some sickness he were forbidden strong wine, he would drink water rather than die of thirst.

Each would drink water sooner than die of thirst.

III. I'll make a poem of sheer nothingness; it will not be about me, or about any other; it will not be of love, or of youth, or of anything else; it was, rather, composed while sleeping on a horse.

I know not in what way I was born; I am neither gay nor downhearted, neither a stranger nor a familiar friend, nor can I do aught else, for thus was I charmed by night, on a high hill.

No sai quora.m suy endormitz,
Ni quora.m velh, s'om no m'o ditz.
Per pauc no m'es lo cor partitz
    D'un dol corau.
E no m'o pretz una soritz,
    Per sanh Marsau!

Malautz suy e tremi murir,
E ren no sai mas quan n'aug dir;
Metge querrai, al mieu albir,
    E no.m sai tau;
Bos metges er si.m pot guerir,
    Mas ja non, si amau.

Amigu'ai ieu, no sai qui s'es,
Qu'anc non la vi, si m'ajut fes!
Ni.m fes que.m plassa ni que.m pes,
    Ni no m'en cau,
Qu'anc non ac Norman ni Frances
    Dins mon ostau.

Anc non la vi et am la fort,
Anc no n'aic dreyt ni no.m fes tort;
Quan non la vey, be m'en deport,
    No.m pretz un jau,
Qu'ie.n sai gensor et bellazor,
    E que mais vau.

Fag ai lo vers, no say de cuy;
E trametrai lo a selhuy
Que lo.m trametra per autruy
    Lay vers Anjau,
Que.m tramezes del sieu estuy
    La contraclau.

William IX

I know not when I sleep, or when I wake, unless someone tells me so; by very little has my heart not broken with a deep sorrow. And I care not a mouse for that, by Saint Martial!

Sick I am and fear to die, and know nothing but what I hear tell of it; I'll seek a doctor, of my way of thinking, and I know not such a one; he'll be a good doctor, if he can cure me, but never, if I grow worse.

I have a loved one, I don't know who she is, for I've never seen her, so help me my faith! She has done nothing to please me, or to grieve me, nor am I bothered about it, for I never had Norman or Frenchman in my house.

I've never seen her and I love her dearly; I've never had right from her, nor has she done me wrong; when I do not see her, I get along quite well, I don't think it's worth a rooster! For I know one more noble and more lovely, and who is worth more.

I've made this poem, I know not of what; and I'll send it to him who will send it on for me by another, yonder, towards Anjou, that he might send back to me, from his own wallet, the key to it.

IV. Pus vezem de novelh florir
Pratz e vergiers reverdezir,
Rius e fontanas esclarzir,
Auras e vens,
Ben deu quascus lo joy jauzir
Don es jauzens.

D'amor non dey dire mas be.
Quar no n'ai ni petit ni re?
Quar ben leu plus no m'en cove;
Pero leumens
Dona gran joy qui be.n mante
Los aizimens.

A totz jorns m'es pres enaissi
Qu'anc d'aquo qu'aimiey non jauzi,
Ni o faray ni anc no fi;
Qu'az esciens
Fas mantas res que.l cor me di:
'Tot es niens.'

Per tal n'ai meyns de bon saber:
Quar vuelh so que no puesc aver;
E si.l reproviers me ditz ver
Certanamens:
'A bon coratge bon poder'—
Qui's ben suffrens.

Ja no sera nuils hom ben fis
Contr'amor, si non l'es aclis,
Et als estranhs et als vezis
Non es consens,
Et a totz sels d'aicels aizis
Obediens.

Obediensa deu portar
A motas gens, qui vol amar,
E coven li que sapcha far
Faigz avinens,
E que.s gart en cort de parlar
Vilanamens.

over

William IX

IV. Since we see flowering anew the fields, and the meadows grow green again, the streams and fountains run clear, the breezes and winds, rightly should each enjoy the joy of which he is (truly) joyous.

I should say nothing of love but good. Why have I so little of it? Most likely because more behoves me not; yet readily it gives great joy to him who well keeps within its bounds.

At all times has it befallen me thus, that never of that which I loved did I have joy; nor will I ever do, nor have I ever done so, for full knowingly I do many things while my heart tells me 'all is nothingness'.

For this do I have less pleasure: I wish for that which I cannot have, and yet the proverb speaks true to me, for sure; 'where there's a will, there's a way'—if one is long-suffering.

No man will ever be gracious to love unless he is submissive to it, and unless he is humble to strangers and those near by, and obedient to all those dwelling within its bounds.

Obedience to many men must he show who would love; and it behoves him to be able to do pleasant deeds, and let him take care not to speak, at court, like a serf.

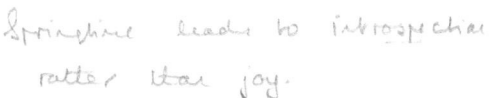

Springtime leads to introspection rather than joy.

Del vers vos dig que mais en vau,
Qui ben l'enten, e n'a plus lau,
Que.l mot son fag tug per egau
Cominalmens,
E.l sonetz, qu'ieu mezeis m'en lau,
Bos e valens.

Mon Esteve, mas ieu no.i vau,
Sïa.l prezens
Mos vers, e vuelh que d'aquest lau
.M sïa guirens.

V. Farai chansoneta nueva
Ans que vent ni gel ni plueva;
Ma dona m'assai'e.m prueva
Quossi de qual guiza l'am,
E ja per plag que m'en mueva
No.m solvera de son lïam.

Qu'ans mi rent a lieys e.m liure,
Qu'en sa carta.m pot escriure,
E no m'en tengatz per yure
S'ieu ma bona dompna am,
Quar senes lieys non puesc viure,
Tant ai pres de s'amor gran fam.

Que plus es blanca qu'evori,
Per qu'ieu autra non azori.
Si'm breu non ai ajutori
Cum ma bona dompna m'am,
Morrai, pel cap Sanh Gregori!
Si no.m bayz'en cambr'o sotz ram.

Qual pro.y auretz, dompna conja,
Si vostr'amors mi deslonja?
Par que.us vulhatz metre monja;
E sapchatz, quar tan vos am,
Tem que la dolors me ponja,
Si no.m faitz dreg dels tortz qu'ie.us clam.

over

Of this poem I tell you that it's worth more if one understands it well, and it receives more praise; for the words are wrought all of one style alike, and the melody, which I myself praise myself for, good and fine.

Before my friend Stephen, though I'm not going, be my poem present; and I want him, concerning this praise, to vouch for me.

V. I'll make a new little song, before the wind and the frost and the rains come; my lady tries me and tests me as to how, in what way, I love her; and never, for any case she might bring against me, would I loose myself from her bond.

I rather yield and render myself to her, that in her charter she may write me down. And do not for this think me drunk, if I love my fine lady, for without her I cannot live, so great has been my hunger for her love.

For she is whiter than ivory, wherefore I adore no other. If soon I do not have help so that my fine lady may love me, I'll die, by Saint Gregory's head! if she does not kiss me in bedroom or in arbour.

What good will it do you, sweet lady, if your love keeps me far off? It seems you would become a nun; but know, for so much I love you, I fear lest the pain should pierce me, if you right not the wrongs I complain to you of.

Qual pro.y auretz s'ieu m'enclostre
E no.m retenetz per vostre?
Totz lo joys del mon es nostre,
Dompna, s'amduy nos amam.
Lay al mieu amic Daurostre
Dic e man que chan e [. . .] bram.

Per aquesta fri e tremble,
Quar de tan bon'amor l'am;
Qu'anc no cug qu'en nasques semble,
En semblan, del gran linh N'Adam.

VI. Pos de chantar m'es pres talentz,
Farai un vers don sui dolens:
Mais non serai obedïenz
En Peitau ni en Lemozi.

Qu'era m'en irai en eisil;
En gran päor, en gran peril,
En guerra laissarai mon fil,
E faran li mal siei vezi.

Lo departirs m'es aitan grieus
Del seignoratge de Peitieus!
En garda lais Folcon d'Angieus
Tota la terr'e son cozi.

Si Folcos d'Angieus no.l socor,
E.l reis de cui ieu tenc m'onor,
Faran li mal tut li plusor
Felon Gascon et Angevi.

Si ben non es savis ni pros,
Cant ieu serai partitz de vos,
Vïas l'auran tornat en jos,
Car lo veiran jov'e mesqui.

over

What good will it do you if I take to the cloister, and you do not retain me for yours? All the joy of the world is ours, lady, if both we love one another. There, to my friend Daurostre I say and command that he should sing and (not) bray.

For her I thrill and tremble, since I love her with such fine love; I think that there was never born her peer in beauty, from all Sir Adam's long line.

VI. Since the desire to sing has come upon me, I'll make a poem of that for which I grieve: no longer shall I render obedience for Poitou and the Limousin.

For now into exile I shall go; in great fear, in great peril, and at war shall I leave my son, and his neighbours will do him harm.

So grievous is for me this parting from the lordship of Poitiers! In wardship I leave to Foulques of Angers all the land, and his cousin.

If Foulques does not help him, and the king from whom I hold my title, they in great numbers will do him harm, the fell Gascons and Angevins.

Unless he is most wise and valiant, when I have parted from you, they soon will have cast him down, for they'll see him young and feeble.

Per merce prec mon compaignon,
S'anc li fi tort, qu'il m'o perdon;
Et il prec En Jesu del tron,
En romans et en son lati.

De pröeza e de joi fui,
Mais ara partem ambedui;
Et eu irai m'en a Sellui
On tut peccador troban fi.

Mout ai estat cuendes e gais,
Mas nostre Seigner no.l vol mais;
Ar non puesc plus soffrir lo fais,
Tant soi aprochatz de la fi.

Tot ai guerpit cant amar sueill,
Cavalarïa et orgueill;
E pos Dieu platz, tot o acueill,
E prec li que.m reteng'am si.

Toz mos amics prec a la mort
Que.i vengan tut e m'onren fort;
Qu'eu ai avut joi e deport,
Loing e pres, et e mon aizi.

Aissi guerpisc joi e deport,
E vair e gris e sembeli.

William IX

In mercy's name I pray to my companion, if ever I wronged him may he forgive me it; and may he pray Lord Jesus on His throne, both in Romance and in what Latin he knows.

I have lived my life in prowess and in joy, but now we both part company, and away I shall go to Him in Whom all sinners find their end.

I have been most gay and lighthearted, but our Lord no more wishes it so; now I cannot bear the burden, so near am I drawn to my end.

All have I quit that I used to love, chivalry and noble pride; and, since it pleases God, all this I accept, and pray to Him to keep me by His side.

All my friends I pray, at my death, to come and to do me great honour, for I have known joy and delight both far and near, and within my own bounds.

Thus I quit joy and delight, rich cloths and precious sable

Jaufré Rudel de Blaye

LIFE. Jaufré Rudel was castellan of Blaye during the second quarter of the twelfth century. With his distant cousin William Taillefer, count of Angoulême, as with other eminent noblemen of the South-West, this minor nobleman seems to have been on cordial terms, due quite possibly to a mutual interest in the developing cult of vernacular lyric poetry as well as to a common pursuit of the crusading ideal. The touching story recounted in his thirteenth-century biography, according to which Jaufré fell in love with the Countess of Tripoli without ever having seen her, put out to sea, fell ill, and died in the arms of his distant love when first brought to her, is generally considered to be no more than a literal interpretation of certain recurrent themes in his own poetry. It is however almost certain that he took part in the Crusade of 1148, and quite possibly he never returned from it, thus providing further material for his mediaeval biographer to transform into legend. In all events, nothing more is known of him after that date. In 1167 another member of his family is attested as holding the fief of Blaye; by then, presumably, Jaufré Rudel was dead.

WORKS. No more than six poems are now attributed to this troubadour, all love-songs, 'with good melodies and poor words' as his early biographer-critic put it. Certainly their range of vocabulary and of general expressive devices is limited, their formal and thematic structures simple. And yet the poetic experience which they formulate is anything but simple; opinions as to the precise nature of their inspiration are almost as numerous as the critics and scholars who have fallen under their enigmatic spell. On the one hand, it is generally agreed that, as in the case of William IX—to whom Jaufré is clearly indebted for much of his formal and thematic material—the poems can be grouped in such a way as to show, successively, an involvement in, a reaction against, and a movement away from a low, furtive, adulterous and humiliating type of love. But, on the other hand, the nature of that 'distant love' towards which the poet moves has been interpreted in extremely divergent ways, ranging from the most down-to-earth, literal, and biographical to the most abstract, symbolizing, and mystical. If anything at all is certain, it is that by the consistent use of a few, simple linguistic structures, the poet has succeeded in giving form to a mystery, the mystery of a love which is known and experienced only as the end of an unending aspiration, and which is made perceptible only in the self-engendered, unique, and utterly isolated reality of the love-song itself.

EDITION. A. Jeanroy *Les Chansons de Jaufré Rudel* (2ᵉ éd. Paris 1924).

SELECTION. Since a chronological grouping is not possible, the four selected poems (Jeanroy nos. 2, 5, 6, 1) have been arranged according to a perceptible thematic development. In the first one, there are no longer any of those episodic, realistic allusions which are used elsewhere (Jeanroy nos. 3, 4) to evoke an adulterous and humiliating liaison; the theme of a noble, distant, unrequited love—alluded to with characteristic ambiguity—is already dominant. The quality of the poet's emotions is still, to some extent, suspect, for their purity is threatened by an inner, psychological conflict between sentimental longing, rational will, and sensuous desire. Allusive though the poem may be, the brief analysis of this conflict endows the thematic material with some kind of objective, realistic substance. This is lacking entirely in the next poem, where even such aspects of the external world as are evoked are wholly transformed into hypothetical reference points to the poet's dream. Undoubtedly the best known of Jaufré's works, this poem is also the most enigmatic, and it is easy to see how critics have variously felt able to identify the poet's distant love with, to mention but a few, the Countess of Tripoli, the Virgin Mary, Jerusalem, or a mystical experience of the divine. It is no less easy to appreciate, however, that no one interpretation is entirely satisfactory; the reader is caught in a cunningly constructed puzzle, so that the more he tries to break through it with one simple interpretation, the more he becomes involved in the mystery. Perhaps, after all, this is what the poet wanted, for the structure of the poem is a masterpiece of ambiguity and allusiveness. The experience of intense abstraction which it formulates is not, however, sustained. In the third selected poem it is resolved into a series of paradoxes by which, although the same theme is dominant, a totally different effect is achieved. The obsessive tension is relaxed and gives way to a more objective, detached mood which at times seems even to approach the humour of self-derision. The fourth poem, finally, deals even more objectively with the same basic theme, at least in its last stanzas which are generally considered as announcing the poet's intention of going on the Crusade of 1148. Since nothing further is known of the poet after this date, it is quite possible that this is indeed his farewell to love, a farewell to the cult of courtly love which he had maintained and furthered in so unique a fashion.

I. Quan lo rius de la fontana
    S'eclarzis, si cum far sol,
    E par la flors aiglentina,
    E.l rossinholetz el ram
    Volf e refranh ez aplana
    Son dous chantar, e l'afina,
    Be's dregz qu'ieu lo mieu refranha.

    Amors, de terra lonhdana,
    Per vos totz lo cors mi dol;
    E no.n puesc trobar mezina
    Si non al vostre reclam,
    Ab maltrait d'amor doussana
    Dinz vergier o part cortina,
    Ab dezirada companha.

    Pus totz jorns m'en falh aizina,
    No.m meravilh si n'ai fam;
    Quar anc genser Crestïana
    Non fo—ni Dieus non o vol—
    Juzïa ni Sarrazina.
    Ben es selh paguatz de mana
    Qui de s'amor ren guazanha!

    De dezir mos cors no fina
    Vas selha ren qu'ieu pus am;
    E cre que volers m'enguana
    Si cobezeza la.m tol.
    Que pus es ponhens d'espina
    La dolors que per joi sana,
    Don ja non vuelh qu'om m'en planha.

    Senes breu de parguamina
    Tramet lo vers que chantam
    En plana lengua romana,
    A.N Hugo Bru, per Filhol;
    Bo.m sap, quar gens Peitavina,
    De Berri e de Guizana,
    S'esgau per lieys, e Bretanha.

I. When the fountain's stream runs clear as it used to do, and the wild rose flower appears, and the nightingale on the bough turns and softens and smooths its sweet song, and refines it, it's indeed right that I should soften mine.

Oh love, of distant land, for you my whole heart aches; and I can find no cure if not in your alluring call, with pangs of sweet love in meadow or within curtained chamber, beside the desired companion.

Since always ease of it forsakes me, I marvel not that I hunger for it; for there was never Christian lady more fair—nor does God wish there to be — nor Jewess nor Saracen lady. He is indeed fed with manna who wins anything of her love!

My heart never ends its longing for her whom I love most; and I fear lest my will should cheat me if urgent desire robs me of her. And sharper than thorn is the pain which by joy is healed and for which I want no one ever to pity me.

Without parchment brief I send off the poem, which we sing in the plain Romance tongue, to Lord Hugo Brun, by Filhol; I am pleased, for the folk of Poitou, of Berry and of Guyenne rejoice in it, and Britanny.

11. Lanquan li jorn son lonc, en may,
M'es belhs dous chans d'auzelhs de lonh;
E quan mi suy partitz de lay,
Remembra.m d'un'amor de lonh;
Vau de talan embroncx e clis,
Si que chans ni flors d'albespis
No.m valon plus qu'iverns gelatz.

Be tenc lo Senhor per veray
Per qu'ieu veirai l'amor de lonh;
Mas, per un ben que m'en eschay,
N'ai dos mals, quar tant suy de lonh.
Ai! car no suy lai pelegris,
Si que mos fustz e mos tapis
Fos pels sieus belhs huelhs remiratz.

Be.m parra joys quan li querray,
Per amor Dieu, l'ostal de lonh;
E, s'a lieys platz, alberguarai
Pres de lieys, si be.m suy de lonh.
Qu'aissi es lo parlamens fis,
Quan drutz lonhdas es tan vezis
Qu'ab cortes ginh jauzis solatz.

Iratz e dolens m'en partray,
S'ieu no vey sest'amor de lonh.
Non sai quora mais la veyrai,
Que tan son nostras terras lonh;
Assatz hi a pas e camis,
E per aisso no.n suy devis—
Mas tot sia cum a lieis platz!

Ja mais d'amor no.m jauziray
Si no.m jau d'est'amor de lonh,
Que melhor ni gensor no.n sai
Ves nulha part, ni pres ni lonh;
Tant es sos pretz ricx e sobris
Que lay, el reng dels Sarrazis,
Fos ieu per lieys chaitius clamatz.

over

II. When the days are long, in May, I'm pleased by the sweet song of birds from afar: and when from that I've turned away, I remember a love from afar. I go, with longing sombre and bowed down, so that neither song nor whitethorn blossom avails me more than icy winter.

The Lord indeed I hold as true through whom I'll see that love from afar; but, for one good that from it befalls me, I have two ills, since I'm so far. Ah! why am I not a pilgrim there, so that my staff and my cloak were beheld by her lovely eyes.

Joy will indeed appear to me when I ask of her, for God's love, shelter afar; and, if it pleases her, I will dwell near her, even though I am from afar. For in this way is the discourse noble, when distant lover is so near that in courtly manner he enjoys sweet solace.

In sorrow and grief will I depart, if I see not that love from afar. I know not when I shall ever see her, for our lands are so far; there are many roads and passes, and for that I'm not separated from her—but be it all as it pleases her!

Never more will I rejoice in love unless I enjoy that [this] love from afar, for I know none more noble or fairer than she, in any part, near or far; so great and supreme is her merit that there in the Saracens' land would I be for her claimed captive.

Dieus que fetz tot quant ve ni vai
E formet sest'amor de lonh,
Mi don poder, que cor ben ai,
Qu'ieu veya sest'amor de lonh
Verayamen, en luec aiziz,
Si que la cambra e.l jardis
Mi resemblon novels palatz.

Ver ditz qui m'apella lechay
Ni deziros d'amor de lonh;
Que nulhs autres joys tan no.m play
Cum jauzimens d'amors de lonh.
Mas so qu'ieu vuelh m'es tant ahis
Qu'enaissi.m fadet mos pairis:
Qu'ieu ames e non fos amatz.

III. No sap chantar qui so non di,
    Ni vers trobar qui motz no fa,
    Ni conois de rima co.s va,
    Si razo non enten en si;
    Mas lo mieus chans comens'aissi:
    Com plus l'auziretz, mais valra.

    Nuils hom no.s meravill de mi
    S'ieu am so que ja no.m veira,
    Qu'el cor joi d'autr'amor non a
    Mas d'aissella qu'ieu anc no vi;
    Ni per nuill joi aitan no ri
    E no sai quals bes m'en venra.

    Colps de joi me fer que m'ausi,
    Et ponha d'amor que.m sostra
    La carn, don lo cors magrira;
    Et anc mais tan greu no.m feri,
    Ni per nuill colp tan no langui,
    Quar no cove, ni no s'esca.

over

Jaufré Rudel de Blaye

God, who created all that comes and goes, and fashioned that love from afar, grant me the power, for I well have the heart, to see that love from afar, truly and in such situation that room and garden may seem to me palace new.

He tells the truth who calls me hungry and desirous for love from afar; for no other joy pleases me so much as enjoyment of love from afar. But that which I want is so opposed to me for my godfather vowed my fate thus: that I should love and should not be loved.

III. He cannot sing who gives no melody, or compose verse who sets down no words, nor does he know how rime goes unless in himself he understands the rules; but my own song begins in this way: the more you hear it the better it will be.

Let no man marvel at me if I love that which will never see me, for in the heart there's joy of no other love but of that one which I never saw; nor am I gladdened so much by any joy, yet I know not what good of it will come to me.

I am stricken by joy which slays me, and by a pang of love which ravishes my flesh, whence will my body waste away; and never before did it strike me so hard, nor from any blow did I so languish, for that is not fitting, nor seemly.

Anc tan soven no m'adurmi
Mos esperitz tost no fos la;
Ni tan d'ira non ac de sa
Mos cors ades no fos aqui.
E quan mi resveill al mati,
Totz mos bos sabers mi desva.

Ben sai c'anc de lei no.m jauzi,
Ni ja de mi no.s jauzira:
Ni per son amic no.m tenra
Ni coven no.m fara de si;
Anc no.m dis ver ni no.m menti,
E no sai si ja s'o fara.

Bos es lo vers, qu'anc no.i falhi,
Et tot so que.i es, ben esta;
E sel que de mi l'apenra
Gart se no.l franha, ni.l pessi;
Car si l'auran en Cäersi
En Bertrans, e.l coms en Tolza.

Bos es lo vers, e faran hi
Calque re don hom chantara.

IV. Quan lo rossinhols el folhos
Dona d'amor e.n quier e.n pren,
E mou son chan jauzent, joyos,
E remira sa par soven,
E.l riu son clar e.l prat son gen,
Pel novel deport que.y renha,
Mi vai grans joys al cor jazer.

D'un'amistat suy enveyos,
Quar no sai joya plus valen
Que d'aquesta, que bona.m fos
Si.m fazīa d'amor prezen.
Que.l cors a gras, delgat e gen,
E ses ren que.y descovenha,
E s'amors bon'ab bon saber.

over

Jaufré Rudel de Blaye

I never so often fell asleep but that my spirit was soon yonder; nor had I so much grief, here, but that my heart was ever there. And when I wake in the morning, all my pleasure fades.

I know well that I never had joy of her, nor will she ever have joy of me; and she will not deem me her lover nor make a promise of herself to me. She never told me the truth nor lied to me, and I know not if she ever will.

The poem is good for I never failed in it, and all that is in it is well in its place; and may he who learns it from me take care not to break it or pull it to pieces, for thus in Quercy will Sir Bertrand hear it, and the Count in the Toulousain.

The poem is good and there they'll do something of which one will sing.

IV. When the nightingale in the thicket bestows its love and seeks and takes it, and pours forth its joyful song in joy, and gazes often on its mate, and the streams are clear and the meadows fair, then for the new delight which reigns there, a great joy goes to nestle in my heart.

For one friendship am I longing because I know no richer joy than this: that she should be good to me, if she made me a gift of her love. And she has a well-fleshed body, soft and fair, with nothing which does not befit it, and her love is good and pleasurable.

D'aquest'amor suy cossiros
Vellan e pueys sompnhan dormen,
Quar lai ay joy meravelhos
Per qu'ieu la jau, jauzitz jauzen;
Mas sa beutatz no.m val nïen,
Quar nulhs amicx no m'essenha
Cum ieu ja n'aia bon saber.

D'aquest'amor suy tan cochos
Que quant ieu vau ves lieys corren,
Vejaire m'es qu'a reversos
M'en torn, e que lay.s n'an fugen;
E mos cavals vai aitan len
A greu cug mais que.y atenha,
S'ilha no.s vol arretener.

Amors, alegre.m part de vos
Per so qu'ar vau mo mielhs queren;
E fuy en tant aventuros
Qu'enqueras n'ay mon cor jauzen.
Mas pero per mon Bon Guiren,
Que.m vol e m'appell'e.m denha,
M'es ops a parcer mon voler.

E qui sai rema deleytos,
E Dieu non siec en Bethlëem,
No sai cum ja mais sïa pros
Ni cum ja venh'a guerimen;
Qu'ieu sai e crei, mon escïen,
Que selh qui Jesus ensenha
Segur'escola pot tener.

In this love I am absorbed, waking and then in dreaming sleep, for then I have wondrous joy because I enjoy it, rejoiced in and rejoicing. But her beauty avails me naught since no friend shows me how I might ever have pleasure of it.

For this love I am so eager that when I go running towards her, it seems to me that in retreat I turn from it and that she goes fleeting away; and my horse moves on so slowly that I scarce believe any more that I might reach her, unless she herself is willing to hold back.

Love, gaily I leave you because now I go seeking my highest good; yet by this much was I fortunate that my heart still rejoices for it. But, for all this, because of my Good Protector who wants me and calls me and accepts me, I must needs restrain my longing.

And if anyone stays back here in his delights and does not follow God to Bethlehem, I know not how he might ever be worthy or come to salvation; for I know and believe that, to my way of thinking, he whom Jesus teaches is sure of certain doctrine.

Marcabrun

LIFE. Marcabrun, the earliest known professional troubadour, was probably born in Gascony about the year 1110, of fairly humble parentage. During the first ten years or so of his career (*c.* 1127–1137) he appears to have enjoyed the patronage of William X, count of Poitou and duke of Aquitaine; Marcabrun espouses his interests in more than one of his poems and associates his death with the decline of *Pretz* and *Valors*—two virtues invariably and almost exclusively attributed to their patrons by professional troubadours. Occasional references in his poetry further indicate that after William X's death in 1137 he visited other great courts of the Midi and of Christian Spain, everywhere seeking, nowhere finding permanent patronage and protection. His latest dateable poems allude to the crusade of 1147–1149 and, in a poem dating from 1157–1158, a later troubadour, Peire d'Auvergne, twice refers to him in the past tense and suggests that he is already 'gitatz a non-cura'—fallen into neglect.

WORKS. Almost as obscure as the material circumstances of his life is the underlying sense of much of Marcabrun's poetry. Many of the forty-two poems attributed to him refer but fleetingly to contemporary events and situations. Many of them, too, affect a style now allegorical, now symbolical, now proverbial and sententious which clearly corresponded to contemporary patterns of thought and expression now no longer current, while on occasion it is suspected that the poet invents new words, or at least new forms and combinations of old words, himself. All this, however, detracts nothing from the impression, created by his poetry, of an immensely strong and forceful personality, having something to say and a mastery of such poetic means as he chooses to say it with. All the resources of the convicted moralist are his: with deep earnestness, scathing irony, or violent invective he condemns the moral corruption which he sees around him, the degeneracy of the nobility, the decline of courtly virtues, and the flourishing of their perverted opposites. Not that he is really the isolated prophet raging in the wilderness which some critics, deceived perhaps by the *persona* which Marcabrun himself adopts, have taken him for. However different his poetry may appear from that of contemporary troubadours, however heavily he relies, for his allegories and symbols, on mediaeval Latin scholastic traditions, his deepest inspiration can be seen to be of the same nature as that of other early poets. They all propose a positive ideal of noble love, oppose it to less noble, coarser patterns of behaviour, and tend all, in varying degrees, to adapt the figures and terminology of religion to their own poetic ends. That Marcabrun stands alone among them is perhaps because, rather than construct an imaginary world of sentiment and emotion in which the positive aspects of the courtly ideal might be realized and made perceptible, he, for the first time, directs his attention to the real world, in order to attribute its vices, weaknesses and scandals to a failure to live up to that same ideal. The reality of the ideal is thus made perceptible by the observable consequences of its absence.

EDITION. J.M.L. Dejeanne *Poésies complètes du troubadour Marcabrun* (Toulouse 1909).

SELECTION. If the mention of the afflicted head, made in the first poem (Dejeanne no. 3) is, as usually supposed, an allusion to the papal schism of the early 1130s, the poem belongs to the early part of Marcabrun's career. The theme of moral degeneration among the great of this world is already dominant, and developed through a complex synthesis of allegory and symbol—much of which is biblical, patristic, and scholastic in origin—with direct, picturesque caricature. The structure of the second poem (Dejeanne no. 35) is, on the other hand, based on a single symbol which, for Marcabrun, seems to figure both the military campaign against the Arabs in Spain (in which the Marquis of Provence and the Knights Templars—*cill del temple Salamo*—were engaged) and the pilgrimage to Santiago. William X, whose death is alluded to, died on just such a pilgrimage, undertaken as an act of penance. In the next two pieces (Dejeanne nos. 40, 5) the figure of Marcabrun as the self-appointed moralist, fully aware of his mission, emerges rather more clearly, while the fifth poem (Dejeanne no. 23) reveals yet another aspect of his personality. Here he speaks as the professional, conscious of his dependence yet proudly recalling to his patron, Alfonso VII of Castile, self-styled 'Emperor' of Spain, his power to make—and break—reputations through his poetry. The note of disenchantment suggests that this poem may belong to a later stage in the troubadour's career when, disappointed with the courts of N. Spain, he returned to the Midi. The last poem (Dejeanne no. 5), by its reference to 'Sir Jaufré Rudel over the sea', dates from the time of the second crusade and must be among the last of his compositions. It is one of his rare attempts to formulate positively, by direct exposition, his own concept of the courtly ideal. That it is dedicated to the castellan of Blaye well indicates the cultural tradition within which Marcabrun is working; a tradition which he himself had developed and expanded in a personal and forceful way which many later troubadours imitated, but never equalled.

I. Al departir del brau tempier
    Quan per la branca pueja.l sucs
    Don reviu la genest'e.l brucs,
    E floreysson li presseguier,
    E la rana chant'el vivier,
    E brota.l sauzes e.l saücs,
    Contra.l termini qu'es yssucs
    Suy d'un vers far en cossirier.

    Cossiros suy d'un gran vergier
    Ont a de belhs plansos mans lucs;
    Gent sont l'empeut, e.l frugs bacucs.
    Selh qu'esser degran sordegier,
    Fuelhs e flors, paron de pomier;
    Son al fruchar sautz'e saücs.
    E pus lo caps es badalucs,
    Dolen son li membr'estremier.

    Mort son li bon arbre primier,
    E.l viu son ramils e festucs,
    Dels fortz assayz los vey damnucs,
    Mas de bordir son fazendier;
    De promessas son bobansier,
    Al rendre sauzes e saücs.
    Don los claman flacs e bauducs
    Ieu e tug l'autre soudadier.

    Quan son la nueg josta.l foguier
    N'Esteves, En Costans, En Ucs,
    [. . .   . . . ucs]
    Mais que Berartz de Monleydier;
    Tota nueg joston a doblier,
    E.l jorn, a l'ombra dels saücs,
    Auziratz nausas e bauducs
    E doblar entr'els l'escaquier.

    Doncs no pairejon li derrier
    En totz bos sens ab los faducs?
    El og—si Cozer'e Sarlucs
    Valon Toloz'e Monpeslier!   *over*

I. Now that the rough weather's gone away, and through the branch rises the sap by which the broom and heather quicken once again, and the peach-trees blossom, and the frog sings in the fishpond, and the willow and elder are in bud, before the hot, dry season comes, I have in mind to compose a poem.

I am mindful of a great orchard, where there are many groves of saplings fair; the parent stocks are fine, and the fruit hollow. Those things which should be among the worst, leaves and blossom, seem to be of apple-trees; when the time comes for the fruit, they turn out to be willows and elders. And, since the head is defective, the furthest limbs are in pain.

Dead are the good old trees, and those that live are twigs and straws. I see them proved worthless in great undertakings, but in idle games they are busy; in promises they are prodigious, in keeping them, willows and elders. Hence we proclaim them weak and feeble-minded, I and all the other retainers.

When, at night, they are by the fire, my lords Stephen and Constant and Hugo, (they boast of achieving?) . . . more than Berart de Mondidier; all night they vie with each other, and, by day, in the shade of the elders, you'll hear the uproar and revelry, and the bids being doubled among them.

These young ones then do not resemble, in all good ways, those who are dead? Indeed yes—if Cazères and Carlux are worth Toulouse and Montpellier!

Qu'ieu sai qual mort foron primier,
E.l mais dels vius son vers saücs;
E podetz dir qu'es benastrucs
Qui troba laur ni olivier!

admiring or cynical?

Neys l'ortalas, ab lo clavier,
Jos ab un vent s'en fuy, huelhs cucs;
Per esclavin'e per trabucs
An laissat mantelh e caussier.
Ni ren non a.i del estatgier,
Tal hira.m fan sautz'e saücs!
Si no.ls ten reys o coms o ducs,
Totz temps seran mais caminier.

Los pros sal Dieus qu'an pretz entier!
Que.l ric malvatz paron saücs,
Per que.l segles es badalucs,
Don malavey'e destorbier.

11. *Pax in nomine Domini!*
Fetz Marcabrus los motz e.l so.
Aujatz que di:
Cum nos a fait, per sa doussor,
Lo Seingnorius celestïaus
Probet de nos un lavador,
C'anc, fors outramar, no.n fon taus,
En de lai deves Josaphas;
E d'aquest de sai vos conort.

Lavar de ser e de maiti
Nos deurïam, segon razo,
Ie.us o afi:
Chascus a del lavar legor.
Dementre qu'el es sas e saus,
Deuri'anar al lavador
Que.ns es verais medicinaus;
Que s'abans anam a la mort,
D'aut en sus aurem alberc bas.

over

Marcabrun

For I know what they were who died long ago, and most of the living are true elder-trees, and you can say that he's lucky who finds laurel or olive-tree.

Even the gardener, along with the keeper, flies off, with the wind, eyes closed; for simple smock and boots they have quit fine mantle and shoes. And there's no trace of the tenant, such grief do willow and elder cause me! If king or count or duke retains them not, they'll be for ever on the road.

May God preserve the valiant who have merit entire! For the mighty wicked are as elder-trees, whereby the world is weak in the head, and hence sick and confused.

11. *Pax in nomine Domini!* Marcabrun fashioned the words and the music. Hear what he says: how in His kindness the heavenly Lord has fashioned for us a wash-place, near at hand, such as there never was except overseas, yonder by Jehosaphat; and by this one here I bring you comfort.

We should wash ourselves evening and morning, by rights, I assure you of this: each has now the chance to do so. Until he is hale and whole, each should go to that wash-place which is our true source of healing. For if, before that, we come to death's door, then from on high we shall be most lowly lodged.

Mas Escarsedatz e No-fes
Part Joven de son compaigno.
Ai! cals dols es
Que tuich volon lai li plusor,
Don lo gazaings es enfernaus!
S'anz non correm al lavador
C'ajam la boca ni.ls huoills claus,
Non i a un d'orguoill tant gras
C'al morir non trob contrafort.

Que.l Seigner que sap tot quant es,
E sap tot quant er, e c'anc fo,
Nos i promes
Honor e nom d'emperador;
E.il beutatz sera—sabetz caus,
De cels qu'iran al lavador?
Plus que l'estela gauzignaus;
Ab sol que vengem Dieu del tort
Que.ill fan sai, e lai vas Domas.

Probet del lignatge Caï,
Del primeiran home felho,
A tans aissi
C'us a Dieu non porta honor;
Veirem qui.ll er amics coraus,
C'ab la vertut del lavador
Nos sera Jhesus comunaus;
E tornem los garssos atras
Qu'en agur crezon et en sort.

E.il luxurïos, corna-vi,
Coita-disnar, bufa-tizo,
Crup-en-cami,
Remanran inz el felpidor;
Dieus vol los arditz e.ls süaus
Assajar a son lavador;
E cil gaitaran los ostaus,
E trobaran fort contrafort,
So per qu'ieu a lor anta.ls chas.

over

But Meanness and Perfidy part Youth from his companion. Ah! what grief it is that most of them all fly there whereof the profit is infernal. If we do not hasten to that wash-place before our lips and our eyes are closed, there is not one so puffed with pride but will find, on dying, the great enemy.

But the Lord Who knows all that is, and knows all that will be and that ever was, promised us, there, honour and imperial fame. And the splendour will be—know you what, for those who go to that wash-place? Greater than the morning star; only provided that we avenge God of the wrong which they do Him hereby, and yonder by Damascus.

So many are there, and such, of Cain's lineage—of that first wicked man—that not one honours God; we shall see who'll be a loyal friend to Him, for, by the virtue of that wash-place, Jesus will be among us. So let us drive back those base wretches who believe in witchcraft and spells.

And the lechers, wine-tipplers, food-gobblers, fireside-squatters, stick-in-the-muds, will all stay behind in their squalor. God seeks to prove at His wash-place the bold and the humble, while the rest will stay lurking in their homes, and they'll find the great enemy; that's why I hound them to their shame.

[handwritten note: Incorporates censure of the infidels and of the social diseases within the faith.]

En Espaigna, sai, lo Marques
E cill del temple Salamo
Sofron lo pes
E.l fais de l'orguoill paganor.
Per que Jovens cuoill avol laus,
E.l critz per aquest lavador
Versa sobre.ls plus rics captaus,
Fraitz, faillitz, de pröeza las,
Que non amon Joi ni Deport.

Desnaturat son li Frances,   cp. 'C. de Roland'
Si de l'afar Dieu dizon no,
Qu'ie.us ai comes.
Antïocha, Pretz e Valor
Sai plora Guïana e Peitaus.
Dieus Seigner, al tieu lavador
L'arma del comte met en paus:
E sai gart Peitieus e Nïort
Lo Seigner qui ressors del vas!

III. Pus mos coratges s'esclarzis
    Per selh joy don ieu suy jauzens,
    E vey qu'Amors part e cauzis,
    Per qu'ieu n'esper estre manens,
    Ben dey tot mon chant esmerar
    Qu'om re no m'i puesca falsar,
    Que per pauc es hom desmentitz.

    Aicel qui fin'Amors cauzis
    Viu letz, cortes, e sapïens,
    E selh, cui refuda, delis
    E met a totz destruzemens;
    Car qui fin'Amor vol blasmar
    Elha.l fai si en folh muzar
    Que, per art, cuid'esser peritz.

    Cill son fals jutg'e raubador,
    Fals molherat e jurador,
    Fals home tenh e lauzengier,   *over*

In Spain, nearby, the Marquis and those of Solomon's temple endure the weight and the burden of pagans' pride through which Youth falls into disrepute. And the outcry concerning this wash-place falls on the mightiest leaders, those broken, forsworn ones, weary of prowess, who love not Joy or Pleasure.

Degenerate are the French if they refuse the business of God's which I've committed to you. Antioch weeps for Merit and Valour, and here, Guyenne and Poitou. Lord God, at your wash-place grant peace to the soul of the Count, and may the Lord Who rose from the tomb here protect Poitiers and Niort!

III. Since my heart grows bright by that joy which I rejoice in, and I see that Love selects and singles out—whereby I hope to be richly endowed—I must indeed make all my song pure so that none might fault me for anything in it, since for little is one belied.

He whom noble Love singles out lives gay, courtly and wise; and he whom it rejects, it confounds, and commits to total destruction. And he who would blame noble Love, it makes him so fondly bemused that, in delusion, he thinks that his end is come.

Such are false judges and thieves, false husbands and perjurors, false impostors and flatterers,

Lengua-loguat, creba-mostier,
Et aissellas putas ardens
Qui son d'autrui maritz cossens;
Cyst auran guazanh ifernau.

Homicidi e traïdor,
Simonïaic, encantador,
Luxurïos e renovier,
Que vivon d'enujos mestier,
E cill que fan faitilhamens,
E las faitileiras pudens
Seran el fuec arden engau.

Ebrïaic et escogossat,
Fals preveire e fals abat,
Falsas recluzas, fals reclus,
Lai penaran, ditz Marcabrus,
Que tuit li fals y an luec pres,
Car fin'Amors o a promes:
Lai er dols dels dezesperatz.

Ai! fin'Amors, fons de bontat,
C'as tot lo mon illuminat,
Merce ti clam, d'aquel grahus
E.m defendas qu'ieu lai no mus.
Qu'en totz luecx me tenh per ton pres;
Per confortat en totas res
Per tu esper estre guidatz.

Mon cors per aquest vers destrenh,
Quar mi plus que.ls autres reprenh;
Que qui autrui vol encolpar
Dregs es que si sapcha guardar
Que no sïa dels crims techitz
De qu'el ieys encolpa e ditz,
Pois poira segurs castïar.

Pero si es assatz cauzitz,
Sel que ben sap dire, e.l ditz,
Que pot, si se vol, remembrar.

hired tongues and convent-plunderers, and those lusting whores who say yes to other wives' husbands; these will reap their harvest in hell.

Murderers and traitors, simonists, sorcerers, lechers and usurers who live by hateful means, and those who cast spells and those stinking witches, they'll be in the burning fire, one and all.

Drunkards and cuckolds, false priests and false abbots, false recluses—men and women—they'll suffer there, says Marcabrun, for all the false ones there have appointed places, and this has noble Love promised: in that place will be the grief of those in despair.

Ah noble Love! fount of all goodness, who have illumined all the world, mercy I beg of you, and from that torment protect me, that I might not tarry there. For in all matters I deem myself your captive; for comfort in all things I hope to be guided by you.

My own self by this poem I constrain, for I take myself to task more than the others, because it is right that he who would accuse another should take care not to be tainted by the crime of which he himself accuses and speaks; then he could in all sureness castigate.

Yet he is indeed well singled out, he who well knows how to say, and says, that which he can, if he wishes, call to mind.

IV. Al son desvïat chantaire
    Veirai si puosc un vers faire
    De fals'amistat menuda,
    C'aissi leu pren e refuda,
    Puois sai ven e lai mercada;
    E morrai si no.m n'esclaire!   *moral urgency*

    Cest'amors sap engan faire,
    Ab engan ses aigua raire,
    Puois, quand l'a ras, se remuda
    E quier autrui cui saluda,
    A cui es douss'e privada;
    Tant que.l fols deven musaire.

    Non puosc dompnas trobar gaire
    Que blanch'amistatz no.i vaire,
    A presen o a saubuda
    N'aja vergoingna perduda,
    Si que la meins afrontada
    N'a laissat cazer un caire.

    Moillerat, per Saint Ylaire,
    Son d'una foldat confraire,
    Qu'entr'els es guerra moguda
    Tals que cornutz fa cornuda,
    E cogotz copatz copada,
    Puois eis la cöa de braire.

    Tals cuid'esser ben gardaire
    De la so'e de l'autrui laire,   *casuistical imagination.*
    C'atretals es devenguda
    D'aicel de sai que la cuida;
    Si l'us musa, l'autra bada,
    E ieu sui del dich pechaire!

    De nïen sui chastïaire,
    E de foudat sermonaire,
    Car puois la flam'es nascuda
    Del fol drut e de la druda,
    Si.l fols art per l'abrasada,
    No.n sui mal meire ni laire.   *over*

IV. Singing on borrowed tune I'll see if I can make a poem about false, mean-minded friendship which takes as readily as it refuses, then sells here and haggles there; and I'll die if I don't speak my mind about it.

This love knows how to practise guile, with guile to shave without water, then, when it's fleeced someone, it moves off and looks for another whom it greets, and to whom it is sweet and intimate, so much that the fool hankers for it.

I can scarce find ladies in whom fair friendship does not vary; none who, in private or publicly, has not lost her shame, so that even the least immodest has dropped some bit of it.

Married men, by Saint Hilary, are all brothers in one folly; among them such war is waged that he who wears horns sets horns on his wife's head, and the cuckold, deceived, deceives his wife, since the tail grows by dint of braying.

Such a one thinks he's guarding well his wife and stealing someone else's who (for her part) is in the same position with him who thinks the same about her; if the husband hankers, the wife gapes, and I'm in the wrong for saying so!

In vain do I castigate and in folly I preach, for once the flame has flared between the fond lover and his mistress, if the fool burns for her who's consumed by fire, I'm not at fault or to blame for it.

Tant cant bos Jovens fon paire
Del segle e fin'Amors maire,
Fon Pröeza mantenguda
A celat et a saubuda,
Mas er l'ant avilinada
Duc e rei et emperaire.

Qu'ieu sui assatz esprovaire
Deffendens et enquistaire,
E vei cum Jovens se tuda,
Per que Amors es perduda,
E de Joi deseretada,
E cum Amors es cujaire.

L'amors don ieu sui mostraire
Nasquet en un gentil aire,
E.l luocs on ill es creguda
Es claus de rama branchuda
E de chaut e de gelada,
Qu'estrains no l'en puosca traire.

'Desirat per desiraire'   (perhaps 'distrairo'?)
A nom qui.n vol Amor traire.

V. Emperaire, per vostre prez
    E per la pröeza qu'avez,
    Sui a vos venguz, zo sabez,
    E no m'en dei ges penedir.

    Meillz m'en degra lo pels sezer
    Car chai vinc vostra cort vezer,
    Qu'eu farai loing e pres saber
    Lo joi que vos es a venir.

    S'anc per vos demenei orguoill,
    Tot m'es tornat en autre fuoill;
    Que tals mena bon fait en l'uoill
    Que no s'en ausa descobrir.   *over*

As long as fine Youth was father of the world and noble Love its mother, Prowess was maintained, in private and public; but now they've degraded it, dukes, kings and emperors.

And I am witness enough, for defence and prosecution, and I see how Youth is extinguished—whereby Love's lost and cut off from Joy—and how Love is lost in delusion.

The love of which I'm speaking was born of a noble line, and the place where it grew is protected by twining branches from both heat and cold, so that the stranger might not take it away from there.

'Desired by desirer' is the name of him who seeks to take love from there.

V. Emperor, for your merit and for the prowess which you have, I am come to you, know this, and I should not at all regret it.

I should be in finer fettle since I came here to see your court, and I'll make known far and near the joy there is coming to you.

If ever, on your account, I acted proudly, now has another leaf been turned for me, for such a one views well a good action who dares not speak his mind about it.

Qui.l sap bon qu'eu sui tant poinenz
Als malvaz et als recredenz,
Per que n'a serradas las denz
E no.n ausa lo criz eissir?

Emperaire, si ben enquers,
Lo reprovers es fis e mers:
Ço que donz dona e plora sers,
Las lacrimas devon perir.

Emperaire, si Dieus me gart,
S'eu me faill al vostre donar,
Jamais a gorc qu'auza lauzar
Non ira Marcabruns pescar,
C'ades cuidarïa faillir.

Per aquella fe qu'eu vos dei,
Anc mes emperador ni rei
Non agron tal marchat de mei
Con vos, e Dieus m'en lais jauzir!

Emperairiz, pregaz per mei,
Qu'eu farai vostre prez richir.

VI.   Cortesamen vuoill comenssar
Un vers, si es qui l'escout'ar,
E puois tant m'en sui entremes,
Veirai si.l poirai affinar,
Qu'eras vuoill mon chan esmerar,
E dirai vos de maintas res.

Assatz pot hom villanejar
Qui Cortezïa vol blasmar,
Que.l plus savis e.l mieills apres
Non sap tantas dire ni far
C'om no li posca enseignar
Petit o pro, tals hora es.

over

And he who is pleased that I'm so ready to attack the wicked and the recreant, why does he keep his teeth tight clamped, and the word of praise dares not come out?

Emperor, if you seek aright, the proverb is fine and true: when the servant weeps for what the master gives away, the tears should go unheeded.

Emperor, so help me God, if I miss your largesse, then nevermore will Marcabrun go to fish in a pool which he hears praised, for he'd always think to miss.

By that faith which I owe you, never did emperors or kings get such a bargain from me as you, and God grant that I benefit from it.

Empress, intercede for me, and I'll make your merit grow greater.

VI. In courtly manner I wish to begin a poem, if there's anyone to listen to it now. And since I'm thus far committed to it, I'll see if I can make it fine, for now I wish to make pure my song and I'll tell you of many things.

He's indeed capable of acting churlishly who seeks to blame Courtliness, for the wisest and most learned man cannot say or do so much pertaining to it but one could still teach him something, great or small, at some time or another.

"Mesura"

De Cortezïa.is pot vanar
Qui ben sap Mesur'esguardar;
E qui tot vol auzir quant es,
Ni tot cant ve cuid'amassar,
Del tot l'es ops a mesurar,
O ja non sera trop cortes.

Mesura es de gen parlar,
E Cortezïa es d'amar;
E qui non vol esser mespres,
De tota vilanïa.is gar,
D'escarnir e de folleiar,
Puois sera savis, ab qu'el pes.

C'aissi pot savis hom reignar,
E bona dompna meillurar;
Mas cella qu'en pren dos ni tres
E per un non si vol fïar,
Ben deu sos pretz asordeiar,
E sa valors a chascun mes.

Aitals amors fai a prezar
Que si meteissa ten a car;
E s'ieu en dic nuill vilanes
Per mal que la.n vueilh encolpar,
Be.ill lauzi fassa.m pro muzar,
Qu'ieu n'aurai so que.m n'a promes.

Lo vers e.l son vuoill envïar
A.N Jaufre Rudel outra mar,
E vuoill que l'aujon li Frances
Per lor coratges alegrar;
Que Dieus lor o pot perdonar:
O sïa pechatz, o merces.

He can boast of Courtliness who knows well how to observe Moderation; and if anyone would hear all that there is, or thinks to assimilate all that he sees, then he must needs observe Moderation in all things, or he'll never be very courtly.

It is Moderation to speak gently, and Courtliness to love; and may he who would not be despised beware of all vulgarity, of mocking and of acting senselessly. Then he'll be wise, provided he bears this in mind.

For thus can the wise man behave, and the fine lady improve; but as for her who takes two or three of them, and would not keep faith with one, her merit and worth must surely decline, month by month.

Such a love is to be prized which holds itself dearly; and if I say anything crude about it through wanting to blame it for some ill, then I approve that it keep me long waiting idly, to have that which it has promised me.

I wish to send this poem and the melody to Sir Jaufré Rudel, over the sea; and I would that the Frenchmen heard it so as to gladden their hearts, for God can grant them this: wherever sin be, may there be mercy.

Bernard de Ventadour

LIFE. Although this poet is now considered to be one of the greatest of the troubadours, little has come down to us concerning the detailed circumstances of his life. A tradition, according to which his parents were humble domestics in the castle of Ventadour, stems from little more than a too literal reading of a remark made in a satirical poem of the late twelfth century. It is, however, most probable that he in fact spent his early years (some time in the 1130s and 1140s) at the court of Ventadour and that he there received, under the guidance of the viscount Eblo his training in the art of lyric poetry. From here, his career as a professional poet, extending over some thirty years or so, took him to a number of courts in the South of France, Toulouse and Narbonne included, and even, on one occasion at least, to the court of Eleanor of Aquitaine, queen of England by her marriage to Henry II and grand-daughter of the first known troubadour. His thirteenth-century biographer, who, in his usual fashion, interprets as amorous liaisons the relations between the professional poet and his various patronesses, reports that Bernard finally withdrew into the Cistercian abbey at Dalon. This last detail is more credible than the others but lacks again, however, any documentary proof.

WORKS. Bernard is one of the earliest of that steadily increasing number of professional troubadours who appear on the scene from about the middle of the twelfth century. In the forty or so poems attributed to him, all but two of which are love-songs, one can see the first full flowering of the troubadours' art, as indeed the period of his literary activity (*c.* 1145–*c.* 1175) coincides with the full expansion of the cult of that art throughout the South of France. By the richness of his poetic imagination, as by his technical mastery, the limited formal and thematic material of his predecessors is magnificently exploited and expanded. It receives its first, classical, formulation which will provide the model for all later poets working in the same tradition.

Less expository than William IX, less intensely abstract than Jaufré Rudel, Bernard dramatises, renders more personally immediate, the ideal aspirations of courtly love. Into the structure of the *canso* he will introduce, for example, temporal, anecdotic and narrative material, while of that structure he will make a pattern of dialectic alternation—*un tremblement affectif* as one critic puts it—by which he formulates an opposition between the objectivity of the courtly ideal and the subjectivity of his own poetic experience. No less than his predecessors, he proposes the ideal of courtly love; his originality lies in the way in which he sets out to demonstrate its authenticity by showing how he, as poet-lover, is involved in an emotional situation created by that ideal. The love-song becomes a dramatic performance; while it lasts, it portrays as real an experience of the courtly ideal. Small wonder that Bernard's biographer credited him with so many passionate affairs; small wonder, too, that in the biographer's wake modern critics tend to ascribe to him the dominant—albeit somewhat problematical—quality of 'sincerity'.

EDITION. C. Appel *Bernart von Ventadorn, seine Lieder* (Halle 1915).

SELECTION. The first poem reproduced (Appel no. 15) is in the nature of a literary manifesto, expounding the poet's concept of love and of poetry, and actually creating the rôle of poet-lover which will be played out in most of his lyrics. Sincerity becomes an artistic attitude—perhaps the hired poet's defence against an anticipated charge of professionalism—and already we see created the tension between an ideal of mutually shared love and desire, and the 'real' situation of the submissive, unrequited, lover. In the second poem (Appel no. 23) the tension breaks into conflict which itself, in the course of the poem, moves to resolution—thanks to the everhelpful motif of the *lauzenger*. The structural pattern, by which the unfolding of the poem itself follows the peripeteia of the poet's emotional drama, is repeated, with variation, in the next two pieces (Appel nos. 29 and 43), while, in the last pieces (Appel nos. 39 and 30), the poet opposes the fixity of his emotional state to all that which, in his fantasy, he desires (no.

5) or to the general instability of time-bound human existence (no. 6). Apparent, too, in all six pieces, is the tremendous technical skill of Bernard de Ventadour, both in the obvious perfection of his stanza-structures and in the more subtle details of sound, rhythm and word-patterns which, with such apparent spontaneity, are made to correspond to the mood which the poet seeks to formulate, be it pathos, anger, distress, or overwhelming joy.

I. Chantars no pot gaire valer
Si d'ins dal cor no mou lo chans,
Ni chans no pot dal cor mover
Si no.i es fin'amors coraus.
Per so es mos chantars cabaus,
Qu'en joi d'amor ai et enten
La boch'e.ls olhs e.l cor e.l sen.

Ja Deus no.m don aquel poder
Que d'amor no.m prenda talans!
Si ja re no.n sabi'aver,
Mas chascun jorn m'en vengues maus,
Totz tems n'aurai bo cor, sivaus;
E n'ai mout mais de jauzimen
Car n'ai bo cor e m'i aten.

Amor blasmen per no-saber
Fola gens, mas leis no.n es dans,
C'amors no.n pot ges dechazer
Si non es amors comunaus.
Aisso non es amors; aitaus
No.n a mas lo nom e.l parven
Que re non ama si no pren.

S'eu en volgues dire lo ver,
Eu sai be de cui mou l'enjans:
D'aquelas c'amon per aver,
E son merchandandas venaus.
Messengers en fos eu e faus!
Vertat en dic vilanamen,
E peza me car eu no.n men.

En agradar et en voler
Es l'amors de dos fis amans.
Nula res no.i pot pro tener
Si.lh voluntatz non es egaus.
E cel es be fols naturaus
Que, de so que vol, la repren,
E.lh lauza so que no.lh es gen.

over

1. Singing cannot much avail, if from within the heart comes not the song; nor can the song come from the heart, unless there be there noble love, heartfelt. Hence is my singing supreme, for in love's joy I hold and direct my mouth, my eyes, my heart, my understanding.

    May God never grant me that power not to take liking for love! Were I never to know how to have aught of it, but that each day pain should come to me from it, still will I have good heart, at least; and thereby I have more cause to rejoice, since for it I have good heart and for it I strive.

    Foolish people blame love, through ignorance, but that's no harm to it; for love can in no way fail for that, if it's not common love. This is not love, such has only its name and semblance, which loves no thing unless it gains from it.

    If I would speak the truth of it, I know well from whom comes the delusion: from those women who love for wealth, and they are common whores. Would that I were a liar in this, and false! I speak the truth of it in uncouth way, and I'm grieved that therein I lie not.

    In accord and in assent is the love of two noble lovers. Nothing can be of profit in it if the will thereto is not mutual. And he is indeed a natural fool who blames her for that which she wishes, and commends to her that which becomes her not.

Mout ai be mes mo bon esper
Cant cela.m mostra bels semblans
Qu'eu plus dezir e volh vezer,
Francha, doussa, fin'e leiaus,
En cui lo reis seria saus,
Bel'e conhd'ab cors covinen,
M'a faih ric ome de nien.

Re mais no.n am ni sai temer,
Ni ja res no.m seri'afans,
Sol midons vengues a plazer;
C'aicel jorns me sembla Nadaus
C'ab sos bels olhs espiritaus
M'esgarda, mas so fai tan len
C'us sols dias me dura cen!

Lo vers es fis e naturaus,
E bos celui que be l'enten,
E melher es, qui.l joi aten.

Bernartz de Ventadorn l'enten,
E.l di e.l fai, e.l joi n'aten.

II. La dousa votz ai auzida
Del rosinholet sauvatge,
Et es m'ins el cor salhida
Si que tot lo cosirer
E.ls mals traihz qu'amors me dona,
M'adousa e m'asazona.
Et auria.m be mester
L'autrui joi al meu damnatge.

Ben es totz om d'avol vida
C'ab joi non a son estatge,
E qui vas amor no guida
So cor e so dezirer;
Car tot can es s'abandona
Vas joi, e refrim'e sona:
Prat e deves e verger,
Landas e pla e boschatge.

Right well have I my good hope placed when she whom I most desire and long to see shows me fair face; pure, gentle, noble and loyal, in whom the king would salvation find, lovely and graceful, with pleasing body, she has made me a rich man from naught.

I love and can fear nothing more than her, and nothing would ever be hardship for me, provided only it come to please my lady; for that day seems Christmas when she with her lovely, spiritual eyes looks on me. But she's so slow to do it that one day alone lasts for me a hundred!

The poem is fine and natural, and good to him who understands it well, and better it is if one hopes for the joy.

Bernard de Ventadour understands it; he recites it, and makes it, and hopes for its joy.

11. I have heard the woodland nightingale's sweet voice, and it has leaped into my heart, so that it soothes and softens all my care and the fell blows which love deals me; and well would another's joy serve me in my distress.

Any man is indeed of base life who has not his dwelling with joy, and who directs not towards love his heart and his desiring, since all that is, gives itself up to joy, and rings and is full of song: meadows and parklands and orchards, heathlands and plains and woods.

Eu las! cui Amors oblida
Que sui fors del dreih vīatge;
Agra de joi ma partida,
Mas ira.m fai destorber;
E no sai on me repona
Pus mo joi me desazona.
E no.m tenhatz per leuger
S'eu dic alcu vilanatge.

Une fausa deschauzida
Traïritz de mal linhatge
M'a traït, et es traïda,
E colh lo ram ab que.s fer.
E can autre l'arazona,
D'eus lo seu tort l'ochaizona.
Et an ne mais li derrer
Qu'eu, qui n'ai faih lonc badatge.

Mout l'avīa gen servida
Tro ac vas mi cor volatge;
E pus ilh no m'es cobida,
Mout sui fols si mais la ser.
Servirs c'om no gazardona,
Et esperansa bretona,
Fai de senhor escuder,
Per costum e per uzatge.

Pois tan es vas me falhida,
Aisi lais so senhoratge,
E no volh que.m si'aizida,
Ni ja mais parlar no.n quer;
Mas pero qui m'en razona,
La paraula m'en es bona,
E m'en esjau volonter,
E.m n'alegre mo coratge.

Deus li do mal'escharida
Qui porta mauvais mesatge!
Qu'eu agra amor jauzida
Si no foso lauzenger.

over

Alas for me, whom Love forgets, for I'm off the proper path! I would have my share of joy but sorrow troubles me, and I know not where I might find rest, when it turns my joy to bitterness. So deem me not frivolous if I say something uncouth.

A false, unseemly, traitress of base lineage has betrayed me, and is herself betrayed, and plucks the switch with which she beats herself. When another arraigns her, she accuses him of her own wrong; and the last to come have more from her than I, who have for her stood waiting long.

I had most nobly served her, till she showed me a fickle heart; and since she's not accorded me, I'm a great fool if I serve her more. Service which is not rewarded, like the Bretons' hope, makes of a lord a squire by custom and habit.

Since she's so faithless to me, I quit then her dominion, and I want her not to be near me, nor do I seek ever to speak of her more; but yet, if one talks to me of her, such talk is pleasant to me, and I rejoice in it readily and gladden my heart thereby.

God grant a wretched fate to him who bears bad tidings! For I would have had love's joy had it not been for tale-tellers.

Fols es qui ab sidons tensona,
Qu'e.lh perdo s'ela.m perdona,
E tuih cilh son mesonger
Que.m n'an faih dire folatge.

Lo vers mi porta, Corona,
Lai a midons a Narbona;
Que tuih sei faih son enter,
C'om no.n pot dire folatge.

III. Lo rossinhols s'esbaudeya
    Josta la flor el verjan,
    E pren m'en tan grans enveya
    Qu'eu no posc mudar no chan;
    Mas no sai de que, ni de cui,
    Car eu non am me, ni autrui.
    E fatz esfortz, car sai faire
    Bo vers, pois no sui amaire!

    Mais a d'amor qui domneya
    Ab orgolh et ab enjan
    Que cel que tot jorn merceya
    Ni.s vai trop umilïan,
    C'a penas vol Amors celui
    Qu'es francs e fis si cum eu sui.
    So m'a tout tot mon afaire:
    C'anc no fui faus ni trichaire.

    C'aissi com lo rams si pleya
    Lai o.l vens lo vai menan,
    Era, vas lei que.m guerreya,
    Aclis, per far so coman.
    Per aisso m'afol'e.m destrui,
    Don a mal linhatge redui,
    C'ams los olhs li don a traire
    S'autre tort me pot retraire.

    Soven me rept'e.m plaideya
    E.m vai ochaisos troban,

over

He's a fool who quarrels with his mistress, so I forgive her if she forgives me, and they are all liars who have made me speak folly of her.

Take for me the poem, Corona, there to my lady in Narbonne; for all her deeds are perfect, and one cannot speak folly of her.

III. The nightingale makes merry by the blossom on the bough, and such great envy takes me that I cannot help but sing; but I know not of what, nor of whom, for I love not myself nor another. And I'm making great efforts, for I can make good verse when I am not in love!

He gains more from love who pays court with pride and deceit than he who is ever suppliant and most humble. For love has no time for one who is frank and noble as I am. This has bereft me of all that was mine to do: that I never was false or deceitful.

But, as the bough bends there where the wind sways it, so was I, towards her who assails me, bent to do her will. For this she crazes and confounds me, whereby she sinks to low-born ways; and I give her both eyes to pluck out if she can blame me for other wrong.

She often indicts and accuses me, and goes making up charges against me;

E can ilh en re feuneya
Vas me versa tot lo dan!
Gen joga de me e.s desdui,
Que d'eus lo seu tort me conclui!
Mas ben es vertatz que laire
Cuida tuih sion sei fraire.

Om no la ve que no creya
Sos bels olhs e so semblan;
E no cre qu'ilh aver deya
Felo cor, ni mal talan,
Mas l'aiga que söau s'adui
Es peyer que cela que brui.
Enjan fai qui de bon aire
Sembla, e non o es gaire.

De tot loc on ilh esteya
Me destolh e.m vau lonhan,
E per so que no la veya
Pas li, mos olhs claus, denan.
Quar selh siec amor qui.s n'esdui,
E cel enchaussa qui la fui.
Ben ai en cor del estraire
Tro que vas midons repaire.

Ja non er, si tot me greya,
Qu'enquer fin e plaih no.lh man,
Que greu m'es c'aissi.m recreya
Ni perda tan lonc afan.
A sos ops me gart e m'estui,
E si non em amic amdui,
D'autr'amor no m'es vejaire
Que ja mais mos cors s'esclaire.

Enaissi fos pres com eu sui
Mos Alvernhatz, e foram dui,
Que plus no.s pogues estraire
D'En Bel Vezer de Belcaire.

Tristan, si no.us es veyaire,
Mais vos am que no solh faire.

over

and when she acts basely in anything, she makes the fault fall on me! Softly she plays and makes sport of me, in damning me with her very own wrong! But indeed it's the truth that the thief believes all are his brothers.

No one sees her but believes in her lovely eyes and her appearance, and he thinks not that she should have fell heart or evil mind. But the water which glides by softly is worse than the noisy one. He deceives who seems of good nature and is not at all.

From every place where she might dwell, I turn and go far off; and, so that I might not see her, I pass by her, eyes shut tight. For he follows love who avoids it, and it pursues him who flees it; I have indeed in mind to forsake it, until it returns to my lady.

It will not be, although she tortures me, but still I'll ask her for a truce and for peace; for it grieves me thus to quit, and to squander such long-suffering. May she keep and confine me for hers and, if we are not both lovers, it seems to me that by no other love will my heart be ever illumined.

Would that my friend Auvergnat were taken as I am, and then we'd be two, for he could no more quit Sir Bel Vezer of Beaucaire.

Tristan, though it seems not to you, I love you more than I used to.

IV. Can vei la lauzeta mover
De joi sas alas contra.l rai,
Que s'oblid'e.s laissa chazer
Per la doussor c'al cor li vai,
Ai, tan grans enveya m'en ve
De cui qu'eu veya jauzion,
Meravilhas ai car desse
Lo cor de dezirer no.m fon.

Ai las, tan cuidava saber
D'amor, e tan petit en sai!
Car eu d'amar no.m posc tener
Celeis don ja pro non aurai.
Tout m'a mo cor e tout m'a me,
E se mezeis e tot lo mon,
E can se.m tolc, no.m laisset re
Mas dezirer e cor volon.

Anc non agui de me poder
Ni no fui meus de l'or'en sai
Que.m laisset en sos olhs vezer,
En un miralh que mout me plai.
Miralhs, pus me mirei en te,
M'an mort li sospir de prëon,
C'aissi.m perdei com perdet se
Lo bels Narcisus en la fon.

De las domnas me dezesper;
Ja mais en lor no.m fiarai,
C'aissi com las solh chaptener,
Enaissi las deschaptenrai.
Pois vei c'una pro no m'en te
Vas leis que.m destrui e.m cofon,
Totas las dopt'e las mescre,
Car be sai c'atretals se son.

D'aisso.s fa be femna parer
Ma domna, per qu'e.lh o retrai,
Car no vol so c'om deu voler
E so c'om li deveda, fai.

over

IV. When I see the lark beating with joy its wings against the ray of the sun until, oblivious, it swoons and drops for the sweetness which enters its heart, ah, such great envy takes me of whatever I see rejoicing, I marvel that on the instant my heart melts not with desire.

Alas, I thought to know so much of love, and I know of it so little! For I cannot help loving her from whom good will never come to me. She has taken from me my heart, and taken myself from me, and her own self and all the world; and when from me she took herself, she left me naught but desire and a longing heart.

I never had mastery of myself, nor was I ever mine from the moment when she let me see into her eyes, into a mirror which pleases me much. Mirror, since I mirrored myself in you, sighs from deep down have slain me, and thus I was lost as, in the pool, the fair Narcissus was lost.

Of ladies I despair, never more will I trust in them; and, just as I used to hold them dear, so will I hold them for naught. Since I see that not one of them gives me help against her who destroys and confounds me, I doubt them all and mistrust them, for I know they are all the same.

By this my lady well shows herself a woman, and hence I reproach her this: that she wants not that which one ought to want, and that which one forbids her, she does.

Chazutz sui en mala merce,
Et ai be faih co.l fols en pon;
E no sai per que m'esdeve
Mas car trop puyei contra mon.

Merces es perduda per ver,
Et eu non o saubi anc mai,
Car cilh qui plus en degr'aver
No.n a ges, et on la querrai?
A, can mal sembla, qui la ve,
Qued aquest chaitiu deziron
Que ja ses leis non aura be
Laisse morir, que no l'äon!

Pus ab midons no.m pot valer
Precs ni merces ni.l dreihz qu'eu ai,
Ni a leis no ven a plazer
Qu'eu l'am, ja mais no.lh o dirai.
Aissi.m part de leis e.m recre;
Mort m'a e per mort li respon,
E vau m'en, pus ilh no.m rete,
Chaitius, en issilh, no sai on.

Tristans, ges non auretz de me,
Qu'eu m'en vau, chaitius, no sai on.
De chantar me gic e.m recre,
E de joi e d'amor m'escon.

V. Can l'erba fresch'e.lh folha par,   *joy in and from nature*
    E la flors boton'el verjan,   *is intoxicating*
    E.l rossinhols autet e clar
    Leva sa votz, e mou so chan,   ↓
    Joi ai de lui, e joi ai de la flor,
    E joi de me e de midons major;
    Daus totas partz sui de joi claus e sens,
    Mas sel es jois que totz autres jois vens.   *over*

I've fallen into bad grace, and have indeed done like the fool on the bridge; and I know not why this happens to me, except because I tried to climb too high.

Mercy is lost, in truth, and that I never once knew; for she who should have most of it has none at all—where then shall I seek it? Ah! how little it appears to one who sees her, that this wretch so full of longing, who will never have good without her, she lets die, and helps him not.

Since with my lady neither prayer nor mercy, nor the right that I have can avail me, and it comes not to please her that I love her, I'll never more tell her so. Thus I part from her, and give up; she has caused my death and by death I answer her and go away, since she does not retain me, a wretch, into exile, I know not where.

Tristan, you'll have nothing from me, for I'm going away, a wretch, I know not where. I quit and give up singing, and from joy and from love I take leave.

V. When the fresh grass and the leaf appears, and the flower blossoms on the bough, and the nightingale raises high and clear its voice and pours out its song, joy I have for it, and joy for the flower, and joy for myself and for my lady yet more: on all sides I am bound and circled by joy, but that is joy which all other joys overwhelms.

Ai las, com mor de cossirar!
Que manhtas vetz en cossir tan,
Lairo m'en poirïan portar
Que re no sabrïa que.s fan.
Per Deu, Amors, be.m trobas vensedor,
Ab paucs d'amics e ses autre senhor.
Car una vetz tan midons no destrens
Abans qu'eu fos del dezirer estens?

Meravilh me com posc durar
Que no.lh demostre mo talan.
Can eu vei midons ni l'esgar,
Li seu bel olh tan be l'estan
Per pauc me tenh car eu vas leis no cor.
Si feira eu, si no fos per päor,
C'anc no vi cors melhs talhatz ni depens
Ad ops d'amar sïa tan greus ni lens.

Tan am midons e la tenh car,
E tan la dopt'e la reblan,
C'anc de me no.lh auzei parlar,
Ni re no.lh quer ni re no.lh man.
Pero ilh sap mo mal e ma dolor,
E can li plai, mi fai ben et onor,
E can li plai, eu m'en sofert ab mens,
Per so c'a leis non avenha blastens.

S'eu saubes la gen enchantar,
Mei enemic foran efan,
Que ja us no saubra trïar
Ni dir re que.ns tornes a dan.
Adoncs sai eu que vira la gensor,
E sos bels olhs e sa frescha color,
E baizera.lh la bocha en totz sens
Si que d'un mes i paregra lo sens.

Be la volgra sola trobar,
Que dormis, o.n fezes semblan,
Per qu'e.lh embles un doutz baizar,
Pus no valh tan qu'eu lo.lh deman.
Per Deu, domna, pauc esplecham d'amor! *over*

Alas, how I die of deep thought! For many a time I am so deep in thought that robbers could carry me off and I'd know naught of what they do. By God, love, you find me indeed easy to conquer, with few friends and no other lord! Why did you but once not constrain my lady, before I was consumed by desire?

I marvel how I can endure not to reveal to her my longing. When I see my lady and behold her, her lovely eyes so well become her that I can scarce hold back from running towards her. So would I, were it not for fear, for I never saw person more well-shaped and fashioned for love to be yet so slow and reluctant.

I love my lady so much and hold her dear, I fear her so much and respect her, that I never dared speak to her of myself, nor seek I anything, nor ask I anything of her. Yet she's aware of my pain and my sorrow, and when it pleases her she does me honour and good, and when it pleases her I am content with less, so that from it there might come to her no reproach.

If I could enchant people, my enemies would be children, so that not one could ever spy out or say anything that might do us harm. Then I know that I would see the most noble one, and her fair eyes and her fresh complexion; and I would cover her mouth with kisses so that for a month the mark would show.

Well would I like to find her alone while she slept or pretended to, that I might steal from her a sweet kiss, since I'm not so worthy as to ask it of her. By God, lady, little of love do we achieve!

Vai s'en lo tems e perdem lo melhor.
Parlar degram ab cubertz entresens
E, pus no.ns val arditz, valgues nos gens!

Be deuri'om domna blasmar
Can trop vai son amic tarzan,
Que lonja paraula d'amar
Es grans enois, e par d'enjan;
C'amar pot om e far semblan alhor,
E gen mentir lai on non a autor.
Bona domna, ab sol c'amar mi dens,
Ja per mentir eu no serai atens.

Messatger, vai, e no m'en prezes mens
S'eu del anar vas midons sui temens.

VI. Lo tems vai e ven e vire
Per jorns, per mes, e per ans;
Et eu, las, no.n sai que dire,
C'ades es us mos talans.
Ades es us e no.s muda,
C'una.n volh e.n ai volguda,
Don anc non aic jauzimen.

Pois ela no.n pert lo rire,
A me.n ven e dols e dans;
C'a tal joc m'a faih assire
Don ai lo peyor dos tans—
C'aitals amors es perduda
Qu'es d'una part mantenguda—
Tro que fai acordamen.

Be deuri'esser blasmaire
De me mezeis, a razo,
C'anc no nasquet cel de maire
Que tan servis en perdo.
E s'ela no m'en chastia,
Ades doblara.lh folia,
Que fols no tem tro que pren.

over

Time goes by and we lose the best of it; we should speak with secret signs and, since boldness avails us not, may guile avail us!

A man should indeed blame his lady when too much she goes putting him off; for long talk of loving is most tedious and equal to deceit. For one can love and make a pretence elsewhere, and smoothly lie there where there's no sure proof. Good lady, if only you deign to love me, I will never be tainted by lies.

Messenger go, and do not esteem me less if I'm afraid of going to my lady.

VI. Time comes and goes and runs its round in days, in months, in years; and I, alas, know not what to say of that, for my longing is ever one. One is it ever and does not change, for one I desire and have desired, of whom I never had joy.

Since she doesn't stop laughing for that, to me comes both grief and harm; and she's made me sit down to such a game whereof I have the worst twice over—for such love is lost that's upheld on one side only—until she make her peace.

I should indeed be mine own accuser by rights, for never was there born of mother one who served so much in vain; and if she does not turn me from it, then doubled will be my folly, for (only) a fool fears not until he suffers.

Ja mais no serai chantaire,
Ni de l'escola N'Eblo,
Que mos chantars no val gaire,
Ni mas voutas ni mei so.
Ni res qu'eu fassa ni dïa
No conosc que pros me sïa,
Ni no.i vei melhuramen.

Si tot fatz de joi parvensa,
Mout ai dins lo cor irat.
Qui vid anc mais penedensa
Faire denan lo pechat?
On plus la prec, plus m'es dura,
Mas si'n breu tems no.s melhura,
Vengut er al partimen.

Pero ben es qu'ela.m vensa
A tota sa voluntat,
Que s'el'a tort, o bistensa,
Ades n'aura pïetat;
Que so mostra l'escriptura:
Causa de bon'aventura
Val us sols jorns mais de cen.

Ja no.m partrai, a ma vida,
Tan com sïa sals ni sas,
Que pois l'arma n'es issida,
Balaya lonc tems lo gras;
E si tot no s'es cochada,
Ja per me no.n er blasmada,
Sol d'eus adenan s'emen.

Ai, bon'amors encobida,
Cors be faihz, delgatz e plas,
Frescha chara colorida,
Cui Deus formet ab sas mas!
Totz tems vos ai dezirada,
Que res autra no m'agrada.
Autr'amor no volh nïen.

Dousa res ben ensenhada,
Cel que.us a tan gen formada
Me.n do cel joi qu'eu n'aten!

Never more will I be a singer, nor of Sir Eblo's school, for my singing is of no avail, neither my trills nor my melodies. And whatever I do or say, I know not how it might profit me, nor do I see in it any chance of improvement.

Though I make a show of joy, my heart, within, is most sad. Who ever once saw penance done before the sin? The more I entreat her, the harder she is to me, but if she changes not soon for the better, it will come to a parting of ways.

Yet it is well that she subjects me to her whole will, for if she's wrong, or delays, she will soon have pity for it; and this the Scriptures declare: on account of good fortune, one single day is worth more than a hundred.

I'll never quit, throughout my life, for as long as I'm hale and whole; for after the soul has gone from it, the flesh flutters long in the wind; and though she has never made haste, she'll never be blamed by me for that, if only from now on she makes amends herself.

Ah, good and desirable loved one, body well-formed, smooth and slender, fresh and fair-complexioned flesh which God fashioned with His hands! All times I have desired you, and no other gives me pleasure. No other love do I want at all.

Sweet and most gracious being, may He who so finely fashioned you grant me that joy which I hope for!

Bernart much more exhaustive and "polished" than his predecessors = casuistic, more concern for verbal ingenuity.

Peire d'Auvergne

LIFE. Peire d'Auvergne, a townsman's son from the diocese of Clermont-Ferrand according to his mediaeval biographer, probably began his career as a professional troubadour in the mid-1150s. His earliest dateable poem shows him already sufficiently well-established to be received, in 1157–1158, at the court of Sancho III of Castile. Other poems indicate his activity in Provence and the Languedoc as well as in N. Spain, while the latest one which can be dated with any degree of certainty shows him taking part in a festive fathering held at or near Puivert (Aude) in the year 1170. Regarding the later part of his life, even his early biographer is vague; there is a suggestion that he entered a religious order, but this, like all other aspects of his last years, remains a matter for speculation.
WORKS. Although relatively limited in number—no more than twenty poems are now attributed to him—Peire d'Auvergne's compositions are remarkably varied in both form and subject-matter. While echoes of his predecessors and early contemporaries, of Marcabrun especially, are numerous, the general impression gained from his work is of a sustained ambition to renew and extend the scope of established poetic traditions. The ethical preoccupations inherent in early courtly poetry, for example, are not unknown to him, but, for the first time, they are clearly rivalled as a source of inspiration by concepts which are purely and simply christian in nature. The result is that in at least four of his poems the *canso* is transformed into a sermon, a prayer, or a hymn. For the first time too, we see in this troubadour's work a more than occasional preoccupation with the subject of poetry itself. Few clearly-defined aesthetic concepts emerge, it is true. Often it is difficult to establish the proper relationship between stated principle and observable practice, while certain affirmations suggest little more than a

desire to outshine, in semi-jocular mood, his professional rivals. It is nevertheless agreed that such preoccupations anticipate the more serious and detailed discussion of poetic styles and functions which will involve many of the most eminent troubadours of the 1170s and 1180s. During this period, poets begin to debate among themselves, in their own verse, the principles of their art; in this process as in others, occupying an intermediary position between such great founding figures as Marcabrun and Bernard de Ventadour and the outstanding troubadours of the later part of the century, Peire d'Auvergne plays a significant rôle, ensuring continuity between the generations and exploring on his own account new areas of creative activity.

EDITION. A. Del Monte *Peire D'Alvernha, Liriche*, (Turin 1955).

SELECTION. Of the four poems selected (Del Monte nos. 3, 11, 15, 16), the first is an accomplished though fairly conventional love-song strongly reminiscent, in its themes, of Bernard de Ventadour but, at the same time, deliberately echoing William IX's *chansoneta nueva* (selection no. 5) by its choice of isolated rime-words in *-am*. The second poem is almost entirely devoted to the subject of poetry; vague in its allusions but fairly specific in its charges, humorously self-assertive in its somewhat exaggerated claims, it also constitutes one of the earliest contributions to the literary controversy which will engage many of Peire's later contemporaries. The next poem, a moral *sirventès*, reveals clearly the influence of Marcabrun in both thematic material and stylistic devices. The immediate pointedness of the Gascon is now, however, somewhat blunted by the poet's manifest preoccupation with sheer formal complexity and technical ingenuity. Certain of Marcabrun's procedures are further apparent in the fourth poem—the garden symbolising earthly life, for instance, and the adoption, for the occasion, of the preacher's tone and attitude—but once again Peire d'Auvergne is seen to be breaking new ground. There is no longer an attempt to fuse together courtly, chivalric, and christian ethical concepts into one aristocratic ideal; traditional christian topics alone provide the subject of this early example of what will later become a typical genre of secular lyric verse.

I. Ab fina joia comenssa
    Lo vers, qui bels motz assona,
    E de re no.i a faillenssa;
    Mas no m'es bon qe l'apreigna
    Tals cui mos chans non coveigna,
    Q'ieu non vuoill avols chantaire,
    Cel qui tot chan desfaissona,
    Mon doutz sonet torn'en bram.

    D'amor ai la sovinenssa
    E.ls bels digz, ren plus no.m dona;
    Mas per bona atendenssa
    Esper c'alcus jois m'en veigna.
    .L segles vol c'om si capteigna,
    Segon que pot sempres faire
    Q'en breu temps plus asazona,
    Q'a pro d'aisso don ac fam.

    Bel semblan n'ai en parvenssa,
    Que gen m'acuoill e.m razona;
    Mas del plus no.m fai cossenssa,
    Ni.s taing que tant aut mi ceigna,
    Ni tan rics jois m'endeveigna
    On coven us emperaire.
    { Pro fai car sol gen mi sona,
    { Ni car sofre q'ieu la am.

    Mout mi fai granda temenssa,
    Car tant pauc si abandona;
    Jois q'enaissi trop bistenssa
    Mout mostra mal'entresseigna.
    Si cum li plaira mi teigna,
    Que tant no.m fai gran mal traire;
    Sel so que no l'encaisona,
    Tant no.m ten en greu liam.

    Ses pechat fis penedenssa,
    Et es tort qui no.m perdona;
    Et ieu fatz long'entendenssa
    Per tal perdon que no.m deigna.

                                over

I. With noble joy the poem begins which rimes fair words together, and there's no fault in anything therein; but it pleases me not that such a one should learn it whom my song does not befit. I've no wish that some wretched singer, the sort who ruins any song, should turn my sweet melody to braying.

I am mindful of love and its fair speech, it gives me nothing more; but by patient waiting I hope that some joy of it may come to me. Life in the world demands that one should act in that way, considering that it can always happen that in a short time things get better, so that one has in plenty that for which one hungered.

I have from her an outward show of favour, for with grace she receives me and addresses me; but of the rest she concedes me nothing, nor is it proper that I should aspire so high, or that such rich joy should befall me as an emperor would find fitting. She does enough in this alone, that with grace she speaks to me and suffers that I love her.

So much does she inspire in me great fear, for she gives of herself so little; joy that is thus too reluctant shows a most disagreeable sign. Just as it pleases her, may she retain me, for she does not make me suffer so much great pain; I'm not the one to reproach her, she does not hold me so much in grievous bondage.

Without sin I did penance, and it's wrong if I'm not forgiven; yet I have long set my heart on such forgiveness as she grants me not.

Assatz cuig que mal m'en preigna,
Que perdutz es desesperaire.
Per c'ai' esperanssa bona,
Pel nostre don mi reclam.

Ben es fis de gran valenssa
Mos cors, s'aqest m'abarona
Per cui totz pretz creis e genssa;
E sap pauc qui so m'enseigna
Que ja nuill'autra.m sosteigna.
Tant bella filla de maire,
Ni tant cum cels plou ni trona,
Non ac tal el ling d'Azam.

Als comtes mand en Pröenssa
Lo vers, e sai a Narbona,
⎰ Lai on pren jois mantenenssa   = ?
⎱ Segon aqels per cui reigna.
E ieu trob sai qi.m reteigna,
Tal dompna don sui amaire;
⎰ Non ges a la lei gascona;   = ?
⎱ Segon las nostras amam.

11. Sobre.l vieill trobar e.l novel
   Vueill mostrar mon sen als sabens,   *technical pride.*
   Qu'entendon be aquels c'a venir so:
   C'anc, tro per me, no fo faitz vers entiers.
   E qui non cre qu'ieu sīa verdadiers,
   Auja dese con estau a razo.

   Qu'ieu tenh l'us—e.l pan e.l coutel
   De que.m platz apanar las gens—
   Que d'est mestier an levat en pairo,
   Ses acordier, que no.s rompa.l semdiers.
   Qu'ieu dic que nier mi mostr'els faitz non niers,
   Qu'a fol parlier ten hom lui e.l sermo.

   C'a un tenen, ses mot borrel,
   Deu de dir esser avinens;   *over*

I think indeed that ill will befall me, for a man without hope is lost; so that I may have good hope, in our Lord's name I appeal.

My person is assured of great worthiness, if this one ennobles me through whom all merit increases and grows more fair; and he knows little who advises me this: that any other lady should ever comfort me. So fair a mother's daughter, by as much as the sky sheds rain, and thunders, there never was in Adam's line.

To the Counts in Provence I commend the poem, and hereby at Narbonne, there where joy has its cult, thanks to those through whom it reigns. And I find here to retain me such a lady whose lover I am; not at all in the Gascon fashion; in our own ways do we love.

11. On the old style of poetry and the new, I would speak my mind to the knowing who well understand those to come; never, until by me, had whole verse been written. And if anyone thinks that I'm not telling the truth, let him hear now how I stand on reason's side.

For I have the experience—both the bread and the knife with which it pleases me to feed folk—which in this art they have held up as model, without collusion, so that the (true) path be not cut off. And I say of him who shows me black in deeds not black, that he with his talk is deemed a stupid chatterer.

For in straightforward fashion, without fill-up phrases, one should be pleasant in one's speech,

Quar qui trassail de Mauri en Miro
Entre.l mieg faill—si no.s pren als ladriers!
Com del trebaill quecs motz fa.s messatgiers,
Qu'en devinaill met l'auzir, de maiso.

E qui qu'en frima ni.n fragel,
Pos qu'es mos trobars tan valens
[... ... ... o;]
Q'ieu soi raïtz, e dic qu'ieu soi premiers
De digz complitz, vensen mos fatz guerriers
Que.m levon critz que ieu no m'en tenh pro.

Donx, com qu'ill sion d'un tropel,
Menton tot gent er per las dens,
Qu'ie.m sen sertas del mieils qu'es e que fo,
Enseguras de mon chant, e sobriers
Ves los bauzas, e sai que dic, qu'estiers
No vengra.l gras don a trop, en sazo.

Quar er m'abelis e m'es bel
Qu'el mieu joi s'enant la jovens;
E s'ieu ren dic que lur an enviro,
Aisi m'en gic, c'uns gaugz mi creis dobliers
D'un dous espic, qu'es joios consiriers,
Don m'an amic hueimais li mal e.ill bo.

D'aisi.m sent ric per bona sospeiso
Qu'en joi m'afic e m'estau volentiers;
Et ab joi pic e gaug mos deziriers,
Et ab joi pic e gaug vueill: Dieus lo.m do!

III. Belh m'es qu'ieu fass'huey mays un vers,
Pus la flors e.lh fuelha brota,
E.l belh temps nos a del lag ters
Que giet'e plou e degota;
E pus l'aura renovelha,
Be.s tanh que renovel mos cors,
Si que flurisc'e bruelh defors
So que dedins mi gragelha.

over

since he who wavers between Mauri and Miro slips down in between—unless he hangs on to the sides! As each word acts as a herald of the labour (behind it), so he turns listening into a puzzle for the whole household.

And no matter who seethes or grumbles about it, since my style of poetry is so fine . . .; for I am the root and say that I'm the first in perfect speech, defeating my stupid assailants who raise against me the outcry that I'm of no use in it.

Therefore, though they are all of one herd, they lie most softly between their teeth, and I feel assured of the best that is and that was, confident in my song and supreme over the deceivers; and I know what I'm saying, for otherwise the grain would not come of which there's plenty, in season.

For now it is fine and pleasing to me that in my joy youth is exalted; and if I say anything which might go against them, I here abjure it, for a twofold joy accrues to me from one sweet bud; that is, joyous thought by which, henceforth, both good and bad have me for a friend.

Hence I feel rich on account of good hope, for in joy I trust and willingly dwell; with joy I peck at and relish my desires, and with joy I peck, and enjoyment I wish for: God grant me it!

III. It pleases me now to compose a poem, when the flower and the leaf are in bud, and the fair weather has rid us of the foul which rains and pours and drizzles; and since the air is thus refreshed, it's fitting that my person be refreshed, so that there flower and burst forth that which within me is stirring.

Hai! Pretz, quon iest mutz, sortz e guers,
E, Pröeza, co.us vey rota,
E menar de tort en travers!
Quar qui que.s vol si.us sabota
Q'una puta gens fradelha,
Que tir'e bat'e pren a mors,
Vos an cofondut e destors,
Que.us afolh'e.us descapdelha.

Greu m'es qu'estiers sera trop paucx
Lo pretz d'aquest segl'äora;
Et ieu suy del castīar raucx
E no.m val ges una mora,
Qu'usquecx a facha gonelha,
Corta, resciza de mal vetz,
Et a.lh fait tant estreit cabetz
Que ja res non lay espelha.

S'als malvatz no fos tan grans guaucx,
Avoleza ja no fora,
Et es tant adubertz lo traucx
Que sobre rocas läora
Selh cuy jais cors, e martelha.
Qu'ayssi.ls ten enredatz lo retz:
Non lur pot escantir lo setz
Ni.l crims, tan los rasc'iselha.

Aquist engres, envers estrait,
Fals e flac filh d'avols paires,
Felo, embronc, sebenc, mal fait,
Sers ressis nat d'avols maires,
Malastros, paubr'escudelha,
Volpillos, blau d'enveja, sec,
Fan que quascus aprent un quec,
Don nays e bruelha.l pustelha.

Peire d'Auvergne

Ah! Merit, how you are muted, deaf and squint, and Worthiness, how broken I see you and dragged to and fro! For whoever wants to so ill-treats you that a vile and wicked people, pulling and pushing and snapping, have confused and perverted you; and this robs you of sense and guidance.

It grieves me, for otherwise scant indeed will be the merit of these present times; and I am hoarse from admonishing, yet it avails me not a whit. For each has fashioned a short tunic, cut from vice, and has made for it such a tight collar that none can ever take example from it.

If for the wicked there were not such great pleasure, baseness there would not be; yet the hole gapes so widely that he ploughs—and hammers—on rocks for whom joy (once) ran freely. And thus the snare holds them ensnared: neither their lust nor their crime can be allayed, so much does corruption harrow them.

This cruel, perverse offspring, false and feeble sons of wicked fathers, felonous, joyless, bastards, ill-formed, weakling serfs born of wicked mothers, brutish, empty vessels, cowards, livid with envy, withered up; they act so that each instructs the other, whence is born and bursts the running sore.

Ara.m tuelh hueymais de lur plait,
Dels forlinhatz d'avols aires;
Ma qui pröeza vol, aguait
Cum pros si'e no.s tric guaires;
Que qui s'esfors'e.s revelha,
Atretan tost, s'anc esser dec,
Sera ben pros hom malvatz lec,
Si no fos d'avol uzelha.

Hueymais si'avols qui.s volra,
O pros, plus als no.n puesc doncas;
Que si pros es, ben i para,
O avols, si ben no.n broncas.
E non sap qu'es calamelha
Qui saüc cuia faire telh,
Ni quant hom en autrui conselh
Si met, qui non l'i apelha.

Peire d'Alvernha mot quera
Qui acoint esquius a concas;
E per aqui hom lo sabra,
Car del fin trobar non roncas;
Ans n'as ben la flor plus belha,
Detorz e l'art e l'aparelh,
E no.i a motz fals que rovelh,
Ni sobredolat d'astelha.

On plus hom mos vers favelha,
Fe que.us deg, on mais valon elh;
E no.y a motz fals que rovelh,
Ni sobredolat d'astelha.

IV. Cui bon vers agrad'a auzir
    De me, lo cosselh qu'el escout
    Aquest c'ara comens a dir;
    Que pus li er sos cors assis
    En ben entendre.ls sos e.ls motz,
    Ja non dira qu'el anc auzis
    Melhors ditz trobatz, luinh ni prop.

Now I betake myself from their plight henceforth, from the misbegotten ones of shameful birth; but he who seeks worthiness, let him watch how he might be worthy, and let him not be deceived. For he who strives and arouses himself will just as quickly, if it were ever to be, become from a wicked lecher a right worthy man, unless he were wicked by custom.

Henceforth let him be wicked who so wishes, or worthy, I can now do no more; for if he is worthy it will be well apparent, or wicked, unless you're deceived. And he knows not what a reed-pipe is who thinks to make lime-tree of willow, or when he sets out to give others advice when he's not asked for it.

Pierre of Auvergne seeks the word which might make known the repulsive by the gallon; and hereby will one know it, for you don't snore for lack of fine verse. You have of it, rather, the fairest flower, I deploy both skill and craft, and in it there's no false word to grow rusty, nor one planed down too smooth.

The more one recites my verse, by my faith, the more worthwhile they are; and in them there's no false word to grow rusty, nor one planed down too smooth.

IV. Anyone for whom fine verse is pleasant to hear from me, I advise to listen to this one which I'm now about to recite; for once his heart is set on hearing well the notes and the words, he'll never say that he ever heard finer things said in verse, near or far.

Ges ben no fai az escarnir,
Qui l'au, ans deu agradar mout,
Si tot l'outracujat albir,
Ab lor nesci feble fat ris,
Tornon so qu'es d'amon de sotz;
E.l be vezem que s'enantis,
E l'esquerns resta de galop.

E per tal fai s'en bon gequir,
Qu'anc esquerns ni coratge.s tout,
Si bruillet no sai vim florir!
E par d'avol respeit jardis
Can vei que la cima ni.l brotz
Non gieta frucha ni tequis,
E l'intrador n'eisson tug clop.

Era.s vol alre devezir:
Qui d'aver sai a gran comout,
Be s'en deurïa far servir;
Qu'en un mueg de marabotis
No.us donarïa döas notz,
Pos a la boca venra.l fis,
Ni.l prestre secodra l'izop.

A quec deurïa sovenir
Que non agues corag'estout
Del be don nos devem jauzir;
Qu'en pauc d'ora es hom conquis,
E can ven als deriers sanglotz,
No li val honcles ni cozis,
Ni metges ab son issarop.

Ben deurïa pensar morir
Qui dreitz huils garda sus lo vout:
Cossi Dieus per nos a guerir
Receup mort, e pos mort aucis,
Celui qui per nos venc en crotz.
Tug morrem, c'avers non gueris
Negun, al temps, plus que fetz Jop.   *over*

Peire d'Auvergne

It's certainly not to be mocked at if one hears it, rather should it be most pleasing, even though the opinions of the overweening, with their stupid, feeble, feckless sniggers, drag down that which is on high; we see that good makes its own way forward, while mockery stays galloping behind.

Hence it is well to ignore it, for never does mockery or spite desist—unless we ever saw here the thicket flowering! And the garden appears of mean promise when I see that neither the tree-top nor the young shoot produces fruit or seed-pod, and those who enter it come out of it all lame.

Now must one speak of other things: whoever has wealth, here, in great abundance, should indeed have it serve him well; for I'd not give you two nuts for a bushel of Spanish coin once the mouth is finally shut and the priest sprinkles the holy water.

Each should remember not to have haughty heart for the goods which we are to enjoy; for in a short space of time is a man laid low, and when he comes to his last gasps then neither uncle nor cousin is of help, nor the doctor with his syrup.

He should indeed think of dying who with steady eyes looks up at the holy image (and sees) how God, to save us, suffered death, and then slew death, He Who for us mounted the cross. We all shall die, and wealth protects none, when the time comes, any more than it did Job.

Mes son intrat en lonc cossir
Cels qui son al derier escout,
C'a la mort no.s pot escremir
Coms ni reis ni ducs ni marquis;
E, s'enantz no.s nedeia totz
Que la mortz li serre lo vis,
Be si pot, si.s vol, trigar trop.

Totz jorns vos poiria legir,
Mas pregem cel qu'es caps e fis
Que.ns garde del enfernal potz,
E que.ns met'el sieu paradis,
Lay on mes Ysach e Jacop.

But now they are plunged in sombre thought who are at the last watch, for against death can neither count nor king, duke nor marquis, defend himself; and unless he wholly purifies himself, before death closes his eyes, then a man might well, if he so wills, delay too long.

I could preach to you for ever, but let us pray to Him Who is beginning and end, that He preserve us from the infernal pit and that He set us in His paradise, there where He set Isaac and Jacob.

Raimbaut d'Orange

LIFE. Born about the year 1144, Raimbaut, lord of Orange, of Courthezon, and of a patchwork of lesser feudal holdings in Provence and Languedoc, was a nobleman of some standing and the first known troubadour originating from Provence proper, although professional poets, such as those whom this brilliant amateur welcomed to his own court, were now beginning to include this region in their itineraries. Extant contemporary documents concerning Raimbaut—wills, records of acts of homage, etc.—tell us little of his public or private life. His parents died while he was still a minor, leaving him under the protection of the lords of Baux and Marseilles, themselves vassals of the counts of Toulouse and Barcelona respectively. In this position of dependence and, to judge from records of his financial transactions, in constant need of ready cash, he seems to have taken no active part in the political events of his day, apparently preferring to enjoy the pleasures and pastimes of court life, in peace and relative luxury. Unlike his predecessor, William IX of Aquitaine, Raimbaut had little chance to prove himself as anything more than a quick-witted, pleasure-loving and artistically talented young nobleman; he died suddenly, in 1173, perhaps a victim of the epidemic which swept across Europe in that year when, as one chronicler records, 'many people coughed out their souls'.

WORKS. Dating from the period *c.* 1162–1173, no less than thirty-nine poems by Raimbaut d'Orange—nearly all love-songs—have been conserved. This fact in itself speaks of the importance which he must have attributed to poetic composition and which tends, perhaps, to be obscured by the dominant quality of his work, best summarized as a playful virtuosity. Every major aspect of the established art of the *canso* is, at some time or another, subjected by him to ingenious modification, of which technical inventiveness and a humorous defiance of convention are the two most recurrent features. More than once, the most basic formal element of the *canso* is itself transformed, the lyric stanza breaking down, for example, into a mixture of verse and prose or giving way to an uninterrupted sequence of verse lines on the model of the mediaeval Latin epistle. Traditional *motifs* of courtly love are often taken as the starting points for elaborately formulated though essentially crude jests; on one occasion the orthodox purity of the poet's feelings is explained by the alleged loss of 'those (two) objects which a man holds most precious' while, on another, the answer to the lady's conventional cruelty is suggested to be a good punch on the nose. But most frequently of all, unoriginal thematic material is re-formulated in complex stanza-forms, intricate rime-schemes, or elaborate series of related images or word-games, in the construction of which Raimbaut clearly shares the artistic preoccupations common to many troubadours of the period. The formal structure of the love-song now undergoes a process of innovation and experiment from which emerges, possibly under the influence of mediaeval Latin literary theory, a concept of three levels or styles of composition, the 'closed' or difficult style, the rich, ornate style, and the clear, light or simple style. Raimbaut is without doubt one of the leading exponents of this concept, seeking perfection and pre-eminence, and inspired as much by a remarkably civilized form of aristocratic pride as by an artist's awareness that poetic creation can itself constitute a game, an adventure, a discovery of new modes of experience.

EDITION. W. T. Pattison *The Life and Works of the Troubadour Raimbaut d'Orange* (Minneapolis 1952).

SELECTION. Typical of much of Raimbaut's work, where the elaboration of one selected formal device largely determines the way in which conventional thematic material is exploited, is the first of the five selected pieces (Pattison nos. 39, 3, 27, 31, 16). Here, the successful maintenance of an extremely complex rime-scheme combining rare rime with grammatical rime, isolated rime with word-rime, must have constituted the main problem of composition. Also typical is the presence of such *motifs* as the lover's confusion bordering on madness, the evocation of urgent and undisguisedly sensual desire, and the notion that the deity plays a special rôle in the poet's love affairs. They all recur in the second poem in which it is again apparent that the choice and quality of the rimes lead the poet to devise a fair number of unusual and far-fetched images, while the regular use of parenthesis—presumably the *razon deviza* of which the poet himself forewarns us—creates a further measure of complexity. In the next poem, the listener's attention is caught and retained by an elaborate network of literary allusions where Raimbaut, as in other poems, is clearly jesting with the theme of adulterous love. The fourth poem, a *tenson* or stanza-by-stanza dialogue with the troubadour Giraut de Borneil,—who addresses him, for the occasion, by the name of a legendary and somewhat promiscuous lover—is largely devoted to a discussion of the respective merits of two poetic styles. Without any great insight or depth, and breaking off inconclusively, this discussion can nevertheless be said at least to touch on that problem of function and purpose which will remain fundamental to the poetic traditions of Western Europe. That Raimbaut's defence of the 'closed' style was inspired, however, by no permanent conviction is immediately apparent in the opening stanza of the last poem where the same general aristocratic outlook seems to motivate his adoption of the contrary style, the plain and simple one. As in several of Raimbaut's poems, complex rime-patterns, and the involved modes of expression which they entail, are replaced, as the distinctive structural feature, by a greater subtlety and variety of line-rhythm. The love-song takes on the light, skipping movements of the dance, bearing along without effort the direct, uncomplicated expression of established themes.

I. Ar resplan la flors enversa
Pels trencans rancx e pels tertres.
Cals flors? Neus, gels e conglapis
Que cotz e destrenh e trenca;
Don vey morz quils, critz, brays, siscles
En fuelhs, en rams e en giscles.
Mas mi ten vert e jauzen joys
Er quan vey secx los dolens croys.

Quar enaissi m'o enverse
Que bel plan mi semblon tertre,
E tenc per flor lo conglapi,
E.l cautz m'es vis que.l freit trenque,
E.l tro mi son chant e siscle.
E paro.m fulhat li giscle.
Aissi.m suy ferm lassatz en joy
Que re non vey que.m sīa croy . . .

Mas una gen fad'enversa
Cum s'eron noirit en tertres,
Que.m fan pro pieigz que conglapis,
Q'us quecx ab sa lengua trenca
E.n parla bas et ab siscles.
E no.y val bastos ni giscles
Ni menassas; ans lur es joys
Quan fan so don hom los clam croys.

Qu'ar en baizan no.us enverse
No m'o tolon pla ni tertre,
Dona, ni gel ni conglapi,
Mas non-poder trop en trenque.
Dona, per cuy chant e siscle,
Vostre belh huelh mi son giscle
Que'm castīon si.l cor ab joy
Qu'ieu no.us aus aver talan croy.

Anat ai cum cauz'enversa,
Sercan rancx e vals e tertres,
Marritz cum selh que conglapis
Cocha e mazelh'e trenca; *over*

I. Now is resplendent the inverted flower along the cutting crags and in the hills. What flower? Snow, ice, and frost which stings and hurts and cuts, and by which I see perished calls, cries, birdsongs and whistles among leaves, among branches and among switches; but joy keeps me green and jovial now, when I see dried up the wretched base ones.

For in such manner do I invert all this that hills seem to me fair plains, and I take the frost for blossom, and the warmth, it seems to me, cuts the cold, and thunderclaps are to me songs and whistles, and the switches appear to me decked with leaves. I am thus firmly bound in joy, for I see nothing which to me is base . . .

except a stupid people, inverted as though they'd been raised on the hills, who do me service worse than frost, for each one cuts with his tongue, and murmurs low and with whistles; and in this matter neither stick nor switch nor threats are of avail, rather it is for them joy when they do that for which one calls them base.

But now from inverting, in kissing, you, neither plains nor hills prevent me, lady, nor ice nor frost, but from it powerlessness cuts me off. Lady, for whom I sing and whistle, your lovely eyes are for me switches, which so chasten me with joy that for you I dare not have base desire.

I have gone like a thing inverted, searching crags and vales and hills, distressed like one whom frost torments and tortures and cuts,

Que no.m conquis chans ni siscles
Plus que folhs clercx conquer giscles.
Mas ar, Dieu lau, m'alberga joys
Malgrat dels fals lauzengiers croys.

Mos vers an, qu'aissi l'enverse
Que no.l tenhon bosc ni tertre,
Lai on hom non sen conglapi,
Ni a freitz poder que.y trenque.
A midons lo chant e.l siscle
Clar, qu'el cor l'en intro.l giscle,
Selh que sap gen chantar ab joy,
Que no tanh a chantador croy.

Doussa dona, amors e joys
Nos ajosten malgrat dels croys.

Jocglar, granren ai meynhs de joy,
Quar no.us vey, e.n fas semblan croy.

11.   Una chansoneta fera
Voluntiers, laner'a dir
Don tem que m'er a murir,
E far l'ai tal que sen sela.
Ben la poira leu entendre
Si tot s'es en aital rima;
Li mot seran descubert
Alques de razon deviza.

Bo.m sap car tan m'apodera
Mon cor, que non puesc sufrir
De mon talan descubrir;
C'ades puech a plena vela,
Qui que veya joy dissendre,
Per que no.y puesc nulh'escrima
Trobar, ans ai trop suffert,
De far parer ma conquiza.   *over*

so that neither song nor whistle had the better of me any more than switch has the better of unruly clerics. But now, God be praised, joy harbours me, despite the false base slanderers.

May my verse go, for I so invert it that neither woods nor hills might hinder it, to there where one feels no frost, where the cold has no power to cut. To my mistress may he sing and whistle it—clearly, that its switches enter her heart—who can sing nobly, with joy, for it befits no base singer.

Sweet lady, may love and joy join us despite the base ones.

Minstrel, I have much less joy, for I see you not, and thereby you seem base.

11. I would willingly make up a little song, simple to say, but of it I fear that I'll die; so I'll make it such that it conceals its sense. She indeed will be able to understand it easily, even though it's on this kind of rime; the things I say will be revealed somewhat incoherently.

I'm glad because she so overwhelms my heart that I cannot help revealing my desire; and now I soar on full sail, no matter who sees joy descending, because I can find no resistance—rather have I refrained too long—against letting my conquest appear.

Pus ma dona m'es tan vera,
Trop miels qu'ieu no.il sai grazir,
S'ieu quier als, tostems m'azir!
Dieus en ira.m met'ab ela,
O.m fassa que be.m tanh pendre
Per la gola d'una sima!
Pro m'a dat; sol lieys no pert,
Dieus m'a pagat a ma guiza.

Ben saup lo mel de la cera
Trīar, e.l miels devezir,
Lo jorn que.m fes lieys ayzir,
Pus, cazen clardat d'estela,
Sa par no.s fay ad contendre
Beutatz d'autra, si be.s lima,
Ni aya cor tan asert
De be s'aribar en Piza.

Domna, can mi colc al sera,
La nueyt, et tot jorn, cossir
Co.us pogues en grat servir.
Cant ieu.m pes, qui.m fer ni.m pela
No.m pot far en als entendre;
Mos cors de gaug salh e guima
Tan ay en vos mon cor sert,
E ma voluntat assiza.

Domna, si no.us alezera
Mos cors, lay on ieu dezir,
Res plus tost no.m pot aucir.
Si.m tarza, pensatz de tela
Al cor c'om no.s pot defendre!
Que.l vida m'es aytan prima,
Soven ai gaug e m'espert
E.m pes: 'Mala l'ai conquiza'.

Doncx, c'ay fag tan long'espera
Que aysi.m degues murir?
Mas un jorn m'es vis que.m tir
Un an; lo pretz d'una mela
Non tenc si no.m pot car vendre!

over

Since my lady is to me so true, far more than I can thank her for, if I seek anything else may she hate me always! May God set me in discord with her, or have me obliged to hang myself by the neck from a tree-top! Much has He given me; provided I don't lose her, God has rewarded me in the way I want.

Well knew He how to separate honey from wax and single out the best, the day when He had her created for me, since by falling starlight no other woman's beauty can rival hers, no matter how polished it be, and no matter how firm her heart be set on arriving safely at Pisa.

Lady, when I lie down in the evening, all night, and all day, I consider how I might serve you to your pleasure. When I thus ponder, then if someone beats me or pulls out my hair he could not make me turn my thoughts elsewhere. My body leaps and bounds for joy, so much is my heart set on you, and my will fixed.

Lady, if my person were not to make you happy there where I desire, nothing can slay me more swiftly. If there's delay, think how a man cannot save himself from cobwebs in the heart! For my life is so finely balanced that often I've joy, and then I despair and think to myself 'To my loss have I won her'.

Why then have I hoped so long, if now I should have to die? But one day seems to me to drag on for a year, and I'm not worth an almond if I cannot sell myself dearly!

Dreitz! per que mos cors m'ensima
C'ades m'estai l'uelh ubert
Vas sela part on l'ay viza.

Deu prec tan de mort m'escrima,
Donna, e m'aia suffert
Tro qu'ie.us embraz ses chamiza.

Qui trob'amor ses escrima,
Ja non deu planher si pert
Domna qu'es vayra ni griza.

III. Non chant per auzel ni per flor
    Ni per neu ni per gelada,
    Ni neis per freich ni per calor,
    Ni per reverdir de prada;
    Ni per nuill autr'esbaudimen
    Non chan, ni non fui chantaire,
    Mas per midonz en cui m'enten,
    Car es del mon la bellaire.

topoi now 'denied' as a means of giving prominence to the mistress

    Ar sui partitz de la pejor
    C'anc fos vista ni trobada,
    Et am del mon la bellazor
    Dompna, e la plus prezada.
    E farai ho al mieu viven,
    Que d'alres non sui amaire;
    Car ieu crei qu'ill a bon talen
    Ves mi, segon mon vejaire.

    Ben aurai, dompna, grand honor
    Si ja de vos m'es jutgada
    Honranssa que sotz cobertor
    Vos tenga nud'embrassada;
    Car vos valetz las meillors cen,
    Qu'ieu non sui sobregabaire.
    Sol del pretz ai mon cor gauzen
    Plus que s'era emperaire!

over

Right! and for this is my heart exalted, that already I stand gazing towards that place where I once saw her.

To God I pray to defend me so from death and, lady, to have suffered me to live, until I hold you, shirtless, in my arms.

Who finds love without resistance should never complain if he loses a lady who is of changing colour or grey.

III. I sing not for bird or flower, not for snow or for ice and not even for cold or for warmth, nor for the meadow's growing green again; and for no other pleasure do I sing, nor have I ever sung, but for my mistress for whom I long, because she is the most lovely in the world.

Now am I parted from the worst that ever was seen or found, and love the fairest lady in the world, and the most esteemed. And this I'll do all my life long for I'm in love with no other, and I believe that she is well-disposed towards me, so it seems to me.

I shall indeed, lady, have great honour if ever the privilege is adjudged me by you of holding you under the cover, naked in my arms, for you are worth the hundred best together, and in this praise I'm not exaggerating; in that merit alone does my heart rejoice more than if I were emperor.

De midonz fatz dompn'e seignor,
Cals que sïa.il destinada,
Car ieu begui de la amor,
Que ja.us dei amar, celada.
Tristan, qan la.il det Yseus gen,
La bela, no.n saup als faire,
Et ieu am per aital coven
Midonz, don no.m posc estraire.

Sobre totz aurai gran valor
S'aitals camisa m'es dada
Cum Yseus det a l'amador,
Que mais non era portada.
Tristan, mout presetz gent presen:
D'aital sui eu enquistaire.
Si.l me dona cill cui m'enten,
No.us port enveja, bels fraire!

Vejatz, dompna, cum Dieus acor
Dompna que d'amar s'agrada:
Q'Iseutz estet en gran päor,
Puois fon breumens conseillada
Qu'il fetz a son marit crezen
C'anc hom que nasques de maire
Non toques en lieis: mantenen
Atrestal podetz vos faire!

ironic use of Tristan myth.

Carestïa, esgauzimen
M'aporta d'aicel repaire
On es midonz qe.m ten gauzen
Plus q'ieu eis non sai retraire.

IV. Ara.m platz, Giraut de Borneill,
Que sapcha per c'anatz blasman
Trobar clus, ni per cal semblan.
Aiso.m digaz
Si tan prezatz
So que es a toz comunal;
Car adonc tut seran egual.

over

My mistress I make my lord and lady, whatever may be the outcome, because I drank of that secret love, so that I must ever love you. Tristan, when noble Iseult, the fair, granted it him, could not do otherwise, and I love by just a such bond my mistress, from it I cannot escape.

Above all men will I have great worth if such a nightdress is given me as Iseult gave to her lover, for it was never worn again. Tristan, you prized much the noble gift: for such a one am I seeking. If she for whom I long gives it me, I bear you no envy, fair brother!

See, lady, how God helps the lady who takes pleasure in loving: for Iseult stood in great fear, then in a moment she was advised and so made her husband believe that no man born of mother had ever laid hands on her. Now you can do the very same thing!

Carestia, bring me some enjoyment from that dwelling where my mistress is who keeps me more joyful than I myself can tell.

IV. Now I'd like, Giraut de Borneil, to know why you go blaming the 'closed' style, and on what grounds. Tell me this, if you prize so much that which is common to all; because all then will be equal.

Seign'En Lignaura, no.m coreill
Si qecs s'i trob'a son talan.
Mas eu son jujaire d'aitan
Qu'es mais amatz
E plus prezatz
Qui.l fa levet e venarsal;
E vos no m'o tornetz a mal.

Giraut, non voill qu'en tal trepeil
Torn mos trobars. Que ja ogan
Lo lauzo.l bon, e.l pauc e.l gran:
Ja per los fatz
Non er lauzatz,
Car non conoisson, ni lor cal,
So que plus car es ni mais val.

Lingnaura, si per aiso veil
Ni mon sojorn torn en affan,
Sembla que.m dopte del mazan.
A que trobatz
Si non vos platz
C'ades o sapchon tal e cal?
Que chanz non port'altre cabtal.

Giraut, sol que.l miels appareil
E.l dig'ades e.l trag'enan,
Mi non cal sitot non s'espan,
C'anc granz viutaz
Non fon denhtatz;
Per so prez'om mais aur que sal,
E de tot chant es atretal.

Lingnaura, fort de bon conseill
Es fis amans contrariān!
E pero si.m val mais d'affan
Mos sos levatz,
C'us enraumatz
Lo.m deissazec e.l diga mal!
Que no.l deing ad home sesal.   *over*

My lord Sir Lignaura, I don't complain if each writes to his liking. But this far I judge, that he is liked more and more esteemed who does so plainly and simply; and don't you take me wrong in this.

Giraut, I don't want my writing to turn into such a jumble. Let henceforth the good ever praise it, both humble and mighty; never by fools will it be praised, for they're not aware of, nor are they concerned by what is most precious and is worth most.

Lignaura, if on that score I lie awake and turn my pleasure into effort, it seems that I fear general acclaim. Wherefore do you write, if you're not pleased that straightway each and every one should know it? For song brings no other success.

Giraut, only provided that I prepare what's best, express it there and then, and bring it forth, I'm not concerned if it's not spread far and wide, for a thing of great cheapness was never a dainty morsel; that's why one prizes gold more than salt, and with any song it's just the same.

Lignaura, of right good advice is the argumentative noble lover! And yet if my piping tune costs me any more effort, then let some croaker garble and sing it badly! for I deem it not fit for a man of property.

Giraut, per cel ni per soleil,
Ni per la clardat que resplan,
Non sai de que.ns anam parlan,
Ni don fui natz,
Si soi torbatz.
Tan pes d'un fin joi natural:
Can d'als cossir, no m'es coral.

Lingnaura, si.m gira.l vermeil
De l'escut cella cui reblan,
Qu'eu voill dir: 'A Deu mi coman!'
C'als fols pensatz
Outracuidatz
M'a mes doptanza deslīal.
No.m soven com me fes comtal?

Giraut, greu m'es, per San Marsal,
Car vos n'anatz de sai Nadal.

Lingnaura, que ves cort rīal
M'en vauc ades, ric' e cabal.

V. Pos trobars plans
Es volguz tan,
Fort m'er greu s'i non son sobrans;
Car ben pareis
※ Qi tals motz fai
C'anc mais non foron dig cantan,
Qe cels c'om tot jorn ditz e brai
Sapcha, si.s vol, autra vez dir.

Mos ditz es sans,
Don gap, ses dan.
Per tal joi soi coindes e vans
Qe mais val neis
Desirs q'ieu n'ai
D'una qe anc no.m ac semblan,
Pels sainz c'om qer en Verzelai,
D'autre joi c'om puesca jauzir.   *over*

Giraut, by the sky and the sun, and by the light that shines, I know not what we're talking about, nor of whom I was born, I am so troubled. I think so much on a fine and natural joy: when I consider aught else, it comes not from the heart.

Lignaura, she whom I woo so turns towards me the scarlet side of the shield that I want to say: 'God save me!'. For in foolish overweening thoughts disloyal doubt has plunged me. Do I not remember how she ennobled me?

Giraut, it grieves me, by Saint Martial, for you're going away. this side of Christmas.

Lignaura, but to a royal court I go now, great and mighty.

V. Since the plain style is in such demand, it will be very hard for me if I don't excel in it; for it seems right that he who composes such words as were never before spoken in song should be able, if he so wishes, to say at another time those which are said and sung every day.

My speech is sound, of that I boast, and flawless. On account of such joy am I gay and lightheaded that even the desire which I have of it from one who never showed me favour is worth more, by the saints one seeks at Vézelay, than any other joy in which one could rejoice.

Son ben aurans,
Car per talan
Solamen, so francs et humans,
De dir ves leis
Ben, ni.m fas gai.
Qe.m val si per lieis trag mal gran?
Si lo mal q'en trac no sap lai,
Mi eis voil d'aitan escarnir.

Ben so trafans
Q'eu eis m'engan.
Car dic aiso tan que vilans.
Cals pros me creis
Si eu mal trai
Per leis, s'il no sapia l'afan?
No m'es doncs pro, e be no.m vai,
Si.m pens qe tan ric joi desir?

Mos volers cans
Qe.m sal denan
Me fai creire qe futz es pans,
Tan aut m'espeis
Mon cor, car sai
Q'enfol; m'aurei donc faz l'efan?
Tot voll cant vei. Respeit segrai.
Respeitz loncs fai omen perir.

Sains Julïans!
Con vauc torban!
Soi serrazis o crestïans?
Qals es ma leis?
Non sai. Qe jai
Me posca, de so qe.il deman,
Et atrestan tost, Dieus, si.l plai,
Co fes vin d'aig'esdevenir!

Pauc soi certans,
Ves qe.us reblan!
Domna, de vos so molt londans.   *over*

I'm indeed mad, for through desire alone to speak well about her I am noble and kind, and become gay. What does it avail me if I suffer for her great pain? Inasmuch as she knows not, there, the pain which I suffer, I'm making a fool of myself.

Indeed I'm treacherous, for I betray myself in saying that just like a churl. What good comes to me if I suffer pain for her and she knew not the anguish? Isn't it then good, and doesn't it go well for me, just to think that I desire such splendid joy?

My burning desire which leaps on ahead of me makes me believe that wood is bread. I'm so deeply befuddled, for I know that I'm going mad; will I then have acted like a child? I want all that I see. I'll keep to my expectation. Long expectation causes a man to perish.

Saint Julian! How troubled I go! Am I Saracen or Christian? What is my faith? I know not. May God, if it please Him, make joy come to me from that which I ask of her, and as quickly as He made wine come from water!

I'm not at all sure of myself; see how I woo you! Lady, I'm very far from you.

Anc no.m destreis
Amors tan mai,
Per q'ieu non creirïa d'un an
C'aissi.us ames, per negun plai,
Si bes no m'en degues venir.

Astrius e ma chanso vos man
Qe dos sautz si rics ar essai;
Lo ters aut on plus pot om dir.

Never before did love distress me so much for I'd not believe in a year that thus I would love you, not on any condition, unless good should come to me from it.

I send you Astrius and my song, so I now try two fine leaps; the third (is) as high as one can possibly say.

Giraut de Borneil

LIFE. Like Bernard de Ventadour, his senior by some twenty years or so, Giraut de Borneil was a professional troubadour, of humble birth, and a native of the Limousin region. Occasional allusions in his work indicate that in the course of his career—which extended from c. 1165 to c. 1200—he visited all the great courts of southern France and northern Spain where the troubadour lyric found favour. While there is no evidence that he spent any length of time at any of these, it does seem most likely that he enjoyed throughout his career the patronage of Adémar v, viscount of Limoges (1138–1199), his immediate overlord and close contemporary. It is normal that he should have begun his career at the local court, it is likely that when, as again indicated in certain of his own compositions, he took part in the Crusade of 1189, it was in the company of the viscount, and his latest dateable poem is a lament on Adémar's death in which Giraut clearly suggests that he had long enjoyed his favour and protection. How long the poet survived him is not known; if, as all the indications suggest, he was born in the mid-1140s, he is not likely to have seen much of the thirteenth century.

WORKS. Giraut's mediaeval biographer affirms that the poet was known in his lifetime and, among the connoisseurs, for long after his death, as the 'maestre dels trobadors' and few modern critics would question his claim to this title. Only one or two troubadours ever produced more than the seventy-six poems now attributed to him, and none equalled his rich variety of structure and style. Both in his forty love-songs and in his thirty or so *sirventès*, Giraut was faced with the constant task of renewing the formulation of thematic material which, since the great poets of the mid-twelfth century, had become fixed by cultural tradition and literary convention. As already apparent in the work of such poets as Peire d'Auvergne and Raimbaut d'Orange, the problems of style and expression had now become dominant. Giraut owes his reputation to the professional mastery with which he solved them. Though he states more than once his approval of the complexities of the *trobar clus*, he yet avoided the extreme manifestations of purely formal virtuosity affected by certain of his contemporaries. His own abilities are more consistently and impressively revealed both in the stylistic richness and structural coherence of the *trobar ric* and in the ease and lightness of rhythm and expression characteristic of the *trobar leu*. Giraut not only took a leading part in the elaboration of these styles; he developed them to their highest point of perfection.

EDITION. A. Kolsen *Sämtliche Lieder des Trobadors Giraut de Borneil*, (2 Vols. Halle 1910–35).

SELECTION. The first poem (Kolsen no. 4) is devoted to what might be called the problem of communication. The ideal of clarity and simplicity—of total communication—proposed in the opening stanzas characterizes the general position adopted by Giraut in the contemporary discussion of poetic ends and means; the conventional dilemma described in the following stanzas is, however, saved from banality only by its association with this more immediate, professional concern. Purely conventional too is the thematic material of the second poem (Kolsen no. 6); it might indeed be considered as a résumé of the principal themes and *motifs* of the courtly love-song, but Giraut has made of it a particularly impressive work, at once highly abstract and deeply intense, intangible yet obsessive—in short, a successful realization of the very essence of the ideal of courtly love. The next three poems (Kolsen nos. 12, 15, 2) are, like the first two, love-songs, and all show how, by the sustained elaboration of one selected device, the poet varies the form and structure of the *canso* in order to revitalize the stock themes with colour, drama, and movement. The sixth poem (Kolsen no. 65) is a moral *sirventès*, and the contrast between the good old days and present troubled times is sketched out with the exaggeration essential to the genre. It is interesting to note, however, that its distinctive qualities led Dante, in his *De Vulgari Eloquentia*, to propose Giraut as the model poet of moral rectitude. The Dalfis of the envoy is surely Dauphin d'Auvergne, count of Clermont and Montferrand, an eminent patron of the troubadours in the late twelfth and early thirteenth centuries; but whether the episode evoked in the last stanza had any grounding in reality is an unsolved and doubtless unsolvable question. The seventh poem, finally (Kolsen no. 54), adapted by Giraut from what is thought to be the folk-song form of the *alba* or dawn-song, is generally considered one of the most perfect compositions in the whole *corpus* of troubadour poetry. The technical skill and the poetic sensitivity with which the conventions of two quite separate literary traditions have been combined are immediately perceptible, rendering all comment superfluous. It is indeed a masterpiece by this the 'maestre dels trobadors'.

I. A penas sai comensar
    Un vers que volh far leuger,
    E si n'ai pensat des er
    Que.l fezes de tal razo
    Que l'entenda tota gens
    E qu'el fass'a leu chantar;
    Qu'eu.l fatz per pla deportar.

    Be.l saupra plus cobert far,
    Mas non a chans pretz enter   trobar leu
    Can tuch no.n son parsoner.
    Qui que.s n'azir, me sap bo
    Can auch dire per contens
    Mo sonet, rauquet e clar,
    E l'auch a la fon portar.

    Ja, pos volrai clus trobar,
    No cut aver man parer—
    Ab so que ben ai mester
    A far una leu chanso;
    Qu'eu cut c'atretan grans sens
    Es, qui sap razo gardar,
    Co mes motz entrebeschar.

    D'als m'aven a consirar,
    Qu'eu am tal que non enquer,
    Per so car del consirer
    Sai be que fatz mesprezo.
    Que farai? C'us ardimens
    Me ve qu'eu l'an razonar,
    E päors fai m'o laissar.

    Be lo.i volrīa mandar,
    Si trobava messatger;
    Mas si.n fatz altrui parler
    Eu tem qu'ilh me n'ochaizo,
    Car non es ensenhamens
    C'om ja fass'altrui parlar
    D'aisso que sols vol celar.   *over*

1. I hardly know how to begin a poem which I want to make light and easy, though I've been thinking about it since yesterday, how I might compose it on such lines that all people may understand it and that it may be easy to sing; for I'm composing it purely for pleasure.

   I could easily make it more obscure, but a song's merit is not complete when all are not partners in it. No matter who's irked by it, I'm glad when I hear my little song sung in contention, rough or clear, and I hear it borne to the public fountain.

   Never, should I wish to write in the 'closed' style, do I think I'd have much company—apart from the fact that I've need enough to compose an easy song; for I think that it's just as much good sense, if one can keep to the point, as to twist my words round each other.

   It behoves me to think on something else, for I love such a one to whom I make no entreaty, because in the thinking itself I know that I'm at fault. What shall I do? for a bold urge comes to me that I should go and plead with her, then fear makes me renounce it.

   I would indeed like to convey this to her, if I found a messenger; but if I make someone else my spokesman I fear that she'll blame me for it, since it's not wise for a man ever to have someone else speak of that which he, on his own, would conceal.

Tan be.m sap lo cor comtar
La beltat e.l pretz sobrer,
Que gran batalha.n sofer
Car no.i vauc ad espero.
Pois m'en ven us espavens
Que m'en fai dezacordar
E mon ardimen baissar.

Ges no la posc oblidar,
Tan me fai gran dezirer;
E volh peitz c'a mo guerrer
Celui que d'als me somo;
Car lai es mos pensamens,
E melhs no.m pot solassar,
Sol que.m lais de leis pensar.

Consirers m'en es guirens
C'anc re tan no.m poc amar,
Pos la vi, ni tener char.

11. Amars, onrars, e char-teners
Umiliars et obezirs,
Loncs merceiars e loncs grazirs,
Long'atendens'e loncs espers
Me degron far viur'ad onor,
S'eu fos astrucs de bo senhor.
Mas car no.m vir ni no.m bïais,
No vol Amors qu'eu sïa gais.

Pero mos sens e mos sabers,
E mos parlars e mos be-dirs,
Mos esperars e mos sofrirs,
E mos celars e mos temers
M'agron totztems onrat d'amor,
S'eu perchasses mo ben alhor.
Mas cilh que.m ten en greu pantais
No vol qu'eu l'am, ni que m'en lais.

over

So well can my heart recount to me her beauty and her sovereign merit, that I endure great strife in not spurring on towards her. Then from that a terror befalls me which makes me change my mind and abate my boldness.

In no way can I forget her, she inspires me with such great desire, and I wish more ill than on my sworn enemy on him who tempts me with anything else; for in that direction is all my thought, and he cannot better entertain me than in simply letting me think of her.

Of that, thought itself is my assurance, for I could never love anything so much, since I saw her, or hold so dear.

II. Loving, honouring and cherishing, acting humbly and obeying, long crying mercy and long seeking to please, long expectation and long hope ought to cause me to live in honour, if I had been blessed with a good liege lord. But, since I veer not nor waver, Love wants not that I should be gay.

Yet my sense and my knowledge, my speech and my eloquence, my hoping and my enduring, and my concealing and my fearing would at all times have honoured me with love, had I saught my good elsewhere. But she who keeps me in grievous torment wants not that I love her, nor that I quit her.

E si.lh plagues mos enquerers,
Ni mos preiars ni mos servirs,
Ja.l trop velhars ni.l paucs dormirs,
Ni.lh mal qu'eu trac matis e sers
No.m pogron ja partir de lor.
Ans m'agra Jois per servidor
E ja no.m fora greus lo fais
Ni.l mals c'al cor me brolh'e.m nais.

Per qu'eu conosc e sai qu'es vers
Que viure.m val menhs que morirs?
Pos que.lh sofranh jois e jauzirs,
E.m falh Amors e sos poders.
Per qu'eu sospir e planh e plor?
Car Jois no.m val ni no.m socor;
Qu'eu sui aquel c'am melhs e mais
E no manei, ni tenh, ni bais.

Era.m combat sobre-volers,
E sobr'amars e loncs dezirs;
E fa.m chassar sobr'enardirs
E foleiars e no-devers
So que no tanh a ma valor.
E s'eu volh trop per ma folor,
Mos sens en par alques savais,
Mas eu remanh fis e verais.

Car ma semblans'e mos parers,
E mos cudars e mos albirs
M'an dich totztems c'altr'enriquirs,
Ni altr'onors ni altr'avers,
No.m podon dar tan de ricor
Com cilh que.m fai viur'ab langor;
C'on plus languisc e dezengrais,
Cut et aten c'a me s'abais.

Domna valens, vostra valor
E vostre pretz e vostr'onor
Poiatz totztems e valetz mais,
Per qu'eu vos sui fis e verais.

And if my wooing pleased her, and my praying and my serving, then neither the wakefulness nor the sleeplessness, nor the pains which I bear morn and evening could ever make me renounce them. Joy, rather, would have me its servant and the burden would never be grievous, nor the pain which in my heart buds and is born.

How do I realize and know it to be true that living is worth less to me than dying? Because it lacks joy and enjoyment, and Love fails me, and its power. Why do I sigh and lament and weep? Because Joy avails me not, nor helps me; for I am he who loves best and the most, yet I caress not, nor hold in my arms, nor kiss.

Now over-wanting assails me, and over-loving and long desire; and overboldness and folly and unseemliness make me pursue that which befits not my worth. And if I want too much, in my folly, my sense appears somewhat paltry, but I remain noble and true.

Since what seems and what appears to me, what I believe and what I judge have always told me that other enrichment, other honour or other possession cannot give me as much wealth as she who makes me live in languor, then the more I languish and pine away, (the more) I believe and expect that she will condescend to me.

Worthy lady, your worth and your merit and your honour you always enhance and increase in worth, wherefore I am to you noble and true.

III. Can lo glatz e.l frechs e la neus
S'en vai, e torna la chalors,
E reverdiz lo pascors,
Et auch las voltas dels auzeus,
M'es aitan beus
Lo dolz tems a l'issen de martz
Que plus sui salhens que leupartz,
E vils non es chabrols ni cers.
Si la bela cui sui profers
Me vol onrar
D'aitan que.m denhe sofertar
Qu'eu sia sos fis entendens,
Sobre totz sui rics e manens.

Tan es sos cors gais et isneus
E complitz de belas colors,
C'anc de rozeus no nasquet flors
Plus frescha, ni d'altres brondeus;
Ni anc Bordeus
Non ac senhor fos plus galhartz
De me, si n.era coltz ni partz
Tan que fos sos dominis sers.
E fos apelatz de Bezers
Can ja parlar
M'auziri'om de nulh celar
Qu'ela.m disses, celadamens,
Don s'aires lo seus cors gens.

Bona domna, lo vostr'aneus
Que.m donetz me fai gran socors,
Qu'en lui refranhi mas dolors,
E, can lo remir, sui plus leus
C'us estorneus;
E sui per vos aissi auzartz
Que no tem que lansa ni dartz
Me tenha dan, n'acers ni fers.
E d'altra part sui plus despers,
Per sobr'amar,
Que naus can vai torban per mar,
Destrecha d'ondas e de vens,
Tan me destreing lo pensamens.

over

III. When the ice and the cold and the snow go away, and the warmth returns and once more it is green Eastertide, and I hear the warblings of the birds, then the sweet time at the end of March so pleases me that I'm more lively than leopard, and neither roebuck nor stag is so nimble. If the fair one to whom I am devoted is willing to honour me so far as to deign to suffer me to be her noble suitor, then above all men am I rich and wealthy.

She is in her person so gay and lively and perfect with lovely hues, that never from rose-bush was flower born more fair, nor from any others; and never had Bordeaux a merrier lord than me, if I were allowed by her and permitted so much as to be her own liege man. And I would be called (a fool) from Béziers if ever one heard me talk of a secret which she had told me, secretly; by this would her noble self be vexed.

Good lady, that ring of yours which you gave me is of great comfort to me, for by it I soothe my sorrows and, when I gaze on it, I'm sprightlier than a starling; and I am for you so bold that I fear not that lance or spear might harm me, nor steel nor iron. Yet, on the other hand, I founder more through over-loving than a ship when it goes tossing on the sea, assailed by waves and winds, so much does deep thought assail me.

Domna, aissi cum us chasteus
Qu'es assetjatz per fortz senhors,
Can la peirer'abat las tors,
E.ls chalabres e.ls manganeus,
Et es tan greus
La guerra devas totas partz
Que no lor te pro genhs ni artz,
E.l dols e.l critz es aitan fers
De cels dedins quez an grans gers,
Sembla.us ni.us par
Que lor ai'obs merce clamar?
Aissi.us clam merce umilmens,
Bona domna, pros e valens.

Domna, aissi com us anheus
Non a forsa contr'ad un ors,
Sui eu, si la vostra valors
No.m val, plus frevols c'us rauzeus,
Et er plus breus
Ma vida, que de cartel chartz
S'oimais me pren negus destartz
Que no.m fassatz drech de l'envers.
Et tu, fin'Amors, que.m sofers,
Que deus garar
Los fis amans de foleiar,
Sïas me chabdeus e guirens
A ma domna, pos aissi.m vens!

Joglars, ab aquestz sos noveus
T'en vai, e.ls portaras de cors
A la bela cui nais ricors;
E digas li qu'eu sui plus seus
Que sos manteus!

Giraut de Borneil

Lady, as when a castle is besieged by grim barons, when the siege-engine topples the towers—and the catapult and the mangonel—and the onslaught is so fierce from every side that neither cunning nor guile avails them, and the suffering and the cries are so terrible of those within who are in great anguish, does it not seem and appear to you that there's need for them to cry mercy? In the same way I humbly cry mercy of you, good lady, noble and worthy.

Lady, as a lamb has no power against a bear, so am I, if your worthiness avails me not, more feeble than a reed; and my life will be shorter for it shrinks by a fourth whenever harm befalls me through your not righting for me what's wrong. And you, noble love, who sustain me, who should protect noble lovers from folly, be you my guide and protector with my lady, since she so overwhelms me.

Minstrel, with these new tunes be off, and you'll bear them swiftly to the fair one in whom greatness is born; and tell her that I am more hers than her own mantle!

IV. Amors,
   E si.m clam de vos,
   Sera.us onors?
   No, per ma fe,
   Car no.s conve,
   Desqu'en vostra mantenensa
   M'aviatz,
   Qu'era.m gecatz;
   Ans pensatz
   Com cela.m volha
   Cui eu volh!

   S'acors
   No.m fai, ve.us me jos!
   C'una dolors,
   Que.m sobreve,
   Me vira.l fre
   Vas leis, si noca l'agensa
   C'om que.lh platz
   Sïa chazatz.
   N'ai? Si.m fatz:
   Can que m'acolha,
   Pro m'acolh.

   Folors
   Fo ma sospeissos,
   C'a trop melhors
   No sofre re
   Cudar de se;
   Be fatz doncs fol'atendensa?
   Trop vïatz
   Me sui chamjatz!
   No.n dïatz
   Qu'ela.s me tolha,
   Qu'eu la.m tolh.

   Pluzors
   Vetz sui consiros
   E.m pren päors
   Qu'en pert l'ale,

over

IV. Love, suppose then I complain of you, will it be to your honour? No, by my faith, because it is not fitting, once you held me in your sway, that you should now reject me; think, rather, on how she might want me whom I want.

If she makes no peace with me, lo! I am lost; for a pain which comes over me turns my steps towards her, though it agrees with her not that a man who pleases her should receive reward. Do I have any? Indeed I do: to whatever extent she accepts me, she accepts me well enough.

A foolish thing was my presumption, for she forbids far better men to expect anything of her; do I indeed then nourish vain hope? I've changed my mind too quickly! Say not that she betakes herself from me; I take her from myself.

Many times am I plunged in thought and fear grips me that I'll stop breathing,

Can me sove
C'a me falh; e me comensa
Frevoltatz,
Que.m tolh solatz.
Grans pechatz
Er qu'eu me dolha,
S'en me dolh.

E sors
Anc res que jois fos
Leu, ni de cors?
Egal ab me,
Qu'era.m n'ave,
En esmai etz en parvensa,
C'oblidatz
M'er söans fatz!
N'er intratz,
Ans que.l rams folha
Port, e.s folh?

Era, can sui en Pröensa,
Vau mesclatz
Entr'ir' e patz;
E sapchatz
Del joi qu'i brolha
Quez eu brolh.

V.   Ailas, com mor!—Quez as, amis?—
Eu sui traïs!—
Per cal razo?—
Car anc jorn mis m'ententio
En leis que.m fetz lo bel parven.—
Et as per so to cor dolen?—
Si ai.—
As enaissi to cor en lai?—
Oc eu, plus fort.—
Est donc aissi pres de la mort?—
Oc eu, plus fort que no.us sai dir.—
Per que.t laissas aissi morir?—   *over*

when I recall how she fails me; and there is born in me a weakness which robs me of comfort. A great sin will it be that I should grieve, if for her I grieve.

Yet did there ever arise a thing of joy, easily and promptly? Like me then, for now it so befalls me, you are, it appears, in dismay, so that silly scorn for me will be forgotten. Will that be started before the branch bears leaf and is leafy?

Now, when I'm in Provence, I go torn between grief and peace; yet know that, with the joy which here bursts into flower, I burst into flower.

V. Alas, how I die!—What's wrong, my friend?—I am betrayed! —For what reason?—Because I once set my mind on her who showed me a sign of favour.—And it's for this that your heart is grieving?—Indeed yes.—And your heart is so set on her?— It is, to the utmost.—And are you thus at death's door?—I am, more than I can tell you.—Why do you thus submit to death?

Car sui trop vergonhos e fis.—
No l'as re quis? -
Eu, per Deu, no!—
E per que menas tal tenso
Tro aias saubut so talen?—
Senher, fai me tal espaven.—
Que.l fai?—
S'amors que.m ten en greu esmai.—
Be n'as gran tort;
Cudas te qu'ela t'o aport?—
Eu no, mas no.m n'aus enardir.—
Trop poiras tu to dan sofrir.

Senher, e cals conselhs n'er pres?—
Bos e cortes.—
Er lo.m dïatz!—
Tu venras denan leis vïatz
Et enquerras la de s'amor.—
E si s'o ten a dezonor?—
No.t chal!—
E s'ela.m respon lach ni mal?—
Sïas sofrens,
Que totztems bos sofrire vens.—
E si.s n'apercep lo gilos?—
Adonc n'obraretz plus ginhos.—

Nos?—Oc be.—Sol qu'ilh o volgues!—
Er.—Que?—Si.m cres.—
Crezutz sïatz!—
Be te sera tos jois doblatz,
Sol lo dichs no.t fassa päor.—
Senher, tan senti la dolor
Mortal,
Per qu'es ops c'o partam egal.—
Er donc tos sens
Que te valh'e tos ardimens.—
Oc, e ma bona sospeissos.—
Garda te que gen t'i razos!— *over*

Giraut de Borneil

Because I am too shy and noble-minded.—You have asked nothing of her?—No, in God's name, not I!—Then why do you carry on this self-torture before you've known what she feels?—My lord, it inspires in me such terror.—What does?—Her love, for which I'm in great dismay.—You're very wrong in this; do you suppose that she'd bring it to you?—No, but I daren't bid boldly for it.—You could suffer your greatest harm.

My lord, what decision is then to be taken?—A good and courtly one.—Now tell it me!—You shall hasten to her presence and ask her for her love.—And if she takes it as a dishonour?—Don't worry!—And if she makes me a cruel and angry answer?—Be patient, for loyal patience always wins through.—And if the jealous one gets to know about it?—Then you'll both proceed more surreptitiously.—

Both?—Yes of course.—If only she wanted it so!—It will be—How?—If you trust me.—Then have my trust!—Your joy will indeed be doubled, provided you be not afraid to speak up.—My lord, I feel the pain so mortal that we must needs share it equally.—Now may your sense serve you, and your ardour!—Yes, and my good hope.—Take care that you plead your case finely!—

Razonar no.m sabrai ja be.—
Dïas, per que?—
Per leis gardar.—
No.n sabras donc ab leis parlar?
Est aissi del tot esperdutz?—
Oc, can li sui denan vengutz . . .—
T'espertz?—
Oc eu, que no sui de re certz.—
Aital fan tuch
Cilh que son per amor perduch.—
Oc, mas eu forsarai mo cor!—
Era non o torns en demor!—

Be m'a aduch
Amors a so, que sabon tuch
Que mal viu qui deziran mor,
Per qu'eu no sai planher mo cor.—

Vas to desduch
Vai, amics, ans c'o sapchon tuch,
Per que no perdas to resor;
Que levet pert om so demor.

VI. Per solatz revelhar
    Que s'es trop endormitz,
    E per pretz, qu'es faiditz,
    Acolhir e tornar,
    Me cudei trebalhar.
    Mas er m'en sui gequitz;
    Per so m'en sui falhitz
    Car non es d'achabar,
    C'on plus m'en ve volontatz e talans,
    Plus creis, de lai, lo destorbers e.l dans.

    Greu es de sofertar;
    A vos o dic c'auzitz
    Com era jois grazitz
    E tuch li benestar.

over

I'll never be able to plead well.—Say now, why?—Out of respect for her.—So you'll not then be able to talk with her? Are you thus so completely at a loss?—Yes, when I'm come before her . . .—You're at a loss?—I am indeed, so that I'm sure of nothing.—All those do so who are through love forlorn.—Yes, but I'll force my heart!—Now don't put it off any longer!—

Love indeed has brought me to this, for all know that he lives ill who dies of desire, wherefore I cannot grieve for my heart.—

Towards your pleasure go, my friend, before all know of it, so that you lose not your resolve; for it's easy to lose what one delays.

VI. To arouse noble pleasure which has fallen sound asleep, and to welcome and bring back merit which is banished, I thought to set to work. But now I've abandoned it; for this have I quit, that it cannot be made to succeed, and the more I have the will and desire for it, the greater, on the other hand, grows the trouble and harm.

It's hard to endure; to you I say it who have heard how joy was once approved, and all that pertained thereto.

Mais no podetz jurar
Qu'egas de fust no vitz,
Ni vilas, velhs, fronitz,
Esters grat chavalgar.
Lachs es l'afars, e fers e malestans,
Don hom pert Deu e rema malanans.

Vos vitz torneis mandar,
E segre.ls gen garnitz,
E pois dels melhs feritz
Una sazo parlar;
Er'es pretz de raubar
E d'ebranchar berbitz!
Chavalers si'aunitz
Que.s met en domneiar
Pos que tocha dels mas moltos belans,
Ni que rauba gleizas ni vïandans!

E vitz per cortz anar
De joglaretz formitz,
Gen chaussatz e vestitz,
Sol per domnas lauzar;
Er no n'auzem parlar,
Tan es lor pretz delitz.
Don es lo tortz issitz
D'elas malrazonar?
No sai de cals, d'elas o dels amans.
Eu dic de totz, que.l pretz n'a trach l'engans!

On son gandit joglar
Que vitz gen acolhitz?
C'a tal a mester guitz
Que solïa guidar;
E pero, ses reptar,
Vai er tals escharitz,
Pos fo bos pretz falhitz,
Que solïa menar
De companhos, e no sai dire cans,
Gen en arnes e bels e benestans.

over

But you cannot swear that you've not seen wooden mares, nor lowborn churls, old and broken, unwilling to act as knights. Such behaviour is ugly and hateful and unseemly, and by it one loses God and remains wretched.

You once saw tourneys proclaimed, and well-equipped men follow them, and then for a time (you heard) talk of the best exploits; now it is merit to steal and snatch sheep from the fold! Shame on the knight who proceeds to pay court after he lays his hands on bleating sheep, and robs churches or travellers on the road!

And you once saw going from court to court skilled minstrels, finely shod and dressed, solely to praise noblewomen; of the latter we now hear no talk, so much is their merit in ruins. Whence comes the fault of speaking ill of them? I know not from whom, whether from them or their lovers. I say from all, and deceit has borne off the prize!

Where have the minstrels fled whom you once saw graciously welcomed? For such a one needs a guide who used to guide, and so, without fault being found, such a one now goes about all alone, since fine merit was betrayed, who used to lead I know not how many friends, all finely equipped and fair and seemly.

Qu'eu eis que solh sonar
Totz pros, om eissernitz,
Estauc tan esbaïtz
Que no.m sai conselhar;
Qu'en loc de solassar
Auch er'en cortz los critz
C'aitan leu s'er grazitz
De l'aucha de Bretmar
Lo comtes, entre lor, com us bos chans
Dels rics afars e dels tems e dels ans.

Mas a cor afranchar
Que s'es trop enduritz,
No deu om los oblitz
Ni.ls velhs fachs remembrar;
Que mals es a laissar
Afars, pos es plevitz,
E.l mal don sui garitz
No.m chal ja mezinar.
Mas so c'om ve, volv'e vir e balans
E prend'e lais e forse d'ams los pans!

D'aitan me posc vanar
C'anc mos ostals petitz
No fo d'els envazitz,
Que.l vei per totz doptar,
Ni no.m fetz mas onrar
Lo volpils ni l'arditz;
Don mos senher chauzitz
Se deurīa pensar
Que no l'es ges pretz ni laus ni bobans
Qu'eu, que.m laus d'els, sīa de lui clamans.

Era no m'ais. Per que? No m'o demans!
Car planchs sera s'aissi rema mos chans.

So di.l Dalfis que conois los bos chans.

And I myself, who used to celebrate all noble men in song, I, a discerning man, stand so confounded that I know not what counsel to take; for in place of noble pleasures, I hear now in courts such a din that the tale of Bretmar's goose would be as readily received among them as a fine song of lofty deeds, of present times and of years gone by.

But to soften the heart which has become indifferent, one should not recall the old, forgotten deeds: and a wicked action is to be left alone, once it is proved so, and the sickness of which I'm cured I'm not concerned with treating. But that (ill) which one sees, let one twist and turn and weigh up, and take and drop and snatch up by both ends!

Of this much can I boast that never was my little house set on by them, for I see it respected by all and neither the cowardly nor the bold did me anything but honour; whence my gracious lord should think to himself that it's not for him a cause of merit or praise or glory that I, who am content with them, should complain of him.

For the moment I'm not worrying. Why? Don't ask me that! For it will be a pity if thus my song is neglected.

This says the Dauphin, a connoisseur of good songs.

VII. Reis glorĭos, verais lums e clartatz,
Deus poderos, Senher, si a vos platz,
Al meu companh sĭatz fizels aiuda;
Qu'eu no lo vi pos la nochs fo venguda,
Et ades sera l'alba.

Bel companho, si dormetz o velhatz,
No dormatz plus, süau vos ressidatz;
Qu'en orĭen vei l'estela creguda
C'amena.l jorn, qu'eu l'ai be conoguda,
Et ades sera l'alba.

Bel companho, en chantan vos apel;
No dormatz plus, qu'eu auch chantar l'auzel
Que vai queren lo jorn per lo boschatge,
Et ai päor que.l gilos vos assatge,
Et ades sera l'alba.

Bel companho, issetz al fenestrel,
E regardatz las estelas del cel!
Conoisseretz si.us sui fizels messatge.
Si non o faitz, vostres n'er lo damnatge,
Et ades sera l'alba.

Bel companho, pos me parti de vos,
Eu no.m dormi ni.m moc de genolhos,
Ans preiei Deu, lo filh Santa Marĭa,
Que.us me rendes per leial companhĭa,
Et ades sera l'alba.

Bel companho, la foras als peiros
Me preiavatz qu'eu no fos dormilhos,
Enans velhes tota noch tro al dĭa.
Era no.us platz mos chans ni ma parĭa,
Et ades sera l'alba.

—Bel dous companh, tan sui en ric sojorn
Qu'eu no volgra mais fos alba ni jorn,
Car la gensor que anc nasques de maire
Tenc et abras, per qu'eu non prezi gaire
Lo fol gilos ni l'alba.

VII. Glorious King, true light and splendour, almighty God, Lord, if it please You, to my companion be a faithful aid, for I've seen him not since night came on, and soon it will be dawn.

Sweet friend, if you sleep or wake, sleep you no more; gently rise again for, in the East, I see the star arisen which brings the day, and I have marked it well; and soon it will be dawn.

Sweet friend, in song I call you; sleep you no more, for I hear the bird sing as it goes seeking the daylight through the woods, and I fear lest the jealous one assail you; and soon it will be dawn.

Sweet friend, go to the window, and look at the stars in the sky! You'll know if I'm your faithful messenger. If you do not, then yours will be the harm; and soon it will be dawn.

Sweet friend, since I left you, I have not slept or got up from my knees, but I've prayed God, the son of Holy Mary, that He might return you to me in loyal friendship; and soon it will be dawn.

Sweet friend, out there by the steps you begged me that I should not be sleepy but should keep watch all night until the day. Now neither my song nor my company pleases you, and soon it will be dawn.

—Sweet, gentle friend, in such a rich dwelling am I that I would it were never more dawn or day; for the most noble woman that ever was born of mother I hold and embrace; hence I heed not the jealous fool, nor the dawn.

Bertran de Born

LIFE. Bertran de Born, a minor nobleman sharing with his brother the castle of Hautefort in the Périgord, was born in the early 1140s; twice married, with five children, by 1192, he later became a monk in the abbey of Dalon where his presence is attested from 1197 to 1202. He died some time between this year and 1215. Though not a professional troubadour, he had relied on his poetic talents to gain the favour of more eminent noblemen, above all of the Plantagenet princes—Henry, crowned king in his father's lifetime, Richard, count of Poitou, duke of Aquitaine and, from 1189, king of England, and Geoffrey, count of Brittany. No doubt Bertran shared the admiration of many of his contemporaries for these princes and profited materially from the relations he cultivated with them but, underlying his attitude, is a more personal, more vital motive, born of his material circumstances, his position in the feudal hierarchy, his ethical convictions and his artistic sensibility. This motive was not exactly a love of domestic strife as Dante suggests and for which, in the *Inferno*, he casts Bertran into hell's eighth circle; it was, more simply, a love of war. War enabled the knight-poet to oust his detested brother from Hautefort, loosed the great nobles' purse-strings, made real the ideals of true chivalry, and delighted the artist's eye and ear. That it also took the form of strife between the sons of Henry II, between the sons and the father, vassal and suzerain, suzerain and sovereign, was for Bertran an historical accident. True, in his verse, he urged on the rebels, claimed even to influence the course of events, but the actual trouble-makers were elsewhere, and Dante's judgement, accepted by many modern critics, seems somewhat exaggerated.

WORKS. Bertran seems to have come to poetry at a fairly late age, for none of his forty or so works can be dated before 1180, while many of them belong to the period 1181–1195. Already in an early group of love-songs, which weave round the strands of conventional courtly *motifs* a tissue of praise in honour of some high-born lady, a preoccupation with the real world contrasts strongly with the timeless abstraction of the classical *canso*. Many of his *sirventès*, which constitute the greater part of his work, formulate reactions to specific political events, while a smaller number outline the poet's concepts of courtly and chivalrous behaviour in the contemporary social context. Whether Bertran is urging on the barons to revolt, reminding his suzerain of some unanswered provocation, deploring the princes' occasional inclinations to peace, or celebrating the splendours of the battlefield, the sharpness and intensity of his feelings are matched only by the vividness with which actual scenes and events are evoked. A simplicity of expression and of formal structure adds further to that unmistakable individuality of style achieved only by the greatest troubadours. By combining the vigour and realism of epic style and theme with the lyric's formal and emotional concentration, Bertran de Born added a new dimension to troubadour poetry, an achievement recognized by Dante when, in his *De Vulgari Eloquentia*, he nominates the castellan of Hautefort the model poet of arms.

EDITION. C. Appel *Die Lieder Bertrans von Born* (Halle 1932).

SELECTION. Bertran's original handling of the *canso* form is well illustrated in the first poem (Appel no. 1). Historical figures are directly addressed or referred to, *Rassa* designating Geoffrey of Brittany, *Mariniers* Henry the Young King, *Bel Senher* some local lady, presumably, while the poet's own suzerain, Richard, is mentioned as the lord who prefers tourneys to war and hesitates to engage with the rebellious viscount (Aimar of Limoges) who is cast, for the occasion, in the role of Maurin, hero of a now lost Provençal epic. Realistic description replaces stereotyped evocation, and the conventional rôle of courtly lover is discarded for the idiosyncratic function of court-poet. In the second poem (Appel no. 40), as near a perfect formulation of Bertran's main theme as can be found, the sights and sounds of the battlefield are impressively presented; its violence too, no doubt, but so also are the ethical values by which the poet gives meaning to the scene and which, from that scene, derive their authenticity. The completeness of the poem, as vision and as self-revelation, is if anything thrown into relief by the final caustic aside which Bertran's minstrel is instructed to make known to Richard Lionheart, the poet's Lord Yes-and-No. More frequent, however, than such general declarations are the comments on political events such as are made in the next three poems (Appel nos. 27, 36, 37). In the first, the poet deplores the treaty of Châteauroux concluded in 1187 between Philip of France and Henry II— then indeed master of the three French duchies of Normandy, Brittany, and Aquitania, as well as of the territories of Maine and Anjou. That kings should settle their differences by the methods of the market-place is contrary to the old knightly ethos which, incarnated for Bertran in the violent and bloody Guerin and his nephew, heroes of the epic poem *Raoul de Cambrai*, is yet associated with the courtly pleasantries addressed, in the envoy, to *Isembart*, thought to be Conon de Béthune, a northern French *trouvère*. In the second, dating from 1194, the return of Richard (from captivity in Germany) is heralded as ensuring renewed military campaigning. Dissociating himself from the dissident local barons, Bertran recalls the origins of his own loyalty by a rapid allusion (st. 5) to the events of 1183 when Richard, having seized the stronghold of Hautefort, restored it ultimately—and exclusively—to him. The particular event which sparked off the third of these political *sirventès* is not known; again the prospect of battle excites the poet's enthusiasm, but he concludes on a somewhat resigned and world-weary note, seemingly anticipating his withdrawal, only a few years later, into the abbey of Dalon. The last poem (Appel no. 43), a lament on the death of Henry the Young King in 1183, is attributed to Bertran by only one of three manuscripts, yet it seems reasonable to append it to the other works of the *cortes soudadier* who, more than any other troubadour, devoted his praises to the first three sons of Henry II, ensuring that their fame should live on not only in the chronicler's dry pages but also in the vigorous and resplendent verse of the poor knight whom they once favoured.

I. Rassa, tan creis e monta e poia
Cela qu'es de totz enjans voia,
Sos pretz a las autras enoia;
Qu'una no.i a que ren i noia,
Que.l vezers de sa beutat loia
Los pros a sos ops, cui que coia.
Que.lh plus conoissen e.lh melhor
Mantenon ades sa lauzor,
E la tenon per la genzor;
Qu'ilh sap far tan entieir'onor,
No vol mas un sol preiador.

Rassa, domn'ai qu'es frescha e fina,
Coinda e gaia mesquina;
Pel saur ab color de robina,
Blancha pel cors com flors d'espina,
Coude mol ab dura tetina,
E sembla conil de l'esquina.
A la fina frescha color,
Al bo pretz et a la lauzor,
Lieu podon trīar la melhor,
Cilh que si fan conoissedor
De me, ves qual part ieu azor.

Rassa, als rics es orgolhosa,
E fai gran sen a lei de tosa,
Que no vol Peitieus ni Tolosa
Ni Bretanha ni Saragosa;
Anz es de pretz tan enveiosa
Qu'als pros paubres es amorosa.
Puois m'a pres per chastīador,
Prec li que tenha char s'amor,
Et am mais un pro vavassor
Qu'un comte o duc galīador,
Que la tengues a desonor.

Rassa, rics om que re no dona,
Ni acuolh, ni met ni no sona,
E que senes tort ochaisona
E, qui merce.lh quier, no perdona,

over

Bertran de Born

I. Rassa! She who is innocent of all guile so grows, increases, and becomes more perfect, her merit offends all others; for there's not one lady whom she harms not in some measure since the sight of her beauty enlists the worthy to her cause, no matter who's aggrieved. And the most knowing and the best maintain all times her praise and hold her to be the most noble; for she is capable of such perfect honour, she desires but one suitor alone.

Rassa! A lady have I who is fresh and pure, a graceful and gay young girl, golden-haired with tints of ruby, with skin as white as hawthorn flower, supple of arm, firm of breast, and like a young rabbit's is her back. By her pure and fresh complexion, by her high merit and by her praise they can easily single her out as the best—they who claim to know in which quarter I adore.

Rassa! She is proud towards the mighty and, like a young girl, acts with much sense, for she wants neither Poitiers nor Toulouse, nor Brittany nor Saragossa; but she is so desirous of merit that she shows love to the worthy without wealth. Since she has chosen me for guide, I pray her that she hold dear her love and love more a worthy vassal than a deceiving count or duke who would hold her in dishonour.

Rassa! The great man who gives naught away, who welcomes not, either by gifts or words, who accuses where there is no wrong, and if one asks him for mercy, pardons not—

M'enoia, e tota persona
Que servizi no guizerdona.
E li ric ome chassador
M'enoian, e.lh buzacador;
Gaban de volada d'austor,
Ni ja mais d'armas ni d'amor
No parlaran mot entre lor.

Rassa, aisso.us prec que vos plassa:
Rics om que de guerra no.s lassa,
Ni no s'en recre per menassa
Tro qu'om si lais que mal no.lh fassa,
Val mais que ribieira ni chassa,
Que bo pretz n'acuolh e n'abrassa.
Maurin ab N'Aigar, so senhor, *[Aimar of Limoges]*
Te om per bon envazidor;
E.l vescoms defenda s'onor,
E.l coms deman la.lh per vigor,
E veiam l'ades, al pascor!

Mariniers, vos avetz onor, *[Henry the Young King]*
E nos avem chamjat senhor—
Bo guerrier per torneiador.
E prec a'N Golfier de la Tor
Mos chantars no.lh fassa päor.

Papïols, mon chantar recor *er? (see notes)*
En la cort mo mal Bel Senhor.

11. Be.m platz lo gais temps de pascor
Que fai fuolhas e flors venir,
E platz mi quan auch la baudor
Dels auzels, que fan retentir
Lor chan per lo boschatge;
E platz mi quan vei sobre.ls pratz
Tendas e pavilhos fermatz, *[slight satire at expense of 'spring'/pastora tradition.]*
Et ai gran alegratge
Quan vei per champanha renjatz
Chavaliers e chavals, armatz.

over

this man offends me, and anyone who rewards not service. And the great men who spend their time in hunting and falconry offend me; they boast of some goshawk's flight but will never, among themselves, speak a word of arms or of love.

Rassa! This I pray you to agree with: for a great man not to weary of war and not to renounce it for any threat till one has desisted from doing him harm, is worth more than river-sports and hunting, for thereby he wins and thereby upholds high merit. Maurin, against his lord Sir Aigar, is deemed a fine warrior; so let the viscount fight for his lands and title, and let the count seek them from him by force, and let us see him here soon, at Eastertide!

Mariner, you have lands and titles, but we've changed lords— a jouster for a fine warrior. And I pray Sir Golfier de la Tour not to be alarmed by my singing.

Papiol, run through my song at the court of my unfair Fair Lord.

11. Well am I pleased by gay Eastertide which makes leaves and flowers come, and I'm pleased when I hear the birds' blitheness as they make their song ring through the woodland; and I'm pleased when over the fields I see tents and pavilions pitched, and I'm greatly cheered when I see lined up on the plain horsemen and horses, armed.

E platz mi quan li corredor
Fan las gens e l'aver fugir,
E platz mi quan vei apres lor
Gran re d'armatz ensems venir:
E platz mi en mon coratge
Quan vei fortz chastels assetjatz,
E.ls barris rotz et esfondratz,
E vei l'ost el ribatge
Qu'es tot entorn claus de fossatz,
Ab lissas de fortz pals serratz.

Et autresi.m platz de senhor
Quan es primiers a l'envazir,
En chaval, armatz, ses temor;
Qu'aissi fai los sieus enardir
Ab valen vassalatge.
E puois que l'estorns es mesclatz,
Chascus deu esser acesmatz
E segre.l d'agradatge,
Que nuls om non es re prezatz
Tro qu'a maintz colps pres e donatz.

Massas e brans, elms de color,
Escutz trauchar e desguarnir
Veirem a l'entrar de l'estor,
E maintz vassals ensems ferir,
Don anaran arratge
Chaval dels mortz e dels nafratz.
E quan er en l'estorn entratz,
Chascus om de paratge
No pens mas d'asclar chaps e bratz,
Que mais val mortz que vius sobratz.

Ie.us dic que tan no m'a sabor
Manjar ni beure ni dormir
Com a quan auch cridar 'A lor!'
D'ambas las partz, et auch ennir
Chavals vochs per l'ombratge,
Et auch cridar 'Aidatz! Aidatz!'

over

And I'm pleased when the skirmishers put people and riches to flight, and it pleases me when I see after them a great mass of armed men come together; and I'm pleased in my heart when I see strong castles besieged, and the ramparts breached and crumbled, and I see the defending host on the bank which is enclosed all round by moats protected by strong palissades.

And I'm likewise pleased by the lord when he's foremost in the attack, on horseback, armed, and fearless; for thus does he make his men grow bold in valiant vassal-service; and then when battle's joined each should be ready to follow him with good heart, for no man's esteemed at all until he's taken and dealt many blows.

Maces and swords, coloured helmets and shields being holed and smashed we shall see when battle is first joined, and many vassals clashing together, from which steeds of the dead and wounded will go riderless. And once he has entered the fray let each man of high birth think of naught but of splitting heads and arms, for better it is to be dead than alive and overcome.

I tell you that for me there's no such pleasure in eating or drinking or sleeping as there is when I hear shout 'Get at them!' from all sides, and when I hear riderless horses whinny in the shade, and I hear shout 'Help! Help!'

E vei chazer per los fossatz
Paucs e grans per l'erbatge,
E vei los mortz que pels costatz
An los tronzos ab los cendatz.

Baro, metetz en gatge
Chastels e vilas e ciutatz,
Enanz qu'usquecs no.us guerreiatz!

Papïols, d'agradatge
A'N Oc-e-No t'en vai vïatz,   *Richard the Lionheart.*
E dijas li que trop estai en patz.

III. Puois als baros enoia e lor pesa
    D'aquesta patz qu'an facha li dui rei,
    Farai chanzo tal que, quan er apresa,
    A cadaü sera tart que guerrei.
    E no m'es bel de rei qu'en patz estei
    Deseretatz, ni que perda son drei,
    Tro la demanda qu'a fach'a conquesa.

Ad ambedos te om ad avolesa
Quar an fach plach don quecs de lor sordei.
Cinc duchatz a la corona francesa
E, si.ls comtatz, son a dire li trei!
E de Gisortz pert lo ces e l'esplei,
E Cäercis rema sai en trepei,
E Bretanha e la terra engolmesa.

Ges aitals patz no melhura pröesa
Com aquesta, ni autra qu'om li grei,
Ni deu sofrir qu'om li bais sa richesa,
Puois Essaudu a tornat deves sei
Lo reis Enrics, e mes en son destrei.
E no.s cuich ges qu'a son ome s'autrei
Si.l fieu d'Angieus li merma una tesa.

Si.l reis engles li fetz do ni larguesa,
Al rei Felip, drechs es qu'el l'en mercei!   *over*

and I see falling alongside the moats both humble and mighty in the grass, and I see the dead who through their ribs have bits of lance with the silk pennons.

Barons! put into pawn your castles and towns and cities sooner than not wage war among yourselves!

Papiol, with good heart go quickly to my Lord Yes-and-No, and tell him that he stands too long in peace.

III. Since the barons are vexed and offended by this peace which the two kings have made, I'll compose such a song that, when it is known of, each one of them will long to be at war. And I'm not pleased by a king who stands in peace, robbed of his heritage, or that he lose his rights, before he's secured by force the demand which he's made.

In both it is considered baseness that they've made a pact by which each of them is worse off. Five duchies has the French crown and, if you count them up, there are three of them missing! and it loses the tax and revenue of Gisors, and Quercy remains, here, in disorder, and Brittany and the land round Angoulême.

Not at all does such peace enhance prowess as this one, or any other which might be forced upon him; nor should he endure that anyone cut down his resources, when King Henry has made off with Issoudun and brought it within his sway. And let him not think at all that the latter would pay him homage if he reduces for him the fief of Angers by a yard!

If the English king bestowed on him gifts and largesse, it's right for King Philip that he should thank him for it!

Que.lh fetz liurar la moneda englesa
Qu'en Franza.n son charcit sac e correi;
E no foron Anjavi ni Mancei,
Que d'esterlis foro.lh primier conrei
Que desconfiron la gen champenesa!

Lo sors Guerics dis paraula cortesa
Quan so nebot vi tornat en esfrei:
Que desarmatz volgra.n fos la fis presa;
Quan fo armatz, no volc penre plaidei.
E no semblet ges lo senhor d'Orlei,
Que desarmatz fo de peior mercei
Que quan el chap ac la ventalha mesa.

A rei armat lo te om a flaquesa,
Quan es en champ e vai querre plaidei.
Ben an chamjat onor per cobeitesa,
Segon qu'auch dir, Borgonho e Francei!
E valgra mais, per la fe qu'ieu vos dei,
Al rei Felip, comenzes lo desrei
Que plaideiar, armatz, sobre la gresa.

not simply the decline of battle, but of noble values.

Vai, Papiols, mo sirventes a drei
Mi portaras part Crespi el Valei
Mon Isembart, en la terra artesa.

E dijas li qu'a tal domna soplei,
Que marves puosc jurar sobre ma lei
Que.lh genser es del mon, e.lh plus cortesa.

IV. Ar ve la coindeta sazos
    Que aribaran nostras naus,
    E venra.l reis, galhartz e pros,
    Qu'anc lo reis Richartz no fo taus.
    Adoncs veirem aur et argen despendre,
    Peirieiras far, destrapar e destendre,
    Murs esfondrar, tors baissar et deissendre,
    E.ls enemics enchadenar e prendre. *over*

For he had the English money delivered to him, so that in France bags and pouches are full of it; and they were not men of Anjou or of Maine, but of pounds sterling, those first battalions which defeated Champagne's forces!

Guerrin the Red spoke fair when he saw his nephew in alarm, saying that, unarmed, he would want a truce concluded; once he was armed, he wanted to make no pact. And he wasn't at all like the Lord of Orleans because, unarmed, he was indeed in worse straits than when he had set his helmet on his head.

In an armed king it is considered weakness, when he is on the field and goes suing for peace. They have indeed exchanged honour for greed, from what I hear say, Burgundians and Frenchmen! And it would have been better for King Philip, in faith, had he joined battle rather than sue for peace, armed, on the river bank.

Go Papiol, you'll bear my sirventes directly, by Crépy-en-Valois, to my Isembart in the Artois.

And tell him I woo such a lady that, without hesitation, I can swear by all I hold right that she is the noblest in the world, and the most courtly.

IV. Now comes the fair season when our ships will put in to port, and the bold and worthy king will come, King Richard, who never was such before. Then we shall see gold and silver spent, siege-machines built, unleashed and sprung, walls collapse, towers topple and fall down, and the enemies taken and enchained.

Ges no.m platz de nostres baros
Qu'an fachs sagramens, no sai quaus;
Per so n'estaran vergonhos,
Com lo lops qu'al latz es enclaus,
Quan nostre reis poira mest nos atendre.
Qu'estiers nuls d'els no s'en poira defendre,
Anz diran tuit 'Me no pot om mesprendre
De nul mal plach, anz mi vuolh a vos rendre'.

Bela m'es pressa de blezos
Cobertz de teintz vermelhs e blaus,
D'entresenhs e de gonfanos
De diversas colors tretaus,
Tendas e traps e rics pavilhos tendre,
Lanzas frassar, escutz traucar, e fendre
Elmes brunitz, e colps donar e prendre
[. . . . . endre].

No.m platz companha de basclos,
Ni de las putanas venaus;
Sacs d'esterlis e de moutos
M'es laitz, quan son vengut de fraus.
E maisnadier eschars deurīa om pendre,
E ric ome, quan son donar vol vendre;
En domn'escharsa no.s deurīa om entendre
Que per aver pot pleiar e estendre.

Bo.m sap l'usatge qu'a.l lëos
Qu'a re vencuda non es maus,
Mas contr'orguolhos es orgolhos.
E.l reis non a baros aitaus;
Anz, quan vezon que sos afars es mendre,
Ponha chascus cossi.l puoscha mesprendre.
E no.us cujetz qu'ieu fassa motz a vendre,
Mas per ric bar deu om tot jorn contendre.

I'm not pleased at all by our barons who have sworn I know not what oaths; for this they'll stand in shame like the wolf which is caught in the trap, when our king can be present in our midst. For in no other way will any of them be able to defend himself from him, but they'll all say 'No one can catch me out in any plot, rather I wish to render myself to you'.

Pleasant to me is a throng of shields covered in blue and scarlet hues, of ensigns and banners likewise of varying colours; tents and bivouacs and splendid pavilions pitched, lances shattered, shields pierced, and burnished helmets split, and blows given and taken. . . .

The company of brigands pleases me not, nor that of venal whores; bags of sterling and French silver repel me, when they've come from fraud. And one should hang a mean captain, and the rich man when he sells what he should give away; nor should a man pay court to a mean mistress whom by wealth he can win over and bring to bed.

The lion's custom appeals to me, who is not cruel to a creature once overcome, but who is proud in the face of pride. And the king has no other such barons; rather, when they see that his cause is worsened, each seeks how he might catch him out. And don't imagine that I compose words for sale, but, for a great lord, one should at all times contend.

V. Miei-sirventes vuolh far dels reis amdos,
    Qu'en brieu veirem qu'aura mais chavaliers
    Del valen rei de Castela, N'Anfos,
    Qu'auch dir que ve e volra soudadiers.
    Richartz metra a muois et a sestiers
    Aur et argen, e te.s a benananza   *ideal of charity.*
    Metr'e donar, e no vol s'afïanza,
    Anz vol guerra mais que qualha esparviers.

    S'amdui li rei son pro ni coratjos,
    En brieu veirem champs jonchatz de quartiers
    D'elms e d'escutz, e de brans e d'arzos,
    E de fendutz per bustz tro als braiers,
    Et arratge veirem anar destriers,
    E per costatz e per pechs mainta lanza,
    E gauch e plor e dol et alegranza;
    Lo perdr'er grans, e.l guazanhs er sobriers.

    Trompas, tabors, senheras e penos,
    Et entresenhs, e chavals blancs e niers
    Veirem en brieu, que.l segles sera bos;
    Que hom tolra l'aver als usuriers,
    E per chamis non anara saumiers,
    Jorn afïatz, ni borges ses doptanza,
    Ni merchadiers qui venha de ves Franza;
    Anz sera rics qui tolra volontiers.

    Mas si.l reis ve, ieu ai en Dieu fïanza
    Qu'ieu serai vius, o serai per quartiers;
    E si sui vius, er mi grans benananza,
    E si ieu muoir, er mi grans deliuriers.

VI. Si tuit li dol e.lh plor e.lh marrimen
    E las dolors e.lh dan e.lh chaitivier
    Qu'om anc auzis en est segle dolen
    Fossen ensems, sembleran tot leugier
    Contra la mort del jove rei engles,
    Don rema Pretz e Jovens doloros,
    E.l mons oscurs e teintz e tenebros,
    Sems de tot joi, ples de tristor e d'ira.   *over*

V. A half-sirventes I would compose concerning both the kings, for soon we'll see who has more knights than the valiant king of Castile, Lord Alfonso, and I hear say that he comes and will want hired men. Richard will spend gold and silver in bushels and gallons, and he considers it his happiness to spend and to give away; nor does he want to treat for peace, rather he wants war more than the hawk the quail.

If both the kings are worthy and brave, we'll soon see fields strewn with fragments of helmets, of shields, of swords, and of saddlebows, and with men split through the trunk down to their breeches, and riderless we'll see chargers go, and many a lance through ribs and through breasts, and rejoicing and weeping, and grief and exultation; the losses will be great, and the winnings splendid.

Trumpets, tabors, banners and pennants, and ensigns and black and white horses we shall see soon, and life will be good, when one takes from the usurers their wealth, and no packhorse goes on the roads even by day in safety, nor townsman without fear, nor any merchant coming from France; rather will he be rich who is ready to plunder.

But if the king comes I have in God my trust, for I'll be alive or I'll be in pieces; and if I'm alive, it will be for me great happiness, and if I die, it will be for me great deliverance.

VI. If all the grief, the tears, and the distress, the suffering, the pain, and the misery which one had ever heard of in this grievous life were put together, they would all seem slight compared with the death of the young English king, for which Merit and Youth are left grieving, and the world dark and sombre and gloomy, empty of all joy, full of sadness and sorrow.

Dolen e trist e ple de marrimen
Son remasut li cortes soudadier,
E.lh trobador e.lh joglar avinen;
Trop an agut en Mort mortal guerrier,
Que tout lor a lo jove rei engles,
Ves cui eran li plus larc cobeitos.
Ja non er mais, ni no crezatz que fos,
Ves aquest dan el segle plors ni ira.

Estenta Mortz, plena de marrimen,
Vanar ti potz que.l melhor chavalier
As tout al mon qu'anc fos de nula gen,
Quar non es res qu'a pretz aia mestier
Que tot no fos el jove rei engles.
E fora mielhs, s'a Dieu plagues razos,
Que visques el que maint autr'enoios
Qu'anc no feiron als pros mas dol et ira.

D'aquest segle flac, ple de marrimen,
S'amors s'en vai, son joi tenh menzongier,
Que re no.i a que no torn en cozen;
Totz jorns veuzis, e val mens uoi que ier.
Chascus si mir el jove rei engles
Qu'era del mon lo plus valens dels pros.
Ar es anatz sos gens cors amoros,
Don es dolors e desconortz et ira.

Celui que plac pel nostre marrimen
Venir el mon nos traire d'encombrier,
E receup mort a nostre salvamen,
Com a senhor umil e drechurier,
Clamem merce, qu'al jove rei engles
Perdo, si.lh platz, si com es vers perdos,
E.l fassa estar ab onratz companhos
Lai on anc dol non ac, ni aura ira.

Bertran de Born

Grieving and sad and full of distress are the courtly retainers left behind, and the poets and the pleasant minstrels; too much have they had in Death a deathly foe, for it has taken from them the young English king, beside whom the most generous were mean. There never more will be, and think not there ever was here below, beside this loss, such lament or sorrow.

Dull, distressful Death, you can boast that you've robbed the world of the best knight there ever was of any nation; for there is nothing which pertains to Merit which was not all in the young English king. It would have been better, had reason pleased God, that he had lived rather than many hateful ones who never caused the worthy aught but grief and sorrow.

If from this mean, distressful world Love goes away, I consider its joy false, for there is nothing which turns not to burning pain; each day grows worse, to-day is worth less than yesterday. Let each one model himself on the young English king who, in the whole world, was the most valiant of the worthy. Now is his noble, lovely person gone, whence there is grief and dismay and sorrow.

To Him Whom it pleased, because of our distress, to come into the world and deliver us from our shackles, and Who suffered death for our salvation, as to a gracious and just lord, let us cry mercy that He might forgive, if it please Him, as He is true forgiveness, the young English king, and that He might set him among the honoured companions, there where there never was grief, nor will be sorrow.

Arnaut Daniel

LIFE. Arnaut Daniel, from the castle of Ribérac in the Périgord, was, like his neighbour Bertran de Born, of noble birth. It is more than possible that the two poets were friends but, whereas in Bertran de Born's work, we can perceive positive traces of the poet's personal situation, such traces are rare indeed in the poetry of Arnaut Daniel. One poem elaborates a jest shared with two minor noblemen of the Quercy, and another claims that the poet had been at many fine courts; on one occasion Arnaut affirms that he was present at the crowning of Philip II of France, and on another he addresses his audience as 'senhor e companhon'. Such fragmentary indications as these, coupled with the almost complete absence from his work of any specifically professional themes, *motifs*, or attitudes, suggest that he may not have been the 'minstrel' which his mediaeval biographer reports him to be; an independent status, moreover, would account for the relatively limited number of his compositions, as indeed for certain of their internal features. As for the chronological details of his literary activity, such limited evidence as his work offers indicates the period *c.* 1180–*c.* 1200, and nothing permits us to suppose that he himself outlived the twelfth century.

WORKS. Of Arnaut Daniel's eighteen extant compositions, one only is not a *canso*; reminiscent of William IX's coarsely erotic humour, it comments in detail on a situation analagous to that in which Absolon found himself in the Miller's tale. The remainder are songs of courtly love, almost entirely free of allusion to external events and situations, and yet, if Arnaut Daniel the man remains a vague and shadowy figure, the artist emerges as a most positive and clear-cut individual. One is aware above all of an exceptionally lively imagination which endows his work with a wealth and variety of imagery drawn not only from traditional literary sources but also from the everyday, practical realities of feudal existence. Closely associated with it is a constant striving after richness and variety of rime and other acoustic effects, and one can see why his early biographer complained that 'he so delighted in rich rime that his songs are not easy to understand'. However, as was already evident to Dante when he proposed Arnaut Daniel as the model poet of love (*De Vulg. Eloq.* II, 2), brilliance of imagery and of versification is no mere external ornament; it is integrated into a coherent unity of structure in which art and inspiration are inseparable. Through his liveliest images is conveyed a certain ecstatic quality of feeling, best experienced in the vigorous and often sensuous celebration of love's joy, while the distinctive character of his rime and sound-patterns expresses not only an obvious emotional plenitude, becoming on occasion obsession and absorption in love's conflicting emotions, but also a less obvious irony or dream-like fantasy in which plenitude, obsession, and absorption are more than once dissolved. This structural unity represents one of the highest achievements of mediaeval Provençal verse; it is surely this which, more than isolated technical detail, so impressed the Italian poets of the thirteenth and fourteenth centuries, which Dante analysed, admired, and imitated, and which led Petrarch in turn to speak of Arnaut Daniel as the 'gran maestro d'amor, ch'a la sua terra ancor fa onor, col suo dir strano e bello'.

EDITION. Gianluigi Toja *Arnaut Daniel, Canzoni* (Florence 1960).

SELECTION. The first piece (Toja no. 12) is unique among the poet's *cansos* by virtue of the *sirventès*-type matter of the final stanza. It is however noticeable that, while the historical figures evoked elsewhere in the poem are readily identifiable —Henry II of England and Sancho IV of Navarre in st. 2, Henry II again and Guy de Lusignan, king of Jerusalem, in st. 6, and Philip II of France (crowned in 1180) in the *tornada* —the allusions made in st. 7 are so vague and imprecise that one feels that the poet himself had but a confused notion of the deeds attributed to Fernando, king of Galicia and Leon. In no other poem does he renew this attempt to comment on the political or social scene. In the second *canso* for example (Toja no. 3) the evocations of 'selh de Pontremble' and of Savoy have no closer connection with the external world than that of Helen and Paris of Troy, their sole function being to meet the demands of rime and stylistic colour. All the more striking, then, is the mention in the *tornada* of the poet's own name; no less than fifteen of the *cansos* are signed in this way, and the device suggests rather the amateur's pride in his work than the professional's self-protective claim to copyright. A comparable note of pride inspires the first stanza of the next poem (Toja no. 10), a pride in craftsmanship closely akin to that expressed by such princely amateurs as William IX and Raimbaut d'Orange. In this *canso* one notices too the typically varied nature of the images; epic in the allusions to the legendary Spanish city of Luserna and to the hero of Monclin, historical in the references to Pope and Emperor—the thrones of both were vacant in 1191—and realistic in the evocation of the woodworker's craft, the usurer's excesses, and the ploughman's labours. But more typical yet of the poet's art and inspiration are the closing lines, where the poet ironically—but aptly—characterizes his strivings as artist and lover. Dante recalls them in the speech he attributes to Arnaut Daniel in his vision of Purgatory (canto XXVI), and they are still vivid in Petrarch's mind, when, on two occasions, he uses the image of hunting 'con un bue zoppo'. The fourth selected poem (Toja no. 15) is distinguished by its structural qualities; its unity, coherence and elegance of thought and expression constitute a convincing and impressive formulation of the courtly ideal. The last poem (Toja no. 18) is a more original and unusual composition; developing to their highest point of complexity a number of his favourite devices of rime and stanza-structure, the poet has created an entirely new lyric form, the sestina. Its technical virtuosity has blinded many critics to its less formal qualities, but the real problem is to appreciate how far the ironic effect, pointed up by the *oncle* rime, was intended to destroy, to dominate, or simply to contend with the mood of emotional intensity created, in particular, by the *arma* and *cambra motifs*. Once again this poet reminds one of an aspect of William IX's art, and once again one recalls that, in the tradition of the troubadour *canso*, a clash of mood and attitude within the same composition, however it appears in cold prose translation, was not necessarily meant to produce a burlesque or comic effect.

1. Doutz brais e critz,
   Lais e cantars e voutas
   Aug dels auzels q'en lur latin fant precs,
   Qecs ab sa par, atressi cum nos fam
   A las amigas en cui entendem.
   E doncas ieu, q'en la genssor entendi,
   Dei far chansson sobre totz de bell'obra,
   Que no.i aia mot fals ni rim'estrampa.

   Ges rams floritz
   De floretas envoutas,
   Cui fan tremblar auzelhon ab lurs becs,
   Non es plus frescs, per q'ieu no volh Röam
   Aver ses lieis, ni tot Jerusalem.
   Pero totz fis, mas juntas, a li.m rendi,
   Q'en liei amar agr'ondra.l reis de Dobra,
   O celh cui es l'Estel'e Luna-pampa.

   Non fui marritz,
   Ni non presi destoutas,
   Al prim q'intriei el chastel, dinz los decs,
   Lai on estai midonz don ai gran fam
   C'anc non l'ac tal lo nebotz Sain Guillem.
   Mil vetz lo jorn en badaill e.m n'estendi,
   Per la bella que totas autras sobra
   Tant cant val mais fis gaugz q'ira ni rampa.

   Ben fui grazitz
   E mas paraulas coutas,
   Per so que ges al chausir no fui pecs—
   Anz volgui mais prendre fin aur que ram—
   Lo jorn qez ieu e midonz nos baisem,
   E.m fetz escut de son bel mantel endi
   Que lausengier fals, lenga de colobra,
   Non o visson, don tan mals motz escampa.

   Dieus lo chauzitz,
   Per cui foron assoutas
   Las faillidas que fetz Longis lo cecs,

Arnaut Daniel

I. Sweet trills and calls, lays and songs and refrains I hear of the birds who in their language plead, each with his mate, in the same way as we do with the loved ones on whom our hearts are set. And I then, whose heart is set on the most noble, should above all make a song finely wrought, so that there be in it no false word or rime unanswered.

The flowering branch decked in blossom, which little birds make tremble with their beaks, is not more fresh, hence I would not have Rouen and be without her, nor all Jerusalem. Thus, most truly, with hands clasped, I give myself to her; for in loving her would the king of Dover have honour, or he to whom belong Estella and Pamplona.

I did not stray, nor took I roundabout ways when I first went, through the outworks, into the castle yonder where dwells my mistress for whom I have a great hunger such as Saint William's nephew had never. A thousand times a day I yawn and stretch with it, on account of the fair one who surpasses all others by as much as pure joy prevails over sadness or rage.

I was welcomed indeed and my words well-received, because I was not stupid in my choosing—I preferred, rather, to take pure gold than copper—the day when I and my mistress kissed, and she shielded me with her lovely blue mantle that they might not see it, the false, snake-tongued tale-tellers by whom so much evil talk is spread.

May the merciful God, by Whom were absolved the faults of blind Longinus,

Voilla, si.l platz, q'ieu e midonz jassam
En la chambra on amdui nos mandem
Uns rics convens don tan gran joi atendi!
Qe.l seu bel cors, baisan, rizen, descobra,
E qe.l remir contra.l lum de la lampa.

Bocca, que ditz?
Q'eu crei qe m'auras toutas
Tals promessas don l'emperaire grecs
En for'onratz, o.l senher de Röam,
O.l reis que ten Sur e Jerusalem.
Doncs ben sui fols, que quier tan qe.m rependi,
Que ges Amors non a poder qe.m cobra,
Ni savis es nuls om qui joi acampa.

Los deschauzitz,
Ab las lengas esmoutas,
Non dupt'ieu ges, si.l seignor dels Galecs
An fag faillir, per q'es dreitz si.l blasmam;
Que son paren pres, romieu, so sabem,
Raimon lo filh al comte, et aprendi
Que greu fara.l reis Ferrans de pretz cobra,
Si mantenen no.l solv e no.l escampa.

Eu l'agra vist, mas estiei per tal obra:
C'al coronar fui del bon rei d'Estampa.

11. Quan chai la fuelha
    Dels aussors entresims,
    E.l freg s'erguelha
    Don seca.l vais'e.l vims.
    Dels dous refrims
    Au sordezir la bruelha,
    Mas ieu soi prims
    D'amor, qui que s'en tuelha.   *over*

grant, if it please Him, that I and my mistress lie together in that room for where we both made a precious tryst of which I expect such great joy! and that I uncover, kissing and smiling, her lovely person, and gaze upon her in the light of the lamp!

Lips, what say you? I fear that you will have robbed me of such promises as the Greek emperor would be honoured by, or the lord of Rouen or the king who rules Tyr and Jerusalem. Now I'm indeed a fool since I ask for so much that I repent, and Love itself has scarce the power to protect me, and no man is wise who puts joy to flight.

The merciless ones, with sharpened tongues, I dread not, though they've made the lord of the Galicians act basely, and it's right if we blame him for it; for he captured his kinsman while he was a pilgrim, this we know, Raymond the Count's son. And I understand that king Fernando will hardly win merit unless straightway he releases and sets him free.

I would have seen it but I stayed here for this business: I was at the crowning of the good king of Etampes.

11. When the leaf falls from the highest twining branches, and the cold grows sharp by which hazel and osier wither, I hear the woodland fall silent of sweet birdsong, but I am sprightly with love, whoever may renounce it.

Tot quant es gela,
Mas ieu non puesc frezir,
Qu'amors novela
Mi fa.l cor reverdir.
Non dei fremir,
Qu'Amors mi cuebr'e.m cela,
E.m fai tenir
Ma valor e.m capdela.

Bona es vida
Pus joia la mante,
Que tals n'escrida
Cui ges no vai tan be;
No sai de re
Coreillar m'escarida,
Que, per ma fe,
Del mielhs ai ma partida.

De drudarïa
No.m sai de re blasmar,
Qu'autrui parïa
Torn ieu en reirazar;
Ges ab sa par
No sai doblar m'amïa,
Qu'una non par
Que seconda no.ill sïa.

No vuelh s'asemble
Mos cors ab autr'amor
Si que ja.il m'emble
Ni volva.l cap ailhor;
Non ai päor
Que ja selh de Pontremble
N'aia gensor
De lieis, ni que la semble.

Ges non es croia,
Selha cui soi amis;
De sai Savoia
Plus belha no.s noiris.

over

All that is, freezes, but I cannot be cold, for a new love makes my heart grow green again. I should not shiver, for Love protects and shields me, and it has me maintain my valour and it guides me.

Life is good once joy sustains it, so such a one blames it when things go not so well; I can for no cause quarrel with my lot, for, by my faith, I have my share of what's best.

In courtship I know of no cause to complain, and to consort with any other I deem a backward step; I cannot match my beloved with her peer, for not one appears but she comes second to her.

I want not my heart to engage in another love so that it should take me from her and head elsewhere; nor do I fear that he of Pontremoli has one more noble than her, or one who even resembles her.

She is not cruel, the one whose lover I am; this side of Savoy there's nurtured none fairer than her.

Tals m'abelis
Don ieu plus ai de joia
Non ac Paris
D'Elena, sel de Troia.

Tant per es genta,
Selha que.m ten joios,
Las gensors trenta
Vens de belhas faisos.
Ben es razos
Doncas que mos chans senta,
Quar es tan pros
E de ric pretz manenta.

'Vai t'en, chansos,
Denan lieis ti prezenta.'
Que s'ill no fos,
No.i meir'Arnautz s'ententa.

envoi does not employ jongleurs: direct approach

III. En cest sonet coind'e leri
Fauc motz, e capuig e doli,
Que serant verai e cert
Qan n'aurai passat la lima;
Q'Amors marves plan'e daura
Mon chantar, que de liei mou
Qui pretz manten e governa.

Tot jorn meillur et esmeri,
Car la gensor serv e coli
El mon—so.us dic en apert.
Sieus sui del pe tro q'en cima,
E, si tot venta.ill freid'aura,
L'amors q'inz el cor mi plou
Mi ten chaut on plus iverna.

Mil messas n'aug e.n proferi,
E.n art lum de cer'e d'oli
Que Dieus m'en don bon issert
De lieis, on no.m val escrima.

over

Such a one delights me of whom I have more joy than Paris—he of Troy—had of Helen.

So very noble is she who keeps me joyous, the thirty most noble she betters in gracious demean. It is indeed right then that she should hear my songs, she is so worthy and with rich merit endowed.

'Be off, my song, and present yourself to her.' Were it not for her, Arnaut would not have put his mind to it.

III. To this light and graceful little air I fashion words, I carve and plane them, so they'll be true and sure when I've given them a touch with the file; for Love soon smooths and gilds my song which is inspired by her who maintains merit and guides it.

Each day I improve and grow more pure, for I serve and worship the most noble in the world—this I can tell you openly. Hers I am from head right down to foot, and even if the cold wind blows, the love that rains within my heart keeps me warm in deepest winter.

A thousand masses I hear and offer for it, and for it I burn lights of wax and of oil, so that thereby God grant me success with her where no striving avails me.

E, qan remir sa crin saura
E.l cors q'es grailet e nou,
Mais l'am que qi.m des Luserna.

Tant l'am de cor e la queri
C'ab trop voler cug la.m toli—
S'om ren per ben amar pert!
Q'el sieus cors sobre-tracima
Lo mieu tot, e non s'eisaura;
Tant a de ver fait renou
C'obrador n'a e taverna.

No vuoill de Roma l'emperi,
Ni c'om m'en fass'apostoli,
Q'en lieis non aia revert
Per cui m'art lo cors e.m rima;
E si.l maltraich no.m restaura
Ab un baisar, anz d'annou,
Mi auci e si enferna.

Ges pel maltraich q'ieu soferi
De ben amar no.m destoli,
Si tot me ten en desert,
C'aissi.n fatz los motz en rima:
Pieitz trac aman c'om que laura,
C'anc plus non amet un ou
Cel de Moncli N'Audierna.

Ieu sui Arnautz, q'amas l'aura,
E chatz la lebre ab lo bou,
E nadi contra suberna.

And, when I gaze on her golden hair and her person which is slender and fresh, I love her more than whoever gave me Luserna.

I love her nobly and long for her so much that, through great desire, I fear that I'll rob myself of her — if one can lose something through loving well! For her heart floods full into mine entirely, and it does not subside; she has in truth practised usury so much that she owns by it worker and workshop.

I'd not have the empire of Rome, nor be made pope of it, if thereby I might not return to her for whom my heart burns and crackles; and if she soothes not my suffering with a kiss before the year's out, she slays me and damns herself.

Scarce for the suffering that I endure do I renounce fine loving, even though it keeps me in solitude, and thus these words thereof I set to rime: I suffer more, a lover, than one who toils at the plough, and never a whit did he of Monclin love more the Lady Audierna.

I am Arnaut, who gathers the wind, and hunts the hare on ox-back, and swims against the rising tide.

IV. Sols sui qui sai lo sobr'afan qe.m sortz
Al cor, d'amor sofren per sobr'amar,
Car mos volers es tant ferms et entiers
C'anc no s'esduis de celliei ni s'estors
Cui encubic al prim vezer e puois.
C'ades ses lieis dic a lieis cochos motz;
Puois, qan la vei, non sai—tant l'ai—que dire.

D'autras vezer sui secs, e d'auzir sortz,
Q'en sola lieis vei et aug et esgar;
E ges d'aisso no.ill sui fals plazentiers,
Que mais la vol non ditz la boca.l cors.
Q'ieu no vau tant chams, vauz ni plans ni puois,
Q'en un sol cors trob aissi bos aips totz,
Q'en lieis los volc Dieus trïar et assire.

Ben ai estat a maintas bonas cortz,
Mas sai ab lieis trob pro mais que lauzar:
Mesur'e sen et autres bos mestiers,
Beutat, joven, bos faitz e bels demors.
Gen l'enseignet Cortesi'e la duois.
Tant a de si totz faitz desplazens rotz;
De lieis no cre rens de ben si'a dire.

Nuills gauzimens no.m fora breus ni cortz
De lieis, cui prec q'o vuoilla devinar—
Que ja per mi non o sabra estiers,
Si.l cors ses digz no.s presenta de fors.
Que ges Rozers, per aiga qe l'engrois,
Non a tal briu c'al cor plus larga dotz
No.m fass'estanc d'amor, qan la remire.

Jois e solatz d'autra.m par fals e bortz,
C'una de pretz ab lieis no.is pot esgar,
Qe.l sieus solatz es dels autres sobriers.
Hai! si no l'ai; las, tant mal m'a comors!
Pero l'afans m'es deportz, ris e jois,
Car en pensan sui de lieis lecs e glotz.
Hai Dieus! si ja.n serai estiers gauzire?

over

IV. I am the only one who knows the over-anguish which wells in my heart, suffering of love through over-loving, for my desire is so steadfast and entire that it never turned nor cut loose from her whom I longed for at first sight and ever after. And ever, far from her, I say to her burning words; then, when I see her, I know not what—I've so much—to say.

To see other women I am blind, and to hear them, deaf, since by her alone do I see and hear and watch; and in that I am no false flatterer to her, for my heart wants her more than my lips declare. And for all that I travel through so many fields, valleys and plains and hills, I find not thus in one person alone all such qualities, for in her God chose to display and establish them fast.

I have indeed been at many fine courts, but here with her I find much more to praise: moderation and sense and other virtues, beauty and youth, fine actions and pastimes fair. Nobly did Courtliness teach and inform her, so far from herself has she banished all unpleasing actions; in her I think that nothing good is lacking.

No pleasure would be brief or short for me, coming from her whom I pray to be pleased to devine it—for she would learn it from me in no other way, unless my heart without words showed itself forth. Even the Rhône, whatever the waters which swell it, flows not so strongly but that, in my heart, a broader stream spreads in a pool of love, when I gaze upon her.

Joy and solace from any other appear to me false and abortive, for no woman can match her in merit, and her solace is supreme above others. Ah, if I have it not; alas, she has so cruelly caught me! Yet the anguish is to me pleasure, smiles and joy, since in thought I am for her greedy and avid. Ah God! will I ever, in some other way, have her joy?

Anc mais, so.us pliu, no.m plac tant treps ni bortz,
Ni res al cor tant de joi no.m poc dar,
Cum fetz aquel, don anc feinz lausengiers
No s'esbrugic, q'a mi sol so.s tresors.
Dic trop? Eu non, sol lieis non si'enois;
Bella, per Dieu, lo parlar e la votz
Vuoill perdr'enans que diga ren qe.us tire.

Ma chanssos prec que no.us sīa enois,
Car si voletz grazir lo son e.ls motz,
Pauc prez'Arnautz cui que plass'o que tire.

V. Lo ferm voler qu'el cor m'intra
No.m pot ges becs escoisendre ni ongla
De lauzengier, si tot per mal dir s'arma;
E quar no l'aus batr'ab ram ni ab vergua,
Sivals a frau, lai on non aurai oncle,
Jauzirai joi, en vergier o dinz cambra.

Quan mi soven de la cambra
On, al mieu dan, sai que nuils hom non intra,
Ans mi son tug plus que fraire ni oncle,
Non ai membre no.m fremisca, ni ongla,
Plus que non fai l'enfas denant la vergua;
Tal pāor ai que.ill sīa trop de m'arma.

Del cors li fos, non de l'arma!
E cossentis m'a celat dinz sa cambra!
Que plus me nafra.l cor que colps de vergua,
Quar lo sieus sers, lai on ill es, non intra;
De lieis serai aisi com carns ez ongla,
E non creirai castic d'amic ni d'oncle.

Anc la seror de mon oncle
Non amei tan ni plus, per aquest'arma!
Que tan vezis com es lo detz de l'ongla,
S'a lieis plagues, volgr'esser de sa cambra;
De mi pot far l'amors qu'ins el cor m'intra
Mieils a son vol c'om fortz de frevol vergua.

over

Never, I pledge you, did any game or sport please me as much, nor could anything give my heart as much joy, as this one did, and no false tale-teller ever revealed it, for to me alone is it a treasure. Do I say too much? Not I, as long as it's no annoyance to her; fair one, by God, I'd sooner lose speech and voice than say anything which might vex you.

I pray that my song be no annoyance to you, for if you are willing to welcome the air and the words, Arnaut cares little who else it might please or vex.

V. The firm desire which in my heart enters cannot be torn from me by tale-teller's beak or nail—albeit he arms himself to speak evilly; and since I dare not beat him with branch or rod, then at least by stealth, there where I'll have no (guardian) uncle, will I enjoy (love's) joy, in bower or bedroom.

When I recall the bedroom where, to my cost, I know no man enters—rather they are all more (hostile) to me than (her) brother or uncle—I've no limb but that trembles—nor fingernail—more than a child does at the sight of the rod; I'm so afraid that I'm hers too much in soul.

Would I were hers in body, not in soul! and that she let me, secretly, into her bedroom! For it wounds my heart more than any blow of a rod, that her servant, there where she is, does not enter. Always I'll be with her as flesh and fingernail, and I'll not heed the warning of friend or uncle.

I never loved my uncle's sister as much, nor more, by this my soul! For as near as is the finger to its nail, if it so pleased her, I'd like to be to her bedroom. The love which in my heart enters can wreak on me better its will than can a strong man on a slender rod.

Pois floris la seca vergua,
Ni d'En Adam foron nebot ni oncle,
Tan fin'amors com cela qu'el cor m'intra
Non cuig qu'anc fos en cors, ni eis en arma;
On qu'ill estei, fors en plan o dinz cambra,
Mos cors de lieis no.s part, tan com ten l'ongla.

C'aisi s'enpren e s'enongla
Mos cors en lieis com l'escors'en la vergua;
Qu'ill m'es de joi tors e palais e cambra,
Ez am la mais no fas cozin ni oncle.
Qu'en paradis n'aura doble joi m'arma,
Si ja nuils hom per ben amar lai intra.

Arnautz tramet son chantar d'ongl'e d'oncle.
Ab grat de lieis que de sa vergua l'arma,
Son Dezirat, c'ab pretz en cambra intra.

Arnaut Daniel

Since there burst into flower the withered rod and from Sir Adam there came nephew and uncle, such pure love as that which in my heart enters I think there never was in body, nor yet in soul. Wherever she be, out in the open or within bedroom, my heart quits her not by so much as the width of a nail.

For thus my heart cleaves and clings with its nail to her, as (close as) the bark to the rod; for she is to me joy's tower and palace and bedroom, and I love her more than I do cousin or uncle. Hence in Paradise will my soul have twofold joy, if ever a man through fine loving therein enters.

Arnaut sends his song of fingernail and uncle, for the pleasure of her who arms him with her rod, to his Desired One, who with merit in bedroom enters.

Peire Vidal

LIFE. Born a furrier's son in Toulouse, Peire Vidal began his poetic career in the early 1180s, at the court of the local count, Raymond V. From here, after some disagreement with his patron, he extended his activities into Provence, where he secured the protection of Barral, Viscount of Marseilles, and into northern Spain, enjoying here the favour of Alfonso II, king of Aragon. The early 1190's, however, marked by the deaths of Raymond (1192), Barral (1194), and Alfonso (1196), must have been for him, as for many troubadours, a difficult period; the disappearance of these three most eminent patrons of their art obliged many to seek favour further afield, and it is to this period that belong Peire Vidal's extensive excursions into northern Italy, attracted, as others, by the brilliant court of Boniface, Marquis of Montferrat. But as in Provence, Languedoc and Spain, he also did the rounds of the minor courts of Lombardy and Piedmont; as he himself once declared, to stay long in one place was for him like being ill. Already in the later 1180s he had gone on a pilgrimage to the Holy Land—under pressure from Raymond V, he himself suggests—and in 1198 he goes to offer his services to the king of Hungary. Early in the new century—*c.* 1204—we find him in Malta, celebrating the exploits of Count Henry, admiral of the Genoese fleet. After Malta, however, all trace of the poet is lost. Even his mediaeval biographer, so rich in other detail, has nothing to say of how Peire Vidal met his death, a silence which in itself suggests that it was sudden and obscure.

WORKS. Of the forty-five poems attributed to Peire Vidal, all but for two *tensons* are either *cansos* or *sirventès-cansos*—a precise classification is in most cases difficult to make since few of the love songs fail to make some reference to contemporary events and persons, while many of what otherwise could be termed *sirventès* devote at least a stanza or two to the themes of courtly love. A more intricate mingling than ever of court poetry with courtly lyric is thus achieved by this poet who constantly alternates the rôle of public spokesman with that of impassioned lover. It is indeed in this varied but sustained self-representation that Peire Vidal's originality lies. Few of his lyrics show that preoccupation with formal refinement so characteristic of his immediate predecessors, but the thematic material by which he creates his own dramatic *persona* is marked by a striking degree of inventive ingenuity. Two devices in particular are exploited; they could be termed the territorial and the self-descriptive *motifs*, and their combined effect is to endow established themes with a more immediate and more realistic setting than had ever before been dared. Though many troubadours had given hints of their real whereabouts, none had so studded his songs with so many precise local references as Peire Vidal, who mingles inextricably the details of his real professional tours with the imaginary details of his heart's adventures. And though imaginative self-revelation underlies the structure of every *canso*, no troubadour so exploited its possibilities, so transformed it to self-portrayal and further yet, on occasion, to self-caricature. Strangely enough, although his success was undoubtedly due to such thematic invention, no later troubadour followed his example. Perhaps it seemed too radical a modification of long-established themes; perhaps the onset of the Albigensian Crusade in 1209, with its disastrous repercussions on court life in the Midi, put an end to all such innovation—a tradition, once threatened, tends to close in on itself. In all events, for all the easy grace and lively humour of his work, for all his picturesque and engaging originality, Peire Vidal stands alone.

EDITION. D. S. Avalle *Peire Vidal, Poesie,* (2 Vols., Milan 1960).

SELECTION. The first selected piece (Avalle no. 20), in courtly fiction a eulogy of the lover's lady, is in effect a justly celebrated song in praise of Provence, well illustrating how the 'territorial' *motif* adds new interest, and new functions, to a conventional form. The second piece (Avalle no. 24) is a characteristic *sirventès-canso*, dating probably from the mid-1180s; after an elegant re-working of conventional material, and a professional nod to his new patron Barral, Viscount of Marseilles, the poet launches into one of his most favoured self-descriptive devices, the *gab* or absurdly enormous boast, adapted no doubt from contemporary epic literature. Next a *canso* (Avalle no. 10), written at the 'imperial' court of Castile —it was Alfonso of Castile's father who had assumed the title of Emperor of Spain —and dating from a little before 1187, the year in which the Bretons' wait for the return of their legendary hero was—at least temporarily—suspended with the birth of Arthur of Brittany. The territorial and the self-descriptive *motifs*, operating on both the literal and imaginative planes, are here subtly inter-woven with an authentic biographical reference if, as has been suspected, the narrative content is indeed a poetic rendering of Vidal's quarrel with the Count of Toulouse. More obviously concerned with public affairs are the two following poems (Avalle nos. 6, 12). The first dates from 1193–1194: Philip of France had slipped away from the third Crusade (1191); Richard Coeur-de-Lion, returning from the Holy Land, was being held prisoner by the German Emperor (1193–1194); the kings of Aragon, Castile, Leon and Navarre were still warring among themselves rather than unite against the Moors while, through the failings of Pope Celestine and his advisers, the Manichean heresy was spreading throughout the Midi. The second poem opens, nonetheless, on a note of renewed enthusiasm for the crusading ideal; in 1201, the Marquis of Montferrat had been named leader of a new Crusade and, at the time of celebrating this, the poet could scarcely have suspected how the conventional moral strictures of his third and fourth stanzas anticipate so well, for us, the perversion of that same Crusade. We note again the nod of respect made to the Spanish kings—though Pedro of Aragon clearly inspires the poet with less enthusiasm than his father Alfonso—and again the scathing reference to Philip of France, the 'reis aunitz' who had lost the Crusader's glory won by his father. The final poem (Avalle no. 19) is one of Peire Vidal's most successful love-songs, coherent, elegant, unified; if the fulsome praises bestowed on the Marquis of Montferrat detract, for some, from its effect, it is to be remembered that even the most tragic of players, swooning to death on the stage, must still rise to bow and beam gratefully to his public.

I. Ab l'alen tir vas me l'aire
    Qu'ieu sen venir de Pröensa;
    Tot quant es de lai m'agensa,
    Si que, quan n'aug ben retraire,
    Ieu m'o escout en rizen,
    E.n deman per un mot cen,
    Tan m'es bel quan n'aug ben dire.

    Qu'om no sap tan dous repaire
    Cum de Rozer tro c'a Vensa,
    Si cum clau mars e Durensa,
    Ni on tant fins jois s'esclaire.
    Per qu'entre la franca gen
    Ai laissat mon cor jauzen,
    Ab lieis que fa.ls iratz rire.

    Qu'om no pot lo jorn mal traire
    Qu'aja de lieis sovinensa,
    Qu'en liei nais jois e comensa.
    E qui qu'en sïa lauzaire,
    De ben qu'en diga, no.i men;
    Que.l mielher es, ses conten,
    E.l genser qu'el mon se mire.

    E s'ieu sai ren dir ni faire,
    Ilh n'aia.l grat, que scïensa
    M'a donat e conoissensa
    Per qu'ieu sui gais e chantaire.
    E tot quan fauc d'avinen
    Ai del sieu bell cors plazen,
    Neis quan de bon cor consire.

Peire Vidal

I. As I breathe I draw in the air I feel come from Provence; all that is from there so delights me that, when I hear good of it spoken, I listen smiling to it and ask, for one word, a hundred, it's so pleasant to me when I hear good said of it.

For one knows of no land so sweet as that between the Rhône and Vence and bound by the sea and the Durance, nor where such pure joy shines bright. Hence among that noble people I have left my joyful heart, with her who makes the downcast laugh.

And one cannot be unhappy the day one brings her to mind, since in her joy is born and has its beginning. No matter who sings her praises, in the good he says of her he lies not, for she is the best, there's no denying, and the most noble to be seen in the world.

And if I am able to say or to do anything, to her be the thanks, for she has given me knowledge and experience whereby I am merry and singing. All that I do pleasantly is inspired by her fair, delightful person, even all that I nobly think of.

11. Baron, de mon dan covit
Fals lauzengiers deslïals,
Qu'en tal domna ai chauzit
Ont es fis pretz naturals.
Et ieu am la de cor e ses bauzïa,
E sui totz sieus, quora qu'ilh sïa mïa.
Qu'a sa beutat e sa valor pareis
Qu'en lieis amar honratz fora us reis;
Per que.m tieng ric, sol que.m deinh dire d'oc.

Anc res tan no m'abellit
Cum sos adreitz cors lïals,
On son tug bon aip complit
E totz bes, senes totz mals.
E pus tot a quan tainh a drudarïa,
Ben sui astrucs, sol que mos cors lai sïa;
E si merces, per que totz bos aips creis,
Mi val ab lieis, be.us puesc dir ses totz neis,
Qu'anc ab amor tant ajudar no.m poc.

Chant e solatz vei fallit,
Cortz e dons e bos ostals;
E domnei no vei grazit—
Si.lh domn'e.l drutz non es fals.
Aquel n'a mai que plus soven galïa,
No.n dirai plus mas cum si vuelha sïa.
Mas peza me quar ades non esteis
Lo premiers fals que comenset anceis;
E fora dreitz, qu'avol eixample moc.

Mon cor sent alegrezit
Quar me cobrara'N Barrals.
Ben aja selh que.m noirit,
E Dieus, quar ieu sui aitals!
Que mil salut mi venon cascun dïa
De Cataluenha e de Lombardïa,
Quar a totz jorns pueja mos pretz e creis
Que per un pauc no mor d'enveja.l reis,
Quar ab donas fas mon trep e mon joc.

over

11. Barons, I defy false, faithless slanderers to harm me, for my choice has fallen on such a one in whom there is noble and natural merit; and I love her truly and without deceit, and am wholly hers no matter when she be mine. Since by her beauty and worth it is clear that, in loving her, a king would be honoured, I therefore deem myself rich, if only she deigned to say 'yes' to me.

Never did anything so delight me as her true and loyal person, in whom are all qualities complete and all good, without any defects. And since she has all that pertains to loving, I am most fortunate, if only I were there with her; and if pity, through which every quality increases, is of help to me with her, then I can indeed say to you, without any reserve, that it could never have helped me so much in love before.

Song and solace I see neglected, court-gatherings and gifts and fine hospitality; and love-service I see not favoured, unless the lady and lover are false. He gains most from it who most often betrays; I'll say no more of it but be it as it will. Yet it grieves me that he didn't perish at once, the first knave who started it all; and it would have been right, for he set a wicked example.

I feel my heart full of happiness, for Lord Barral will again have me with him. Fortune favour him who raised me, and God, that I am such as I am! For a thousand love-letters come to me each day from Catalonia and Lombardy, and every day my merit grows and increases, so that the king is almost dying of envy, and with the ladies I dance and play as I will.

Ben es pröat et auzit
Cum ieu sui pros e cabals;
E pus Dieus m'a enriquit,
No.s tanh qu'ieu sīa venals.
Cent domnas sai que cascuna.m volrīa
Tener ab se, si aver me podīa—
Mas ieu sui selh qu'anc no.m gabei ni.m feis,
Ni volgui trop parlar de mi meteis;
Mas domnas bais e cavaliers desroc.

Mainht bon tornei ai partit
Pels colps qu'ieu fier tan mortals,
Qu'en luec non vau qu'om no crit:
'So es En Peire Vidals,
Selh qui manten domnei e drudarīa,
E fa que pros per amor de s'amīa;
Et ama mais batalhas e torneis
Que monje patz, e sembla.l malaveis
Trop sojornar et estar en un loc.'

Plus que non pot ses aigua viure.l peis,
Non pot esser ses lauzengiers domneis,
Per qu'amador compron trop car lur joc.

III. Mout es bona terr'Espanha,
E.l rei qui senhor en so
Dous e car e franc e bo,
E de corteza companha;
E s'i a d'autres baros,
Mout avinens e mout pros,
De sen e de conoissensa,
E de faitz e de parvensa.   *over*

It's well-proven and commonly known how worthy and outstanding I am; and since God has so well endowed me, it's not right that my price be low. A hundred ladies I know who each would like to have me for hers, if she could—but I've never been one to boast or make pretences, and I never wanted to talk much about myself; instead I kiss ladies and unhorse knights.

Many a fine tourney have I decided with the blows I deal so deadly, so that in no place I go but they all shout: 'Here's my lord Peire Vidal, the man who upholds courtship and fine loving, and acts with prowess for his lady's love, and likes battles and tourneys more than a monk likes peace, and for whom it's like a sickness to dwell and stay long in one place.'

No more than the fish can live without water, love-service cannot be without slanderers, hence lovers pay dearly for their joy.

III. Most fine is the land of Spain, and the kings, who are its lords, gentle and dear, noble and good, and of courtly company. And there are other noblemen there too, most seemly and most worthy in sense and experience, in deeds and in outward show.

Per que.m platz qu'entr'els remanha
En l'emperial reyo,
Quar ses tota contenso
Mi rete gent e.m gazanha
Reis emperaires N'Anfos,
Per cui Jovens es joyos,
Quez el mon non a valensa
Que sa valors no la vensa.

Fach ai l'obra de l'aranha
E la muza del Breto,
Per qu'ieu mezeis no sai co
M'en rancur ni m'en complanha;
Que.l ver dir m'es angoissos
E.l mentir no m'es nuls pros;
Daus totas partz truep falhensa
En la sua benvolensa.

Mout m'a tengut en greu lanha,
Quar l'ai servid'en perdo;
E servirs ses gazardo —
Crei que chaptals en sofranha!
Que vielhs, paubres, sofrachos,
Venc entre.ls rics, vergonhos;
Per qu'om deu sercar garensa
Ans que torn en decazensa.

E pus ma dona m'estranha
De so que no.l platz que.m do —
S'amor, tart veirai Orgo
Ni.l rial castell d'Albanha.
E ja tan pauc orgulhos
Amic, ni tan amoros,
Non auran mais part Durensa,
En la terra de Provensa.

Peire Vidal

For this I am pleased to stay among them in the imperial realm, for without any ado he retains me graciously and wins me over, the king-emperor Lord Alfonso for whom Youth is joyful, and in the world there's nothing valorous but his valour overwhelms it.

I have toiled like the spider and waited long like the Breton, yet thereof I know not myself how I might complain, nor how I might lament; for to speak the truth is painful to me, and lying profits me not. On all sides I find failings in my lady's goodwill.

She has held me in most grievous affliction, and so I have served her to my loss, and service without reward—I think there's no benefit in that! And so, old, poor, and needy, I came among the rich, and full of shame, for one has to seek protection sooner than come to ruin.

And since my lady deprives me of that which she's pleased not to give me—her love, I'll not see Orgon soon, nor Aubagne's royal castle; and they'll never more have so humble a friend, nor one so full of love, there by the Durance in the land of Provence.

IV. A per pauc de chantar no.m lais,
    Quar vei mort Jovent e Valor,
    E Pretz, que non trob'on s'apais,
    C'usquecs l'enpeinh e.l gieta por;
    E vei tant renhar malvestat—
    Que.l segl'a vencut e sobrat—
    Si qu'apenas truep nulh päes
    Que.l cap non aj'a son latz pres.

    Ar, com an vout en tal pantais
    L'Apostolis e.lh fals doctor
    Sancta Gleiza, don Dieus s'irais!
    Que tan son fol e peccador
    Per que l'eretge son levat;
    E quar ilh commenso.l peccat,
    Greu es qui als far en pogues—
    Mas ieu no.n vuelh esser plaies.

    E mou de Fransa totz l'esglais,
    D'els qui solon esser melhor,
    Que.l reis non es fis ni verais
    Vas Pretz ni vas Nostre Senhor;
    Que.l Sepulcr'a dezamparat,
    E compr'e vent e fai mercat
    Atressi cum sers o borzes;
    Per que son aunit siei Franses.

    Totz lo mons torn'en tal bïais
    Qu'ier lo vim mal et huei peior;
    Et anc, pus lo guit de Dieu frais,
    Non auzim pueis l'Emperedor
    Creisser de pretz ni de bontat.
    Mas pero s'ueimais laiss'en fat
    Richart, pus en sa preizon es,
    Lor esquern en faran Engles.

over

IV. For a little I'd give up singing because I see Youth and Valour dead, and Merit too which finds nowhere to pasture for each one repels and rejects it; and I see wickedness so hold sway—it has conquered and overcome the world—that I scarcely find any country which has not its head caught in its snare.

Now, how the Pope and the false doctors have cast Holy Church in such confusion that God Himself is grieved! It's because they're so foolish and sinful that the heretics have sprung up; and since they're the first to sin, it's hard for one to do anything else—but I don't want to be their advocate.

And all the trouble comes from France, from those who used to be the best, for the king is neither noble nor true to Merit, nor to Our Lord; and he's quit the Sepulchre, and he buys and sells and haggles just like a peasant or townsman, whereby his Frenchmen are put to shame.

All the world's coming to such a pass that yesterday we saw it bad and, today, worse; and ever since he broke God's command, we hear not of the Emperor increasing in merit or virtue. And yet if henceforth he leaves Richard to his fate, now that he's in his prison, the English will vent their scorn on him.

Dels reis d'Espanha.m tenh a fais
Quar tant volon guerra mest lor;
E quar destriers ferrans ni bais
Trameton als Mors, per päor,
Que lor erguelh lor an doblat,
Don ilh son vencut e sobrat.
E fora miels, s'a lor plagues,
Qu'entr'els fos patz e leis e fes.

Mas ja non cug hom qu'ieu m'abais
Pels rics, si.s tornon sordeyor,
Qu'us fis jois me capdell'e.m pais,
Qui.m te jauzent en gran doussor,
E.m sojorn'en fin'amistat
De lieis que plus mi ven a grat.
E si voletz saber quals es,
Demandatz la en Carcasses.

Et anc no galïet ni trais
Son amic, ni.s pauzet color —
Ni.l cal, quar selha qu'en leis nais
Es fresca cum roz'en Pascor.
Bell'es sobre tota beutat,
Et a sen ab joven mesclat,
Per que.s n'agrado.l plus cortes,
E.n dizon laus ab honratz bes.

V. Baron! Jhesus, qu'en crotz fon mes
Per salvar crestïana gen,
Nos mand'a totz comunalmen
Qu'anem cobrar lo saint päes
On venc per nostr'amor morir.
E si no.l volem obezir,
Lai on feniran tuit li plag
N'auzirem maint esquiu retrag.

Peire Vidal

As for the kings of Spain, I deem it grievous that they so much want war among themselves; and because they send to the Moors fine chargers, bay and grey, out of fear, they've therefore doubled for them their pride whereby they themselves are conquered and overcome. And it would be better, if it pleased them, that among them there should be peace, and justice, and faith.

But let no man ever think that I'm abased because of the great ones, though they become more vile; for a noble joy guides and sustains me, which holds me, rejoicing, in great sweetness, and has me dwell in noble love of her who is most pleasing to me. And if you would know who she is, ask for her in the Carcassonne country.

She never deceived or betrayed her lover, nor put on false colouring—she has no need to, for the one with which she was born is as fresh as a rose at Easter. Lovely is she above all loveliness, and she has sense mingled with youth, wherefore the most courtly delight in her and speak, in her praise, of her honoured good.

V. Barons! Jesus, who was put on the cross to save all christian people, summons us all in common to go and recover that holy land where He came for our love to die. And if we would not obey Him, then there where all disputes will end shall we hear for it many a bitter reproach.

Que.l saint paradis que.ns promes,
On non a pena ni tormen,
Vol ara liurar francamen
A sels qu'iran ab lo Marques
Outra la mar, per Dieu servir.
E cill qui no.l volran seguir,
No.i aura negun, brun ni bag,
Que no.n puesc'aver gran esglag.

Ar veiatz del segle quals es:
Que qui.l sec plus al pieitz s'en pren.
Pero no.i a mas un bon sen:
Qu'om lais los mals e prenda.ls bes;
Que pus la mortz vol assalhir,
Negus non pot ni sap gandir.
Doncs, pus tuit morem atrazag,
Ben es fols qui viu mal ni lag.

Tot lo segle vei sobrepres
D'enjan e de galïamen;
E son ja tan li mescrezen
C'apenas renha dreigz ni fes,
Que quasqus ponha en traïr
Son amic per si enriquir.
Pero.lh trachor son aissi trag
Cum selh qui beu tueissec ab lag.

Catalan et Aragones
An senhor honrat e valen,
E larc e franc e conoissen,
Humil et adreg e cortes.
Mas trop laissa enmanentir
Sos sers—cui Dieus bais e azir!—
Qu'a totz jorns estan en agag
Per far en cort dan et empag.

over

Peire Vidal

For the holy paradise which He promised us, where there's neither pain nor torment, He's willing now to give freely to those who'll go with the Marquis overseas to serve God. And of those who'll not want to follow him, there'll not be one, dark or fair, but that can be sure to have great dismay.

Now see what the world is: who follows its ways the most undertakes the worst of all. Still there is but one good way: let a man quit evils and take up good works; for once death is ready to attack, no one can or knows how to escape. And so, since we all shall surely die, he's indeed a fool who lives badly or basely.

I see the whole world in the grip of guile and treachery; and so many are the unbelievers that right and good faith scarce hold sway, for each one is eager to betray his friend so as to enrich himself. Yet the betrayers are as much betrayed as he who drinks poison with milk.

Catalans and Aragonese have an honoured and valiant lord, generous and noble and wise, modest and upright and courtly. But he allows his servants to grow too rich—may God strike down and vex them!—and they're always on the watch to stir up trouble and strife at court.

Reis aunitz val meins que pages
Quan viu a lei de recrezen,
E plora.ls bes qu'autre despen,
E pert so que.l paire conques.
Aitals reis fari'ad aucir,
Et en lach lueg a sebelhir,
Qui.s defen a lei de contrag,
E no pren ni dona gamag.

Domnas vielhas non am ieu ges,
Quan viven descauzidamen
Contr'Amor e contra Joven;
Quar fin paratg'an si mal mes,
Fer es de comtar e de dir,
E fer d'escotar e d'auzir;
Quar franc domnei an si tot frag
Qu'entre lor no.n trob'om escag.

Dona, si.m tenetz en defes
Que d'al re non ai pessamen
Mas de far vostre mandamen;
E s'en grat servir vos pogues
Entre.l despulhar e.l vestir,
Ja mais mals no.m pogra venir,
Quar vostre dig e vostre fag
M'an sabor de roza de mag.

Reis de Leon, senes mentir,
Devetz honrat pretz reculhir,
Cum selh qui semen'en garag
Temprat d'umor ab douz complag.

A king put to shame is worth less than a peasant, when he lives like a recreant and deplores the wealth which another spends, and loses that which the father won. Such a king deserves to be slain and buried in a loathsome place, who stands up for himself like a paralytic, neither taking nor dealing a blow.

I've no liking for old noblewomen, when they live gracelessly, hostile to Love and to Youth, for they've so neglected true nobility it's hard to tell and recount, and hard to hear of and listen to; they've so utterly destroyed fine courtship that among them one finds no trace of it.

My lady, you so hold me in subjection that I have no thought of anything else but of doing your bidding; and if I could serve you to your pleasure between the time of undressing and dressing, then no ill could befall me, for your words and your deeds have for me the fragrance of the rose of May.

King of Leon, without a lie, you should reap honoured merit, as one who sows in a meadow watered with sweet pleasure.

VI. Per mielhs sofrir lo maltrait e l'afan
Que'm don' Amors don ieu no.m puesc defendre,
Farai chanso tal qu'er leus per aprendre,
De motz cortes et ab avinen chan.
E fas esfors, quar n'ai cor ni talan
De far chanso, qu'ades planh e sospire
Quar no vei lei don mos cors non s'azire.
Quar tant m'es luenh la terr'e.l dous païs
On es selha vas cui ieu sui aclis,
Per qu'ai perdut joi e solatz e rire.

A lieis m'autrei ab ferm cor ses enjan,
Quar totz sui sieus, ses donar e ses vendre;
E vuelh trop mais en bon esper atendre
Lieis cui soplei, don jois me vai tarzan,
Que d'autr'aver bel fait e bel semblan.
Qu'inz en mon cor m'a fait Amors escrire
Sa gran beutat don res non es a dire,
E son gent cors ben fait e ben assis;
Per qu'ieu li sui hom francs, fizels e fis,
E, per s'amor, a las autras servire.

Dieus, quan veirai lo jorn ni.l mes ni l'an
Qu'elha.m vuelha del mal gazardon rendre!
Qu'ieu non l'aus dir—mielhs m'auzarïa pendre—
Mon coratge, quant ieu li sui denan.
Mas assatz pot conoisser mon talan,
Qu'ilh es la res el mon qu'ieu plus dezire,
E per s'amor suefri tan greu martire
Que la dolors m'a ja del tot conquis,
E.l deziriers, que m'aura tost aucis;
Et a.n gran tort, mas ieu no.lh o aus dire.   *over*

VI. So as better to endure the pain and the anguish inflicted on me by Love, against whom I cannot defend myself, I'll compose a song such as will be easy to learn, with courtly words and pleasant melody. And I'm forcing myself since I've neither heart nor mind to compose, for always I lament and sigh because I see her not with whom my heart cannot be vexed. Because I'm so far from the land and the sweet country where she is to whom I am subject, I've therefore lost joy and solace and laughter.

To her I yield myself with sure and guileless heart, for I am wholly hers—there's no giving or selling; and I would much rather wait in good hope for her whom I entreat, though joy thereby comes tardily to me, than have from another fair deed or show of favour. For in my heart Love has had me inscribe her great beauty, from which there's nothing lacking, and her graceful person, well-fashioned and formed; hence I am her liege man, frank, faithful, and true, and, for her love, servant to all other ladies.

God, when shall I see the day, the month, the year when she will repay me for my pains! For I dare not reveal to her my heart—I'd sooner dare hang myself—when I am in her presence. But she can know well enough my mind, for she is the thing in the world I most desire, and for her love I suffer such grievous torment that the pain has already quite overwhelmed me, and the desire, it soon will have slain me. She does wrong in this, but I dare not tell her so.

E si merces ab lieis mi valgues tan
Qu'ela.m volgues lo sieu bell bratz estendre,
Ja del tirar no.m feira escoissendre
De tost venir, humilmen merceyan,
Vas lieis que m'a trastot en son coman;
Que.m pot donar joi o del tot aucire,
Que non ai ges poder qu'alhors me vire.
E si.l plagues que pres de si m'aizis,
Be.m tenc per sieu, mas mielhs m'agra conquis,
E feira.m ric e de gran joi jauzire.

Al pro Marques qu'a pretz, e valor gran
Manten, e sap gen donar e despendre,
E sos rics pretz fai los autres dissendre,
Vas Monferrat, chansoneta, te man;
Que.l sieu ric fait son dels autres trïan,
E per melhor lo pot hom ben eslire,
Qu'el es la flors de totz, a cui que tire,
E de totz bes comensamens e fis.
E s'aissi fos cum ieu vuelh ni devis,
Corona d'aur li vir'el cap assire.

And if mercy availed me with her this much, that she would hold out her lovely arms towards me, I'd scarcely need to be painfully dragged, but would come swiftly, humbly praying for mercy, to her who has me entirely at her command; for she can give me joy or utterly slay me, and I have no power at all to turn elsewhere. And if it pleased her to lodge me by her side, though I deem myself hers, she would have better won me, and would make me rich and in enjoyment of great joy.

To the worthy Marquis who has merit, who maintains great worth, and knows how to give and spend graciously, and whose great merit lowers that of all others, to Montferrat, my little song, I send you; for his great deeds stand out from all others, and one can indeed elect him as the best, for he is the flower of all men, no matter whom that offends, and of all good the beginning and the end. And if things were as I wish and foretell, I'd see a crown of gold set on his head.

Aimeric de Péguilhan

LIFE. Péguilhan is a small village in the Haute-Garonne, but it seems that Aimeric himself was born in Toulouse, where his father was a merchant of some standing. It was at the court of Count Raymond VI of Toulouse that, towards the end of the twelfth century, Aimeric made his professional début, but already before 1200 he had set out for Spain where for some ten years or so he was to cultivate the patronage of the kings of Castile and Aragon. The major part of his career, however, was spent in northern Italy which, with its numerous, flourishing, and culturally ambitious courts, was in the early thirteenth century becoming the favourite haunt of many troubadours. After a brief call at the court of Montferrat, Aimeric moved on to Ferrara and Malaspina, and it was under the protection of these two marquisates that he spent, throughout the second decade of the thirteenth century, the richest, most productive, and no doubt the most comfortable years of his career. It was above all to the Marquis William Malaspina that Aimeric owed his gratitude, and one can well understand the dismay expressed by the poet at his patron's death in 1220; he was never again to secure any such lasting protection. One of his last compositions, an exchange of couplets with the young Italian poet Sordello, dates from the mid-1220s, and the reference in it to Aimeric's advanced years, though made in jest, was undoubtedly true. His mediaeval biographer reports that he died in Lombardy, without indicating when; it was, in all probability, about the year 1230.

WORKS. Aimeric's forty-nine compositions fall into three distinct groups, *cansos, sirventès*, and poetic exchanges in the form of *coblas* or *partimens*, but one feature is common to them all: the predominant influence of the poet's professional status. Few of his love-songs lack some flattering reference or dedication to actual or potential patrons; few venture beyond the most widely accepted formal and thematic conventions, and such attempts at innovation as are made tend, by their very isolation, to underline a general lack of originality. Not that professionalism, of itself, precluded inventiveness, but its effects were reinforced by the fact that the major part of Aimeric's career was spent in Italy. Here, in the early thirteenth century, the *canso* was still rather an imported luxury than the spontaneous product of a native culture; as such, it appears that the closer it remained to pre-established models, the more accessible it was to its new public. In the *sirventès*, professionalism operates more specifically on the thematic level. Four *planhs* lament the deaths of various Italian patrons, and one of their most dominant *motifs* is the poet's concern for his own material prospects, a concern which inspires two other poems of this group, one being an attack on the 'new minstrels' flocking to the Italian courts, the other a song of praise by which Aimeric manifestly hoped to gain the favour of the Emperor Frederick II. The third group of compositions is made up of *coblas* and *partimens*. The former, being exchanges of single couplets with one or another of the poet's colleagues, represent little more than snatches of minstrel gossip, one interesting feature of which, however, is the personal contact they reveal between the Provençal poets and their early Italian imitators. The *partimens*, or stanza by stanza debates with another poet on some, usually amorous, dilemma, are rather more ambitious in scope but, as in the *coblas*, the figure of the poet as passionate lover or earnest spokesman clearly gives way to that of simple public entertainer. This feature too is in some measure determined by the conditions which the professional troubadour found in Italy; indeed the principal interest of Aimeric's work might be said to be the extent to which it is involved in, and hence reflects, the processes whereby troubadour poetry, already in its native land approaching its decline, was being established in an area where it was to put down fresh roots and flourish anew.

EDITION. W. P. Shepard and F. M. Chambers *The Poems of Aimeric de Péguilhan* (Evanston 1950).

SELECTION. The first selected piece (Sh.-Ch. no. 19) is a typical *partimen*, shared in this case with Guilhem de Berguédan, a Spanish nobleman who probably helped Aimeric gain access to the royal courts in Spain. It is an early composition —

Guilhem died *c.* 1200—and in more than one later poem Aimeric was to take up again the attitude defended here of the 'desamatz amoros'. There follow two *cansos* (Sh.-Ch. nos. 12, 15), the elegant banality and facile smoothness of which represent the poet's highest artistic achievement. The abundant word-play, accumulation, and relatively elaborate imagery are characteristic of Aimeric's style; no less characteristic are the double dedication of the one and the fulsome flattery which concludes the other, here addressed to Frederick II. Aimeric composed the fourth poem (Sh.-Ch. no. 11) on the occasion of Innocent III's launching of yet another crusading campaign in 1213; straightforward, direct, and wholly traditional in theme and expression, it also exploits the possibilities inherent in the genre of praising the poet's protectors and criticizing those more remote princes too occupied in their own quarrels to hear the call to holy war, in this case the kings of France and England and the rival claimants to the imperial throne. The last poem (Sh.-Ch. no. 10) is a *planh* lamenting the death of William Malaspina in 1220; the very frankness with which the poet speaks of his own situation leaves little doubt as to the sincerity of the sentiments expressed; he never did find 'replacement or consolation' for his late patron and possibly felt, as we do, that this poem marks the beginning of the end of his career.

1. De Berguedan, d'estas dōas razos
    Al vostre sen chausetz en la meillor,
    Q'ieu mantenrai tant ben la sordejor
    Q'ie.us cuich vensser, qui dreich m'en vol jutgar:
    Si volrīatz mais desamatz amar,
    O desamar e que fossetz amatz?
    Chausetz vīatz cella que mais vos platz.

    N'Aimerics, doncs aurīa sen de tos
    Si eu lo mieills non chausīa d'amor.
    Totz temps vuoill mais qe.m teignan per seignor
    E que desam e c'om mi teigna car;
    C'anc en amor non vengui per musar,
    Ni anc non fui d'aqels desfasendatz;
    Qe.l gazaing vuoill de dompnas e de datz.

    De Berguedan, nuils hom desamoros,
    Al mieu semblan, non a gaug ni honor;
    C'aissi cum sens val mais sobre follor,
    Val mais qui serv e.n fai mieills ad honrar,
    C'aicel qe vol penre e non donar.
    Per q'ieu vuoill mais esser paubres, honratz,
    C'avols, manens e desenamoratz.

    N'Aimerics, tot enaissi o faitz vos
    Cum fetz Rainautz qand ac del fruich sabor,
    Que s'en laisset non per autre temor
    Mas car non poc sus el cereis montar.
    E blasme.l fruich car aver ni manjar
    Non poc, e vos etz ab lui acordatz,
    C'aisso que non podetz aver blasmatz.

    De Berguedan, car vos etz malgignos,
    Cuidatz qez eu sīa d'aital color?
    Non sui, q'en loc de gauch pren la dolor,
    Mas bos respieitz m'aiud'a sofertar.
    Per qu'eu vuoill mais ses consegr'enchaussar
    Que conseguir so don non fos pagatz,
    Car mil d'autres val us bens desiratz.

                                                                    over

I. De Berguédan, of these two ways of thinking choose the one which to your mind is better, then I'll uphold so well the worse that I think I'll beat you, if in this one would judge me aright: would you prefer to love, unloved, or not to love while loved? Choose quickly now the one which pleases you more.

Sir Aimeric, I'd for sure have the mind of a child if I were to choose not the better part in love: at all times I prefer to be deemed lord, and that I love not while one holds me dear. For never to love came I to waste my time, and I was never one of your idle bystanders; so I want the winnings from ladies as from dice.

De Berguédan, no man who's not in love, it seems to me, has ever joy or honour; for just as good sense is worth more than folly, so he is worth more who serves, and is more to be honoured, than he who wants to take and not to give. Wherefore I prefer to be a poor man, honoured, than a base fellow, wealthy and disenamoured.

Sir Aimeric, you're acting just like Reynard the fox when he caught a whiff of the fruit, for he gave it up from no other fear but this, that he could not climb into the cherry-tree. He scorned the fruit since he could not get it and eat it, and you're of one mind with him since you scorn what you cannot have.

De Berguédan, because you're unsophisticated, do you believe that I'm of the same complexion? I'm not, for in place of joy I accept sorrow, but fair hope helps me to wait patiently. Hence I'd rather chase without catching, than catch that with which I'd not be satisfied, because one good thing, desired, is worth a thousand others.

N'Aimerics, mainz de gaillartz e de pros
N'ai vistz faillir tot per aital error.
Qe.l cors d'En Ot del caval milsoudor
En fo vencutz car no.l laisset brochar,
Que si de prim l'agues faich enanssar,
Cel qe.l venqet fora per el sobratz.
Per c'om deu far, quan pot, sas volontatz.

De Berguedan, cella q'ieu teing plus car
Vuoill mil aitans mais amar, desamatz,
C'ab autra far totas mas volontatz.

Bar N'Aimerics, ja no.us cuidetz gabar!
Que s'amassetz aissi cum vos vanatz,
No.us foratz tant de Tolosa loignatz.

11. Atressi.m pren quom fai al joguador
Qu'al comensar jogua mayestrilmen
A petits juecs, pueis s'escalfa perden,
Que.l fai montar tan qu'es en la folor:
Aissi.m mis ieu pauc e pauc en la vïa,
Que cujava amar ab mayestrïa
Si qu'en pogues partir quan me volgues,
On sui intratz tan qu'issir non puesc ges.

Autra vetz fui en la preizon d'Amor,
Don escapei, mas äora.m repren
Ab un cortes engienh tan sotilmen
Que.m fa plazer mo mal e ma dolor;
Q'un latz me fetz metr'al colh ab que.m lïa,
Don per mon grat mai no.m deslïarïa;
E nulhs autr'om que fos lïatz non es,
Qui.l deslïes, que ben no li plagues.

Anc mais nulh temps no trobei lïador
Tan ferm lïes ab tan pauc lïamen,
Que.l lïams fo d'un dous bays solamen,
Don non truep sai qui.m desli, ni alhor.

over

Sir Aimeric, I've seen many fine men and true failing by just such an error. And Sir Otto's race with the priceless horse was lost because he did not give it its head, whereas, if from the start he had let it run, he who beat him would have been overcome by him. Hence a man should, when he can, fulfil his desires.

De Berguédan, the one whom I hold most dear I prefer a thousand times to love, unloved, than with another fulfil all my desires.

Noble Sir Aimeric, don't think you can boast like that! For if you loved in the way which you're now vaunting, you'd not have come so far from Toulouse.

11. It is so with me as it is with the gambler who, at the start, plays masterfully for small stakes and then becomes heated, when losing, which makes him raise his game until he is deep in folly; so I once set out, step by step, along that road—thinking to love with mastery so that I could quit whenever I wanted—to which I am now so committed that I cannot leave it at all.

Once I was in Love's prison and I escaped from it, but now it recaptures me with a courtly device so subtly that it makes pleasing to me my pain and my sorrow; for it had me put a leash around my neck with which it might bind me and from which, by my own will, I'd never unbind myself, and there is no other man, were he bound, who if one unbound him would not be pleased indeed.

At no time did I ever find a captor who bound so strongly with such little binding, for the bond was formed of one sweet kiss alone, and from it I find none, here or elsewhere, to unbind me.

Enlïamatz sui tan que, si.m volïa
Deslïamar, ges far non o poirïa;
Qu'Amors, que lai m'enlïamet e.m pres,
M'enlïama sai plus fort per un tres.

A ley del fer que va ses tirador
Vas l'azimen que.l tira vas si gen,
Amors, que.m sap tirar ses tiramen,
Mas tirat m'a sivals per la melhor.
Quar si d'autra melhuirar me sabïa,
Tant am lo mielhs que be.m melhuirarïa,
Mas melhuirar no cre que m'en pogues;
Ve.us per que m'a, part las melhors, conques!

Na Gentils Cors, formatz plus gen que flor,
Aiatz de me qualacom chauzimen,
Quar muer per vos, d'envey'e de talen—
E podetz o pröar a ma color,
Quan vos remir, que.s trasva e.s cambïa.
Per que fora almorn'e cortezïa
Q'humilitatz merceyan vos prezes
D'aquest cochat, sofrachos de totz bes.

Be.m platz Guillems Malespina.l marques,
Quar conquier pretz, e Pretz a lui conques.

Na Beatritz d'Est, lo bes qu'en vos es
Fa melhuirar las autras ab lors bes.

I am so bound that, were I to seek to unbind myself, I could not do so at all; for Love, who there took me and bound me, here binds me three times more strongly.

In the manner of iron which moves, with no one pulling, towards the lodestone which gently pulls it towards itself, Love, which can pull me without any pulling, has at least pulled me most by virtue of her who is best. For if by another lady I could grow better, I so love what's best that I would for sure grow better, but I think not that I could thereby be better; now see you by whom, from among the best, Love has conquered me!

My Lady Fair-in-Person, more gracefully formed than a flower, have for me some measure of indulgence since for you I die of longing and desire—this you can prove by my complexion which, when I behold you, changes and fades away. Wherefore it would be charity and courtliness that humility should take you, showing mercy to one afflicted and deprived of all things good.

I'm well pleased by William Malaspina, the Marquis, for he conquers merit and Merit has conquered him.

My Lady Beatrice of Este, the good that is in you makes other ladies, with the good in them, grow better.

III. Cel qui s'irais ni guerreia ab Amor
Ges que savis non fai, al mieu semblan,
Car de guerra vei tart pro e tost dan,
E guerra fai tornar mal en pejor.
En guerra trob, per q'ieu no la volrīa,
Viltat de mal e de ben carestīa.
Mas fin'Amors, sitot mi fai languir,
A tant de joi qe.m pot leu esjauzir.

Qe.ill plazer son plus qe.il enoi d'Amor,
E.il ben qe.il mal, e.il sojorn qe.il afan,
E.il gaug qe.il dol, e.il leu fais qe.il pesan,
E.il pro qe.il dan son plus, e.il ris qe.il plor.
Non dic aissi del tot que mal no.n sīa,
E.l mals c'om n'a val mais que si.n garīa;
Car qui ama de cor non vol garir
Del mal d'Amor, tant es dolz per sofrir.

Ancaras trob mais de ben en Amor,
Qe.l vil fai car, e.l nesci gen-parlan,
E l'escars larc, e leial lo trüan,
E.l fol savi, e.l pec conoissedor.
E l'orgoillos domesg'et homelīa,
E fai de dos cors un, tant ferm los līa.
Per c'om non deu ad Amor contradir,
Pois tant gen sap esmendar e fenir.

S'ieu l'ai servit, pro n'ai canje d'Amor,
Ab que ja puois non agues mas aitan;
Q'en mains luocs m'a faich tant aut e tant gran
Don ja ses lieis non pogr'aver honor;
E maintas vetz m'engart de vilanīa
Que ses Amor gardar no m'en sabrīa,
E mains bons motz mi fai pensar e dir
Que ses Amor no.i sabrīa venir.

Bona dompna, de vos teing e d'Amor,
Sen e saber, cor e cors, motz e chan;
E s'ieu ren dic que sīa benestan,
Devetz n'aver lo grat e la lauzor,
Vos et Amors, qe.m datz la mäestrīa. *over*

III. He who grows vexed or wages war with Love behaves, it seems to me, scarce like a wise man, since from war I see advantage coming slowly and harm swiftly, and war makes bad turn to worse. In war I find—wherefore I'd want it not—a deal of evil and of good a dearth. But noble Love, although it makes me languish, has so much joy that it can soon make me rejoice.

For the pleasures are more than the pangs of Love, the good than the bad, the solace than the anguish, the joys than the sorrows, and the gay moments than the grievous; the advantages than the harms are more, and the smiles more than the tears. I do not say by this at all that therein is no ill, but the illness one has of it is worth more than if one were cured; for he who loves nobly seeks not to be cured of Love's ill, so sweet it is to suffer.

I find still more good in Love, for it makes what is common precious, the blockhead eloquent, the mean man liberal, and trustworthy the rogue, the fool wise and the ignorant learned. It tames and humbles the haughty, and makes of two hearts one, it binds them so strongly. On this account one should not gainsay Love, since it can so well make better and more fine.

If I have served it, I've much in exchange from Love, even if I had never again so much as this; for in many a place it has made me so high and great where, without it, I never could have had honour; and many a time it keeps me from lowly actions when, without Love, I could not have refrained therefrom, and many fine words does it cause me to think and utter which, without Love, I could not have come upon.

Good Lady, I hold from you and from Love sense and knowledge, heart and body, words and song; and if I say aught that is seemly, you should have the thanks and the praise for it, you and Love, who give me the mastery.

E si ja plus de ben no m'en venïa,
Pro n'ai cambi segon lo mieu servir;
E si fos plus, ben saubra.l plus grazir.

Chanssos, vai t'en de ma part e d'Amor,
Al bon, al bel, al valen, al prezan,
A cui servon Latin et Alaman,
E.l sopleion cum bon Emperador;
Sobre.ls majors a tant de majorïa,
Larguez'e pretz, honor e cortesïa,
Sen e saber, conoissens'e chausir—
Ric de ricor per ric pretz conquerir.

IV. Ara parra qual seran enveyos
D'aver lo pretz del mon e.l pretz de Dieu,
Que be.ls poiran guazanhar ambedos
Selh que seran adreitamen romieu
Al Sepulcre cobrar. Las! qual dolor,
Que Turc aian forsat Nostre Senhor!
Pensem el cor la dezonor mortal,
E de la crotz prendam lo sanh senhal
E passem lai, que.l ferms e.l conoissens
Nos guizara, lo bos Pap'Innocens.

Doncs, pus quascus n'es preguatz e somos,
Tragua s'enan e senh s'e nom de Dieu,
Qu'en la crotz fo mes entre dos lairos,
Quan, ses colpa, l'auciron li Juzieu.
Quar si prezam leialtat ni valor,
Son dezeret tenrem a dezonor;
Mas nos amam e volem so qu'es mal,
E söanam so qu'es bon e que val;
Que.l viures sai, qu'es morirs, non es gens,
E.l morirs lai, viures sades, plazens.

No deurïa esser hom temeros
De suffrir mort el servizi de Dieu,
Qu'elh la suffri el servizi de nos,
Don seran salf, essems ab Sant Andrieu,   *over*

And if no more good were ever to befall me, I have much in exchange for my service; and if there were more I could well, for that more, give thanks.

Song, go now in my name and in Love's, to the good, the fair, the valiant and the praiseworthy, to him whom Latins and Germans serve, to whom they bow down as to a good Emperor; above the most eminent he has such eminence, liberality, merit, honour and courtliness, wisdom and knowledge, judgement and discernment—great in that greatness by which great merit is won.

IV. Now will it be clear which men are desirous of having the world's merit and the merit of God, for they'll indeed be able to gain them both who straightway set forth to recover the Sepulchre. Alas! what grief, that the Turks have done violence to Our Lord! Let us think in our hearts on the mortal dishonour, and take up the sacred sign of the cross, and journey yonder; for he, the strong, the wise, will guide us, the good Pope Innocent.

So then, since each is asked and summoned thus, let him step forth and take the holy sign in the name of God, Who was put on the cross between two thieves when, for no fault, the Jews killed Him. For, if we prize loyalty and valour, His disinheritance we shall deem a dishonour; but we love and desire that which is evil, and scorn that which is good and worthwhile. While living here, which is dying, is not noble, to die yonder is life sweet and pleasant.

No man should be afraid to suffer death in the service of God, for He suffered it in our service, and for this reason they will be saved, in company with St Andrew,

Selh que.l segran lai vas Monti-Tabor.
Per que negus non deu aver päor,
El vïatge, d'aquesta mort carnal;
Plus deu temer la mort esperital
On seran plors ez estridors de dens,
Que Sanhs Matieus o mostr'e n'es guirens.

A! vengutz es lo temps e la sazos
On deu esser pröat qual temon Dieu;
Qu'elh non somo mas los valens e.ls pros,
Quar silh seran totz temps franchamen sieu
Qui seran lai ferm bon combatedor,
[. . . .]
E franc e larc e cortes e leyal;
E remanran li menut e.l venal,
Que dels bos vol Dieus qu'ab bos fagz valens
Se salvon lai—ez es belhs salvamens!

E si anc Guillems Malespina fon bos
En est segle, ben o mostra en Dieu,
Qu'ab los prumiers s'es crozatz voluntos
Per socorre.l Sant Sepulcr'e son fieu.
Don an li rey colp'e l'emperador,
Quar no fan paz ez acort entre lor
Per desliurar lo regisme reyal,
E.l lum, e.l vas, e la crotz atretal,
Qu'an retengut li Turc tan longuamens
Que sol l'auzirs es us grieus pessamens.

Marques de Monferrat, vostr'ansessor
Agron lo pretz de Suri'e l'onor;
E vos, senher, vulhatz l'aver aital.
El nom de Dieu vos metetz lo senhal
E passatz lai, que pretz ez honramens
Vos er el mon, et en Dieu salvamens.

Tot so qu'om fai el segl'es dreitz nïens,
Si, a la fi, non l'äonda sos sens.

they who follow Him yonder to Mount Tabor. Wherefore no man should fear on the journey this death of the flesh; he should fear more the death of the spirit wherein will be weeping and gnashing of teeth, as St Matthew propounds it and to it bears witness.

Ha! now is the time and season come when it is to be proved what men fear God. For He summons none but the brave and the worthy since they will always be His, in freedom, who yonder are good strong fighters (. . .) and free and generous and courtly and loyal; and the mean and the venal will stay behind, for of good men alone does God wish that, by fair deeds of valour, they should be saved—and a fine salvation it is!

And if ever William Malaspina was good in this earthly life, he now shows it well in God's; for with the first he has willingly taken the cross to save the Holy Sepulchre and its fief. On this account are the kings at fault, and the emperors, for they do not make peace and accord among themselves so as to deliver the royal kingdom, the light, the tomb, and the cross as well, which the Turks have retained for so long now that only to hear of it is a grievous sorrow.

Marquis of Montferrat, your forebears had the merit and glory of Syria; and may you, Lord, be willing to have it too. In the name of God put on the holy sign and journey yonder, for merit and honour will be yours in this world, and, in God, salvation.

All that a man does in this world is pure nothingness if, at the end, his good sense helps him not.

V. Era par ben que Valors se desfai,
E podetz o conoisser e saber,
Quar selh que plus volïa mantener
Solatz, domney, larguez', ab cor veray,
Mezur'e sen, conoissens'e parïa,
Humilitat, orguelh ses vilanïa,
E.ls bos mestiers totz ses menhs e ses mai,
Es mortz! Guillems Malespina marques,
Que fo miralhs e mayestre dels bes.

De bos mestiers el mon par non li say,
Qu'anc no fon tan larcs, segon mon parer,
Alexandres, de manjar ni d'aver,
Qu'elh non dis 'non' qui.l quis, ni trobet plai;
Ni ges Galvains d'armas plus non valïa,
Ni non saup tan Ivans de cortezïa,
Ni.s mes Tristans d'amor en tan d'essay.
Hueymais non er castïatz ni repres
Negus, si falh, pus lo miralhs no.y es.

On son eras siei dig plazent e guai,
E siei fag plus poderos de poder,
Que.ls autres fagz fazïan desvaler?
Oi Dieus! cum son escurzit li clar rai
Qu'alumnavan Toscan'e Lombardïa,
Per que quascus anava e venïa
Ab lo sieu lum, ses dupt'e ses esmai,
Qu'aissi saup Pretz guizar, tan fon cortes,
Cum l'estela guidet los reys totz tres.

Per cui venran soudadier de luenh sai,
Ni.l ric joglar que.l venïan vezer,
Qu'elh sabïa honrar e car tener
Plus que princeps de sai mar ni de lai,
E manhta gen ses art, ses joglarïa?
Per lo sieu don, on negus no falhïa,
Que manh caval ferran e brun e bay
Donava plus soven, ez autr'arnes,
De nulh baron qu'ieu anc vis ni saubes.

over

V. Now indeed is it clear that Valour is undone, and this you can see and know for sure, for he who sought most, with true heart, to uphold pleasure, courtship, liberality, moderation and reason, knowledge and friendship, humility, pride without baseness, and all good qualities with nothing more and nothing less—he is dead, the Marquis William Malaspina, who was mirror and master of virtues.

In good qualities I know not his equal in the world, for never so liberal, so it appears to me, was Alexander in sustenance or riches, for he never said 'no' if one asked him, nor found cause to quibble; and Gavain was not at all more valiant in arms, and Ivain not so versed in courtliness, nor did Tristan prove himself so much in love. Henceforth none will be blamed or reproached if he does wrong, for the mirror is here no more.

Where are they now, his gay and pleasant words, and his deeds more mighty than might itself, which rendered other deeds of little worth? Ah God! how are the bright rays dimmed which lighted Tuscany and Lombardy where, by his light, each came and went without fear and without dismay, for thus he could guide Merit, he was so courtly, as the star guided once the three kings together.

For whom will come paid warriors here from afar, and the fine minstrels who came to visit him and whom he honoured and held dear more than any prince this side of the sea or the other, and many folk too, without art, without minstrelsy? They came for his gifts whereof none went lacking, as he gave away more readily many a steed, grey, brown, or bay, and other equipment too, than any baron I ever saw or knew.

Belhs senher cars, valens, ieu que farai?
Ni cum puesc sai vius ses vos remaner,
Que.m saubes tan dir e far mon plazer
Qu'autre plazers contra.l vostre.m desplai?
Que tals per vos m'onrav'e m'aculhīa
Que m'er estrans cum si vist no m'avīa.
Ni ja nulh temps cambi no.n trobarai,
Ni esmenda del dan qu'ai per vos pres,
Nez ieu non cre qu'om far la m'en pogues.

Lo Senher qu'es us en personas tres
Vos valh'aissi cum ops ni cocha.us es.

Fair, dear, noble lord, what shall I do now? How can I stay here, alive, without you who caused me such pleasure in words and deeds that in contrast with yours other pleasure displeases me? Such men there are who for your sake honoured and welcomed me, who now will spurn me as if they had not seen me. And at no time will I ever find replacement or consolation for the loss which I've suffered in you, nor do I think that one could do so for me.

May the Lord Who is one in three persons help you as is your need and ardent desire.

Sordello

LIFE. Sordello, one of the first Italian poets to cultivate the troubadour lyric, and the most justly celebrated, was born at Goito, near Mantua, in the early years of the thirteenth century. The son of a poor knight, he frequented in his youth the courts of Lombardy where we first find traces of him in the mid-1220s, already enjoying some notoriety among the troubadours now flocking to the region and with whom he exchanged his first verses. In 1229, however, being deeply implicated in certain scandalous affairs, including the kidnapping and possible seduction of Count Ricciardo di San Bonifacio's wife in Verona, he fled the country. There followed a rather obscure period spent as a wandering minstrel, until he eventually found refuge at the court of Provence. Here, beginning in the early 1230s, Sordello enjoyed the patronage of Count Raymond Bérenger IV and, after the latter's death in 1245, of his successor Charles of Anjou. From 1241 to 1269 a series of original documents attest that he acquired an increasingly important position as court functionary and when, in 1265, Charles first undertook his extensive military campaigns in Italy, Sordello, now a knight and referred to by the Count as his *dilectus familiaris et fidelis*, was able at last to return to his native land. In 1268 and 1269, for services rendered, he was rewarded with a number of feudal holdings in the conquered kingdom of Naples; not that it profited him much for in August 1269 they are made over to another knight in Charles' service. No reason for the re-allocation is given and in no further relevant document is Sordello's name mentioned; one can only presume that by late 1269 he was dead.

WORKS. Of the general characteristics of Sordello's work, consisting of forty-three compositions in all, the most obvious are a considerable variety of genre and, within that variety, a numerical predominance of minor forms—*coblas, tensos, parti-*

mens, etc.—over the major forms of *canso* and *sirventès*. Many of the minor compositions belong either to the poet's early years in Italy, or to that period of his life when, in the service of Charles of Anjou, he was entrusted with more important functions than those of simple court minstrel. Their interest is mainly biographical, their artistic merit slight. The major part of his work, including the *cansos* and *sirventès*, date from the 1230s and early 1240s when he most actively pursued the career of professional troubadour. The twelve *cansos* form a fairly coherent group, unadventurous in their verse-form and remarkable in their style only by a relative simplicity of expression well-suited to a poet not working in his native tongue. Their thematic material, however, although generally rather limited, conventional, and repetitive in nature, is distinguished by one important feature. That is the sustained exploitation of the theme of honour, conceived of as both the highest reward to which the lover might aspire and the greatest attribute of the lady which no concession to love or the lover's pleas should taint. Not only does this theme most distinctively individualize Sordello's love-poetry, it marks an important step in the process by which the sensualism of the classical troubadour *canso* is transformed into the spirituality of the *dolce stil nuovo*. It is further touched on in Sordello's minor, possibly fragmentary, compositions and provides the main subject of his *Ensenhamen d'Onor*, a long didactic poem which catalogues those courtly virtues which constitute true honour. As for Sordello's eight *sirventès*, three are personal satires, two are devoted to a general deploration of the moral state of the world, and the remaining three deal, in the same spirit, with rather more specific historical circumstances. Although they are formally less ornate than the *cansos*, and lack the vigour and sharpness achieved by such eminent practitioners of the genre as Bertran de Born or Peire Cardenal, it is undoubtedly to them that Sordello owed his lasting fame. Dante certainly had them in mind when, in the *Purgatory*, he assigns to him the rôle of critic of kings and princes, and it is on the basis of Dante's presentation, combined with local tales of his youthful exploits, that the legend of Sordello was to thrive for centuries to come. Unfortunately, for all its rich fantasy, this legend serves only to obscure the real interest and importance of Sordello's poetry.

EDITION. M. Boni *Sordello, Le Poesie* (Bologna 1954).

SELECTION. Such is the uniformity of the art and inspiration of Sordello's *cansos* that any selection from among them will represent in most aspects the complete group; in the three *cansos* first selected here (Boni nos. 2, 4, 9), one can well appreciate the poet's elegance and simplicity of expression, his successful attempts at relatively elaborate simile, the restricted scope of the stanza-structure and, associated with a number of purely conventional *motifs*, the distinctive part played by the theme of honour. The same formal qualities are to be seen in the fourth selected piece (Boni no. 22), a moral *sirventès* dedicated, like the first *canso*, to *Na Agradiva*, thought to be Guida of Rodez, wife of a Provençal baron. The somewhat ambiguous envoy to James I of Aragon almost certainly echoes Raymond Bérenger's desire to secure more firmly a rather problematical alliance with the Spanish monarch. The next poem, the second of three personal *sirventès* directed against the poet Peire Bremon Ricas Novas, is one of the more elegant examples of an increasingly cultivated genre by which, with a low, music-hall type of humour, the professional troubadours sought to amuse their noble public. Lastly, a political *sirventès* (Boni no. 26) which, in the guise of a funeral lament for a Provençal nobleman, castigates the failings and weaknesses of most of the crowned heads of W. Europe. Composed *c.* 1237—as is indicated by the fairly transparent historical allusions—this is generally considered to be Sordello's most successful composition, and it is certainly his most famous. Several imitations of it were soon produced, and it is this poem above all which led Dante, already an admirer of Sordello's work, to make of him the splendidly impressive figure who stalks through cantos 6, 7 and 8 of the *Purgatory*.

I.   Aitant, ses plus, viu hom quan viu jauzens,
     C'autra viure no.s deu vid'apellar;
     Per q'ieu m'esfors de viur'e de reinhar
     Ab joi, per leys plus coratjozamens
     Servir q'ieu am; quar hom que viu marritz
     Non pot de cor far bos faitz ni grazitz;
     Doncx er merces si.m fai la plus grazida
     Viure jauzens, pus als no.m ten a vida.

     Tant pes en lieys e tan l'am coralmens
     Que nueyt e jorn tem mi falh'al pensar,
     Quar de beutat ni de pretz non a par,
     Per que.l devon esser obediens
     Las plus prezans, quar enaissi es guitz
     Per dreg guidar, sos gens cors ben aibitz,
     Las pros en pretz, cum las naus en mar guida
     La tramontana e.l fers e.lh caramida.

     E puys guida.l ferm'estela luzenz
     Las naus que van perillan per la mar,
     Ben degra mi cil, qi.l sembla, guidar,
     Qu'en la mar suy per lieys profondamens
     Tant esvaratz, destreitz, et esbaïtz,
     Qe.i serai mortz ans que.n hiesc'e peritz,
     Si no.m secor, quar non truep a l'yssida
     Riba ni port, gua ni pont, ni guerida.

     Dura merces e trop loncx chauzimens
     Me fan murir per sobre-dezirar,
     Quar ieu non puesc ses lo joy vius durar
     Qu'ie.l quier, sirven, aman, ab tals turmens
     Que.l jorn mil vetz volri'esser fenitz,
     Tan mi destreing lo dartz don sui feritz
     Al cor d'Amor, per qe.l mortz m'es ayzida,
     Car il non es tot eissamen ferida.

     Las! Don li ven de mi aucir talens,
     Pos q'ill no.m pot en nulh forfach trobar,
     E ja per mal que.m sapcha dir ni far
     Non puosc esser de lieis amar partens?
     Doncx, e que.lh val si.m fai mal ni.l me ditz?   *over*

I. Inasmuch, no more, does a man live as he lives joyously, and to live otherwise should not life be called; wherefore I strive to live and to dwell in joy, so as to serve with greater heart her whom I love. For the man who lives sadly cannot with heart do fine deeds or fair; hence it will be mercy if she, the most gracious, has me live joyously, since aught else I deem not life.

So much do I think of her and love her so in my heart that, night and day, I fear that by thinking I fail, because in beauty and merit she has no peer. For this should ladies who merit most be obedient to her, that in the same way is her gracious and perfect person a guide, truly to guide in merit those ladies of worth, as the pole-star or magnet or lodestone guides ships on the sea.

And since the constant, shining star guides ships that go in peril on the sea, she should indeed, who is like it, guide me who for her am so deeply at sea, so lost, distressed and in dismay that I'll be dead before I emerge from it, and perished, unless she helps me; for I find not at journey's end a shore, or haven, ford or bridge, or shelter.

Obdurate mercy and long-delayed indulgence make me die of over-desiring, for I cannot live without the joy which I seek of her, serving, loving, in such torment that a thousand times a day I would my life were ended. So much does Love's dart, by which I'm stricken in heart, torment me that death is near, because she is not by it likewise stricken.

Alas! Whence comes to her the wish to slay me, since she can find me in no fault, and never, for any ill which she might say or do me, can I quit loving her? What then does it avail her if she says or does me ill?

C'aissi.l sui ferms, autreiatz, e plevitz
Qu'enans sera m'arma del cors partida
Qu'ieu me.n parta, tan l'am d'amor complida.

N'Agradiva, dompna de pretz razitz,
De cor, de cors, e de faitz e de ditz
Suy vostres totz, quar etz la mielhs aybida,
Net'e plazens, süaus et yssernida.

Per Dieu, aiatz merce, dompna grazida,
De me, qu'en vos es ma mortz e ma vida.

11.   Bel m'es ab motz leugiers a far
    Chanson plazen et ab guay so,
    Que.l melher que hom pot trïar,
    A cuy m'autrey e.m ren e.m do,
    No vol ni.l plai chantar de mäestrïa;
    E mas no.lh plai, farai hueymais mon chan
    Leu a chantar e d'auzir agradan,
    Clar d'entendre e prim, qui prim lo trïa.

    Gen mi saup mon fin cor emblar
    Al prim qu'ieu mirey sa faisso,
    Ab un dous amoros esguar
    Que.m lansero siey huelh lairo.
    Ab selh esgar m'intret en aisselh dïa
    Amors pels huelhs al cor d'aital semblan,
    Que.l cor en trays e mes l'a son coman,
    Si qu'ab lieys es, on qu'ieu an ni estïa.

    Ai, cum mi saup gent esgardar—
    Si l'esgartz messongiers no fo—
    Dels huelhs que sap gent envïar
    Totz temps per dreg lai on l'es bo!
    Mas a sos digz mi par qu'aiso.s cambïa,
    Pero l'esgar creirai, qu'ab cor forsan
    Parl'om pro vetz, mas nulh poder non an
    Huelh d'esgardar gen, si.l cor no.ls envïa.   *over*

For so I am bound to her, devoted and pledged, that my soul will have left my body sooner than I had left her, so much do I love her in perfect love.

Lady Delightful, root of all merit, I am in heart, in body, and in deeds and words entirely yours, for you are the most perfect, pure and pleasing, gentle, and discerning.

In God's name have mercy, gracious lady, on me, for in you is my death and my life.

11. I'm happy to make with easy words a pleasant song, and with gay melody, for the best lady that a man can choose, to whom I devote and yield and render myself, neither desires nor is pleased by the elaborate style of singing; and since she is not pleased by it, I'll make from now on my song easy to sing and agreeable to hear, clear and simple to understand, for one who chooses it simple.

Gently she knew how to steal my pure heart from me, when first I beheld her, with a sweet loving glance which her thieving eyes cast me. With that glance, on that day, love entered through the eyes into my heart, and in such guise that it drew my heart from me and placed it at her command, so that it is with her wherever I go or dwell.

Ah! How she knew how to glance gently at me—unless that glance was a liar—with eyes which she can gently turn always directly there where it pleases her! But from her words it appears to me that all that is now changing, yet I'll believe her glance; for many a time can one speak with constrained heart, but the eyes have no power to cast a gentle glance unless the heart directs them.

E quar am de bon pretz ses par,
Am mais servir lieys en perdo
Qu'autra qu'ab si.m degnes colgar.
Mas no la sier ses guazardo,
Quar fis amicx no sier ges d'aital guïa,
Quan sier de cor en honrat loc prezan;
Per que l'onors m'es guazardos d'aitan
Que.l sobreplus non quier, mas be.u penrïa.

Vailla.m ab vos merces, dolz'enemïa;
No m'auzïez s'eu vos am ses enjan.
Qe me suffratz qe.us serv'ab ferm talan:
Tal don deman, ni estre non deurïa.

III. Qan plus creis, dompna, .l desiriers
Don languisc, quar no.m faitz amor,
De lauzar vostre pretz ausor
Creis plus mos cors, car jois entiers
No.m pot ges vinir, amija,
De vos, si.l pretz s'en destrija;
Q'aitan car teing vostre fin pretz valen
Com am ni voill vostre cors car e gen.

Aital m'autrei, fis, vertadiers,
A vos q'etz ses par de valor,
Q'eu am mais morir ab dolor
Qe de vos mi veng'aligriers
Q'al fin pretz q'en vos s'abrija
Puesca dan tener; e si ja
Mais me trobatz vas vos d'autre talen,
Ja non aiaz merce ni chausimen.

Q'amar non pot nuls cavaliers
Sa dompna ses cor trichador,
S'engal lei non ama sa honor.
Per qe.us prec, bels cors plazentiers, *over*

And because I love in fair and peerless merit, I would rather serve her in vain than any other who might let me lie with her. Yet I do not serve her without reward, for the noble lover serves not in such manner when he serves with his heart in an honoured and praiseworthy place; wherefore the honour is such ample reward for me that I seek not the rest, though I would gladly take it.

May mercy avail me with you, sweet enemy; pray do not slay me if I love you without guile. That you suffer me to serve you with steadfast desire: such is the gift which I ask for, nor should there be denial.

III. The more, my lady, that the longing grows of which I languish since you show me no love, the greater heart I have to praise your highest merit, since joy entire cannot come to me from you, beloved, if that merit is thereby destroyed; for I hold dear your noble, worthy merit as much as I love and desire your dear and gentle self.

Such do I yield myself, noble and true, to you who are peerless in worth, that I would rather die in grief than that any pleasure should come to me from you which, to the noble merit which dwells in you, might be of harm. And if ever you find me otherwise disposed towards you, then may you never have mercy or indulgence.

For no knight can love his lady without deceitful heart unless as much as her he loves her honour. Wherefore I pray you, fair and gracious one,

Qe pauc ni gaire ni mija
Non fassatz de re qe.us dija,
Q'esser puesca contra.l vostr'onramen.
Gardaz s'ie.us am de fin cor, leialmen!

Per merce.us prec, bell'amija,
Qez ab una qualqe brija
Del joi d'amor mi secoraz breumen,
Si far se pot salvan vostr'onramen.

Q'estiers non posc aver nul jauzimen,
Si pïetatz e merces no.us inpren.

IV. Qui be.is membra del segle qu'es passatz,
Con hom lo vi de toz bos faitz plazen,
Ni com hom ve malvatz ni recrezen
Aquel d'aras, ni com ja restauratz
Non er per cel qi vendra, plus malvatz,
Totz hom viura ab gran dolor, membran
Cals es, ni fo, ni er d'aissi enan.

Mas non es dreitz c'om valentz ni prezatz
Si recreza per aital membramen,
Anz taing s'esforz tot jorn plus vivamen
Com sofra.l fais de pretz, qu'es mesprezatz,
Car cel n'a mais que plus fort n'es cargatz,
E car es dreitz que s'esforço.il prezan
De ben, on plus l'avol s'en van laissan.

En plus greu point non pot nuills esser natz
Com cel que pert Dieu e.l segl'issamen;
Tot aital son li trist malvatz manen,
C'an mes a mort domnei, joi, e solatz.
Tant los destreing non-fes e cobeitatz
C'onor e pretz en meton en söan,
E Dieu e.l mon en getan a lur dan.

over

Sordello

to do not a whit, no mite or iota, of whatever I tell you which could counter your honour. Behold how I love you with pure heart, loyally!

For Pity's sake I pray you, fair beloved, that with some little crumb of love's joy you come to my help, swiftly, if that can be done saving your honour.

For otherwise I can have no joy, unless pity and mercy take you.

IV. If one well remembers the times that are gone, how one saw them graced with all fine deeds, and how one sees present times wicked and faithless, and how they will never be made up for by times to come, more wicked still, then any man will be in great grief, remembering what times they are, and what they were, and what they will be henceforth.

Yet it's not right that the man of worth and of merit should lose faith through such remembrance; it rather behoves him to strive every day more keenly to take on the burden of merit which is despised, because he has more of it who is by it more heavily burdened, and because it is right that the praiseworthy strive after good the more the worthless abandon it.

In more grievous state can no one be born than he who loses God and the world together; in just such a state are the wretched, wicked rich who have put to death courtship, joy, and pleasure. So much do faithlessness and greed grip them that they neglect thereby honour and merit, and they despise thereby God and the world.

Ai! com pot tan esser desvergoignatz
Nuls hom gentils, que an enbastarden
Son lignage per aur ni per argen?
Qe l'avers vai leumens, e la rictatz,
E.ill vid'es breus e la mortz ven vïatz;
Per c'om degra lïalmen viure, aman
Deu, retenen del mon grat, gen regnan.

Dels maiors mou tota la malvestatz,
E pois apres de gra en gra dissen
Tro als menors, per que torna a nïen
Jois e pretz, si que, qui pretz vol ni.l platz,
Pot n'aver leu, car tan n'es gran mercatz
Que per cinc solz n'a hom la pez'e.l pan,
Si.l tenon vil li ric malvatz trüan!

N'Agradiva, qui quez estei malvatz,
Per vos azir malvestat et enjan,
Et am valor e joi e pretz e chan.

Al rei tramet mon sirventes vïatz,
Cel d'Aragon, que.l fais lo plus pesan
Sosten de pretz, per que.l ten en treman.

V. Lo reproviers vai averan, so.m par,
    D'om'escaudat qui tem tebe ancse,
    C'us fals volpills qe.is fai a det mostrar
    —Tant fort se feing—a pres de sobre se
    Mon sirventes, de cui qez eu faich l'aia,
    Car en son cor sap totz los mals qe.i son;
    E pois per sieu lo pren, qui qu'el retraia,
    Far l'ai l'onor qu'a lui l'autrei e.l don.

    Ges no.m degra de bausïa reptar,
    Q'ieu sui leials, et el tant fals, q'en re
    Non ausarïa ad un gat tornas far,
    Ni.s farïa el, del dreich c'aurïa, be. *over*

Ah! How can any man of good birth be so unashamed as to bastardize his lineage for gold or silver? For wealth goes quickly, and riches; and life is short and death comes swiftly. Wherefore one should live loyally, loving God, retaining the world's approval, behaving nobly.

From the most eminent does this wickedness spring, and thereafter, step by step, it descends to the least; hence joy and merit come to naught, so that he who desires merit, he whom it pleases, can easily have it for it's going at such a bargain that, for five halfpence, one has a whole suitlength of it and more, so cheap do the great ones, wicked and criminal, hold it.

Lady Delightful, no matter who lives wickedly, for you I hate wickedness and deceit, and I love valour and joy and merit and song.

To the king I send my sirventes swiftly, he of Aragon who sustains the heaviest burden of merit, and thus holds it in some trepidation.

V. The proverb's proving true, it seems to me, about the scalded man who fears ever after what's warm, for a foxy knave who's attracting attention—he gives himself such airs—has taken as about himself my sirventes, no matter about whom I wrote it, because in his heart he knows all the evils there are there; and since he's taken it as about himself, no matter whom it portrays, I'll do him the honour of according and giving him it.

He should by no means accuse me of trickery, for I am loyal and he so knavish that he wouldn't dare quarrel with a cat, nor defend even the right that he might have.

C'om que anc jorn non fetz colp ni pres plaia
No m'es semblan pogues far nuill faich bo;
Car aitant tost cum el s'arma, s'esglaia,
C'anc hom d'aital fantonïa non fon.

Ben a gran tort, car m'apella joglar
C'ab autre vau, et autre ven ab me!
E don ses penre, et el pren ses donar,
Q'en son cors met tot qant pren per merce.
Mas eu non pren ren don anta m'eschaia,
Anz met ma renda e non vuoill guizerdon
Mas sol d'amor; per qe.m par q'el dechaia
Et eu poje, qui nos jutg'a razon.

Car sol si sap peigner et afaitar,
E car se feing tot jorn non sap de que,
E car se sap torser e remirar,
Cre qe.is n'azaut tota dompna de se!
Mas eu non crei que pros dompna s'atraia
Vas tant vil cors per tant vil ochaison,
Mas car als crois si taing dompna savaia,
Trobar la pot sus el castel Babon.

En luoc d'ausberc fai camis'aredar,
E per caval vol amblan palafre,
Et en luoc d'elm fai capiron fresar,
E per escut pren mantel—e.l rete;
E si per so.ill don Amors ren qe.il plaia,
Reptar pot hom Amor de tracïon.
Mas non o fai mas per semblansa gaia
Lo fals feignens, car alres no.il ten pron.

Gen l'a saubut lo valens coms onrar
De Tolosa, si co.is taing ni.s cove,
C'a Marseilla l'a faich azaut tornar,
Per que laisset son seignor e sa fe.
Mas el no tem vergoigna, ni s'esmaia
Don degr'estar marritz tota sazo,
Lo fals volpills q'a nom, car pauc s'essaia,
'Cor de conill ab semblan de leon'.

Sordello

And the man who never dealt a blow or received wound (in battle) could not, it seems to me, do any fine deed; for as soon as he puts on arms he's scared to death, and never was there a man of such cowardliness.

He is most certainly wrong when he calls me a minstrel, for he follows others while others follow me; I give without taking and he takes without giving and keeps to himself all that he takes by favour. But I take nothing by which shame might befall me; I rather spend all that I gain and seek no other reward but that of love alone. Hence it appears to me that he is on the way down, and that I'm rising high, if one judges us rightly.

Simply because he knows how to paint and adorn himself, and because all day long he fancies himself he knows not about what, he thinks every lady finds him to her liking! But I think that no worthy lady is attracted to such a base fellow for so base a reason; but, since for knaves a worthless lady is fitting, he can find one up in Babon's castle (in the low quarter of Marseilles).

Instead of a breastplate he has a soft shirt prepared, and for a charger asks for an ambling palfrey; instead of a helmet he has a riding-hood stitched, and for a shield he takes—and keeps— a cloak. And if for that Love gives him anything which pleased him, then one can accuse Love of betrayal; but he has such only in gay appearance, this knavish impostor, for anything else is of no advantage to him.

The worthy Count of Toulouse knew well how to honour him as was fitting and suitable, for to Marseilles he properly made him turn back, since he had quit his lord and his pledged faith. But he fears no shame nor is moved by that for which he ought to be downcast the whole year through, this foxy knave who's called, since he undertakes little, 'Rabbit's heart in lion's guise'.

VI. Planher vuelh En Blacatz en aquest leugier so,
Ab cor trist e marrit, et ai en be razo,
Qu'en luy ai mescabat senhor et amic bo,
Et quar tug l'ayp valent en sa mort perdut so.
Tant es mortals lo dans qu'ieu non ai sospeisso
Que jamais si revenha, s'en aital guiza no:
Qu'om li traga lo cor e que.n manjo.l baro
Que vivon descorat—pueys auran de cor pro!

Premiers manje del cor, per so que grans ops l'es,
L'emperaire de Roma, s'elh vol los Milanes
Per forsa conquistar; quar luy tenon conques,
E viu deseretatz, malgrat de sos Tïes.
E deseguentre lui manje.n lo reys frances:
Pueys cobrara Castella que pert per nescïes;
Mas, si pez'a sa maire, elh no.n manjara ges,
Quar ben par, a son pretz, qu'elh non fai ren que.l pes.

Del rei engles me platz, quar es pauc coratgos,
Que manje pro del cor; pueys er valens e bos,
E cobrara la terra, per que viu de pretz blos,
Que.l tol lo reys de Fransa, quar lo sap nüalhos.
E lo reys castelas tanh qu'en manje per dos,
Quar dos regismes ten, e per l'un non es pros;
Mas, s'elh en vol manjar, tanh qu'en manj'a rescos,
Que si.l mair'o sabïa, batrïa.l ab bastos.

Del rey d'Arago vuelh del cor deia manjar,
Que aisso lo fara de l'anta descarguar
Que pren sai, de Marcella e d'Amilau, qu'onrar
No.s pot estiers per ren que puesca dir ni far.
Et apres vuelh del cor don hom al rei navar,
Que valïa mais coms que reys, so aug comtar;
Tortz es quan Dieus fai hom'en gran ricor poiar,
Pus sofracha de cor lo fai de pretz bayssar.

over

VI. I would lament Sir Blacatz in this simple melody, with sad and sorry heart, and I have indeed reason for it, since in him have I lost a lord and good friend, and all worthy qualities have with his death disappeared. So mortal is the loss that I have not the faintest hope that it might ever be made good, unless in this way: that his heart be cut out and the great nobles eat of it, who now live disheartened—then they'll have heart enough!

Let there first eat of it, because his need is great, the Emperor of Rome, if he wants to conquer the Milanese by force; for they deem him conquered, and he lives deprived of his heritage, in spite of his Germans. And straight after him let the French king eat of it, then he'll recover Castile which he's losing through his stupidity; but if it annoys his mother, he'll not eat of it at all, for it well appears, from his repute, that he does nothing which might annoy her.

Of the English king I would that, since he is uncourageous, he eat a good deal of the heart; then he'll be fine and worthy, and he'll recover the land on account of which he lives without merit, and of which the king of France robs him since he knows him to be fainthearted. And it behoves the Castilian king to eat of it twice over, since he has two kingdoms and he's not worthy by one; but if he would eat of it, it behoves him to eat of it in secret, for if his mother knew it, she'd beat him with sticks.

I would that the king of Aragon should eat of the heart, for that will relieve him of the shame which he incurs here, for Marseilles and Millau, since in no other way can he win honour through anything that he might do or say. And next I would that one gave of the heart to the king of Navarre, for he was more worthy as a count than now as a king, so I hear say; it's wrong when God causes a man to rise to great eminence, then lack of heart makes him decline in merit.

Al comte de Toloza a ops qu'en manje be,
Si.l membra so que sol tener ni so que te;
Quar si ab autre cor sa perda non reve,
No.m par que la revenha ab aquel qu'a en se.
E.l coms pröensals tanh qu'en manje, si.l sove
C'oms que deseretatz viu, guaire non val re;
E si tot ab esfors si defen ni.s chapte,
Ops l'es manje del cor pel greu fais qu'el soste.

Li baro.m volran mal de so que ieu dic be,
Mas ben sapchan qu'ie.ls pretz aitan pauc quon ilh me.

Belh Restaur, sol qu'ab vos puesca trovar merce,
A mon dan met quascun que per amic no.m te.

For the Count of Toulouse there's need to eat well of it, if he remembers that which he used to possess and that which he now possesses; for if with another heart he doesn't make good his loss, it does not seem to me that he'll make it good with the one he has in him. And it behoves the Provençal Count that he eat of it, if he recalls that the man who lives deprived of his heritage is worth hardly anything; and even though with great striving he defends and maintains himself, there's need for him to eat of the heart for the great burden which he sustains.

The great nobles will wish me ill for that which I say well, but let them know rightly that I prize them as little as they me.

Fair Recompense, only provided that with you I could find mercy, I scorn each man who holds me not his friend.

Guilhem de Montanhagol

LIFE. In the thirty years or so during which, following the end of the Albigensian Crusade in 1229, the political, social, and cultural autonomy of the Midi was being eroded, Guilhem de Montanhagol was one of the few troubadours still striving to maintain there the art of the courtly lyric. Of obscure origin, possibly belonging to the lower rank of the nobility, he consequently depended on the patronage of more eminent nobles, although the limited number of his compositions makes it unlikely that his services were exclusively literary in nature. Many of his poems, including the earliest dating from 1233–1234, reveal a close attachment to Raymond VII, Count of Toulouse and, apart from a brief visit to the court of Aragon in 1238, Guilhem did not quit the Midi until after Raymond's death in 1248. A small group of poems indicate his presence at the court of Alfonso X of Castile from 1252 to 1257, but after this last date all trace of the poet is lost. One of the rare *planhs* composed on the death of a troubadour was written to lament his death, but its author, a certain Pons Santolh of Toulouse, gives no chronological details. In all probability, Guilhem de Montanhagol died in Spain, in the late 1250s.

WORKS. Five *sirventès*, seven *cansos*, a *partimen* shared with Sordello and an exchange of double *coblas* with the troubadour Blacasset make up Guilhem's total poetic output. As much of his life centred on the court of Toulouse, so a great deal of his poetry is closely linked with the political fortunes of his suzerain. Thus, from the period 1233–1242, during which Raymond was actively resisting both the Inquisition and the incursions of French royal authority in his domains, we have a first group of *sirventès* inspired by this resistance; they echo Raymond's grievances, encourage his allies, revile those who defect from his cause, and generally deplore the decline of prowess and generosity which, for Guilhem, survive only in the person of his patron. However, the collapse of Raymond's revolt in 1242 marks the end of this first period; it was followed by one of outward submission and retrenchment during which Raymond bids desperately to ensure some measure of territorial integrity and dynastic continuity. Guilhem now composes a group of *cansos* in which he, for his part, seeks to defend and conserve the forms and ideals of courtliness. A consequent feature of them is an insistence on the moral values of love, on such concepts as honour, virtue and purity which, though not unknown to earlier troubadours, are now redefined with a new precision and a new dialectical coherence. A second feature is the poet's recognition of a long-established cultural tradition, the sense of a real and more glorious past which already prefigures an attitude common to poets and romancers of the later Middle Ages. The third group of Guilhem's compositions belongs to the period following Raymond's death in 1248, when the cause of freedom from French domination in the Midi was shattered, and, with it, the cultural conditions in which the courtly lyric had once thrived. These last poems, composed at the court of Castile, and in which the didactic, theorizing and discursive tone is dominant, represent a final bid to resume, to make known, and so to ensure the survival of what Guilhem conceived to be the essence of the courtly ideal. In a way, they are no less partisan than the most outspoken of his political *sirventès*, but what he, the expatriate troubadour, is now resisting is the total disappearance of an art which in its native land was already on the point of extinction.

EDITION. P. T. Ricketts *Les Poésies de Guilhem de Montanhagol* (Toronto 1964).

SELECTION. The first poem (Ricketts no. 1), Guilhem's earliest composition, is a *sirventès* dating from 1233–34. The Inquisition had just been entrusted to the Dominican friars, and a measure of the dread which it inspired is suggested by the poet's own cautious affirmation (st. 2) of the two fundamental orthodox beliefs denied by the Albigensian heretics. The criticisms made by Guilhem of both the regular clergy and the preaching friars, for all their generality, correspond in fact precisely to the attitude of Raymond VII, whose humiliating submission imposed at the end of the Albigensian Crusade is recalled in the *tornada*; it was he who, late in 1233, complained to the Pope of the excesses and arbitrary judgements of the Inquisitors, and he who, in March of the following year, protested to Louis IX against the greedy acquisition of lands and property by abbots and bishops in his domains. The second poem (Ricketts no. 4), an equally partisan *sirventès*, dates from mid-October 1242 when some of Raymond's allies had already submitted to the French king, when Henry III of England was still recovering in Bordeaux from the defeats of Saintes and Taillebourg, and when James I of Aragon still showed no sign of joining in an offensive alliance with Raymond against the French. The next two poems (Ricketts nos. 8, 6) are *cansos* belonging to Guilhem's middle period—the ladies to whom they are dedicated, not positively identifiable, may well be the wives of two of Raymond's vassals. That both songs are of identical stanza-structure is but one indication of the poet's relative indifference to the more formal aspects of his art. For him, the thematic material of the *canso* has become all-important—an innovation of which he seems fully aware—and the thematic material itself tends now to be formulated as abstract theoretical concept rather than subjective emotional experience. This tendency is even more marked in the fifth piece (Ricketts no. 12) which dates from Guilhem's stay with the scholar-king Alfonso X of Castile. Its versification is even plainer, the style more colourless, while the rationalizing, discursive register now is predominant. The sixth poem (Ricketts no. 14), Guilhem's last work, is a moral *sirventès* dating from 1257, the year of Alfonso's election to the Imperial throne and of the threat to Europe of Mongolian invasion. The vast disillusion which it so eloquently expresses is scarcely tempered by the formulation of an ideal of social justice which, in all its simplicity, nevertheless serves to recall that, for the troubadours, courtliness had been not only an ideal of heterosexual relationships but a total concept of life in feudal society.

1. Del tot vey remaner valor,
   Qu'om no.s n'entremet, sai ni lai,
   Ni non penson de nulh ben sai,
   Ni an lur cor mas en läor;
   E meron mal clerc e prezicador,
   Quar devedon so qu'az els no.s cove:
   Que hom per pretz non do ni fassa be.
   E hom que pretz ni do met en söan,
   Ges de bon loc no.l mou, al mieu semblan.

   Quar Dieus vol pretz e vol lauzor,
   E Dieus fo vers hom, qu'ieu o sai;
   E hom que vas Dieu res desfai,
   E Dieus l'a fait aitan d'onor
   Qu'al sieu semblan l'a fag ric e major,
   E pres de si mais de neguna re—
   Doncx ben es fols totz hom, que car no.s te:
   E que fassa en aquest segle tan
   Que, sai e lai, n'aya grat, on que.s n'an.

   Ar se son fait enqueredor,
   E jutjon aissi com lur plai.
   Pero l'enquerre no.m desplai,
   Anz me plai que casson error,
   E qu'ab bels digz plazentiers, ses iror,
   Torno.ls erratz desvïatz en la fe,
   E qui.s penet que truep bona merce,
   E enaissi menon dreg lo gazan
   Que tort ni dreg no perdan—so que.y an.

   Enquer dizon mais de folor:
   Qu'aurfres a dompnas non s'eschai.
   Pero si dompna piegz no fai,
   Ni.n leva erguelh ni ricor,
   Per gen tener no pert Dieu ni s'amor;
   Ni ja nulhs hom, s'elh estiers be.s capte,
   Per gen tener ab Dieu no.s dezave,
   Ni ja per draps negres ni per floc blan
   No conquerran ilh Dieu, s'alre no.y fan.

   over

I. I see worthiness wholly in decline, for no man makes it his business near or far, and here none think of any good thing, nor have their hearts set on aught but gain; and clergy and preaching friars are ill deserving, because they forbid that which it behoves them not to: that a man should for merit's sake give and act generously. Yet if a man scorns merit and generosity, it springs from no good motive, to my mind.

For God is in favour of merit and of praiseworthiness, and God became in truth a man, I know this; and the man who wrongs God when He has done him such honour as to make him, in His image, great and supreme, and nearer Him than any living thing—every such man is then indeed a fool, for he has no self-esteem; let him in this world do so much that, near and far, he may have approval for it wherever he may go.

Now they have set themselves up as Inquisitors, and so give judgement as it pleases them. Yet the Inquisition does not displease me; rather, it pleases me that they should pursue error, and with fair pleasant words, without anger, lead the lost heretics back to the faith, and that he who repents should find sweet mercy and that they should so conduct their business rightly that they neglect not right or wrong, such as they have in it.

Still more folly do they speak, saying that cloth of gold does not befit ladies. Yet, if a lady does no worse and feels neither pride nor haughtiness for that, then through fine apparel she loses neither God nor His love; and no man, if in other ways he behaves well, is ever through fine apparel at variance with God, nor, through wearing black cassocks or white friars' robes, will they ever find God, if to that end they do nothing else.

Tug laisson, per Nostre Senhor,
Nostre clerc lo segle savai,
E no pessan mas quan de lai;
Aissi.ls gart Dieus de dezonor
Cum elhs non an ni erguelh ni ricor,
Ni cobeytatz no.ls enguana ni.ls te,
Ni no volon re de so qu'hom bel ve.
Res no volon? Pero ab tot s'en van,
Pueys prezon pauc, qui ques i aya dan!

Sirventes, vay al pro comte dese
De Toloza; membre.l que fag li an,
E gart se d'elhs d'esta ora enan.

11. Bel m'es quan d'armatz aug refrim
De trompas, lai on om s'escrim,
E trazon prim
L'arquier melhor—
Nostri e lor—
E vey de senhas bruelha;
Adoncx trassalh
Cor de vassalh,
Tro que sos cors s'erguelha!

Coms de Tolza, on plus esprim
Los ricx, vos vey de pretz al cim;
E vuelh qu'aissi.m
Don Dieus s'amor
Cum, part lauzor,
Vostre ricx pretz capduelha—
Sol qu'a un talh,
Qui ara.us falh
May ab vos no s'acuelha.

La Marcha, Foys e Rodes vim
Falhir ades als ops de prim!
Per qu'ieu.ls encrim
De part honor
E de valor,

over

Guilhem de Montanhagol

May our clerics, for Our Lord's sake, all abandon this wicked world, and may they have no thought but for the next; and may God by as much preserve them from dishonour as they have neither pride nor haughtiness, as greed deceives them not and does not possess them, and as they desire naught of what one deems fair. Desire naught? Yet they go off with all, and then care little, no matter who loses thereby!

Sirventes, go swiftly to the worthy Count of Toulouse; remind him of what they have done to him, and let him beware of them from this time forth.

II. It's pleasant to me when I hear the call of armed men's clarions, there where there's fighting, and when the best archers—ours and theirs—shoot sharp, and I see a forest of banners; then let the heart of the vassal thrill, till his body is filled with pride!

Count of Toulouse, the more I consider the great ones, the more I see you at the peak of merit; and I would that God granted me as much His love as, beyond praise, your great merit reigns supreme—only provided that, by the same token, whoever now fails you be not received in your presence again.

La Marche, Foix, and Rodez have we seen fail in the first hour of need! For this I accuse them in the name of honour and valour,

Don quasqus si despuelha;
Qu'en tal sonalh
An mes batalh,
Don non tanh pretz los vuelha.

Ja mais no cug que.s desencrim,
Quar trop s'a levat peior crim,
Que.l de Caïm,
Hom qui l'amor
Del ric senhor
De Toloz'era.s tuelha;
Quar, qui defalh
Ni a senhor falh,
Greu er que no s'en duelha.

Si.l reys Jacmes, cuy no mentim,
Complis so qu'elh e nos plevim,
Segon qu'auzim,
En gran dolor
Foran ab plor
Frances, qui qu'o desvuelha;
E quar defalh
Qu'ades no salh,
Totz lo mons lo.n reiruelha.

Engles, de flor
Faitz capelh o de fuelha!
No.us detz trebalh,
Neis qui.us assalh,
Tro qu'om tot vos o tuelha!

III. Non an tan dig li primier trobador
Ni fag d'amor,
Lai el temps qu'era guays,
Qu'enquera nos no fassam, apres lor,
Chans de valor,
Nous, plazens e verais;
Quar dir pot hom so qu'estat dig no sïa,
Qu'estiers non es trobaires bos no fis   *over*

of which each of them is stripped bare; and they've rung out such a tune on their bells that it is not fitting that merit should want anything to do with them.

I think that he'll never prove himself guiltless, for he has committed a crime worse than Cain's, he who rejects now the love of the great lord of Toulouse; because, if anyone defects and fails his lord, then it will hardly be that he does not regret it.

If King James, whom we have not belied, accomplished that which he and we did pledge, then from what we hear the French would be in great pain and in tears, no matter who disavows it. But since he fails to sally forth straightway, everyone turns a scornful eye on him.

You English, go on making hats of leaves or flowers! Don't trouble yourselves, not even if you're attacked, till all has been taken from you!

III. The early troubadours have not said and composed so much on the subject of love, in the past when times were gay, that we may not still, after them, compose songs worthwhile, new, pleasant, and true; for one can say what may not have been said, and in no other way is a troubadour good or fine

Tro fai sos chans guays, nous e gent assis,
Ab nöels digz de nova mäestrïa.

Mas en chantan dizo.l comensador
Tant en amor
Que.l nous dirs torn'a fays.
Pero nou es, quan dizo li doctor
So que alhor
Chantan no dis hom mais,
E nou, qui ditz so qu'auzit non avïa;
E nou, qu'ieu dic razo qu'om mais no dis,
Qu'amors m'a dat saber, qu'aissi.m noiris
Que s'om trobat non agues, trobarïa.

Be.m platz qu'ieu chan, quan pes la gran honor
Que.m ven d'amor,
E.n fassa ricx essais,
Quar tals recep mon chan e ma lauzor
Que a la flor
De la beutat que nays.
Pero be.us dic que mielhs creire deurïa
Que sa beutatz desus del cel partis,
Que tan sembla obra de paradis
Qu'a penas par terrenals sa conhdïa.

D'una re fan donas trop gran follor,
Quar lor amor
Menan ab tan loncx plays
Que quascuna, pus ve son amador
Fi, ses error,
Falh si l'alonga mais.
Quar hom no viu tan quan faire solïa,
Doncx convengra que.l mals costums n'issis
Del trop tarzar, qu'ieu no cre qu'om moris
Tan leu com fai, si d'amor si jauzïa.

Trop fai son dan dona que.s do ricor
Quant hom d'amor
La comet, ni.s n'irays,
Que plus bel l'es que sofran preyador
Que si d'alhor

over

Guilhem de Montanhagol

but in making his songs gay, new, and nobly fashioned, with new things to say with new art.

But in song the first poets say so much inspired by love that to say anything new becomes difficult. Yet new it is when the experts say that which nowhere else has been said in song before, and new if someone says what he has never heard; and new when I say things which no one has said, for love has given me the knowledge and so instructs me that, had no one made poetry, I would a poet be.

It pleases me well that I sing, now when I think of the great honour which comes to me from love, and that I give fine proof of it, because such a one receives my song and my praise who has the flower of beauty, newly-born. On this account I tell you indeed that I ought rather to believe that her beauty came from heaven above, for it seems so like the work of paradise that scarce does her loveliness appear terrestrial.

In one thing do ladies commit too great a folly, because they spin out their love with such lengthy procedures that each one of them, once she sees that her lover is noble and without fault, does wrong if she then protracts it further. Because men live not so long as they used to, it would be fitting that the low practise of long delay should disappear, for I believe that men would not die as soon as they do, if they had joy of love.

Great harm to herself does the lady who puts on fine airs when a man woos her in love, and who thereat takes offence, for she finds it better that humble suppliants should suffer than if, from elsewhere,

* it is better for her that the aspirants should be patient with her aspirants

Era.l peccatz savais.
Que tals n'i a, quays qu'om non o creirïa
Ab que fos dig, qu'en fan assais fraydis;
Per qu'amors falh entr'elas e vilsis,
Quar tenon mal en car lor carestïa.

Ieu am e blan dona on ges non cor
Enjans d'amor,
Per que no m'en bïays,
Ni o dey far, qu'om la te per melhor
E per gensor;
Per qu'amors m'i atrays,
Qu'amans es fols quant en bon loc non trïa,
Quar qui ama vilmen se eis aunis,
Qu'a las melhors deu hom esser aclis,
Don nais merces, valors e cortezïa.

N'Esclarmonda, qui etz vos, e Na Guïa,
Quascus dels noms d'ambas o devezis;
Que quecx dels noms es tan cars e tan fis,
Qu'om que.l mentau pueys non pren mal lo dïa.

IV. No sap per que va son joy pus tarzan,
Ni fug ni gan
Dompna son amador,
Pus lo conoys be per bo servidor,
Senes error
En fag et en semblan.
Quar trop tarzar en dompney es follïa,
Que mans amicx ne ven en dezesper,
Quar pueys no.s deu dompna de ren temer,
Pus ve l'amor ses fench'e ses bauzïa.

Bona dompna, ab bel cors benestan,
Vos tray enan
Beutatz part la gensor,
E.us fai valer Valors part la melhor.
Pro.us fan d'onor:
Per so faitz lur coman.   *over*

there were wicked sin. And there are such, though one would not believe it even if it were said aloud, who of this give hateful proof; wherefore love fails among them and is debased, for wrongly they prize too high their preciousness.

I love and serve a lady in whom love knows no guile, and hence I turn not from her, nor should I do so for she is considered the best and the most noble; on this account love draws me to her, for the lover is foolish who does not choose where there is good, since he who loves cheaply brings shame on himself, and one should be devoted to the best ladies, from whom are born mercy, worth, and courtliness.

My lady Esclarmunda, who you are, and lady Guida, each of your names reveals; for each of these names is so precious and noble that he who is mindful of them cannnot then come to harm, the day long.

IV. No lady has reason to delay her lover's joy, to flee and to avoid him, once she well knows him to be a good servant, without fault in deed or semblance. For great delay in courtship is folly, and many a lover comes thereby to despair, because a lady should not fear anything when once she sees love without feint or deceit.

Good lady, fair and comely of person, Beauty sets you above the most noble, and Worthiness affirms your worth above the best. They do you much honour: do therefore as they bid you.

Valors vos ditz que fassatz ben tot dīa,
Et Amors vol qu'ametz, non per dever,
Mas lo plus fi, ab qu'aya meyns poder;
Qu'on meyns er rics, mais vos o grazirīa.

Trīat vos ai, dompna, mi ses enjan,
De bon talan
Que ben gar vostr'onor,
Si cum trīet si ad emperador,
Senes temor,
Ja Fredericx antan;
Si eis s'i mes, quar hom tan no.y valīa.
Atressi.us dic qu'om mi no.y pot valer,
Quar res, dompna, tan no.us ama, per ver;
Per so.us valh mais ieu qu'autre no farīa.

Ben pot chauzir dompn'un sol fin aman,
Ses malestan,
Son par o pauc major;
Pero no falh si chauzis en menor,
Si.l ve valor,
Sol non pes lo baran.
Quar lo plus bas li grazis tota vīa
Mais que.l plus ricx ni.l pars, si.l fa plazer,
Per que.l deu mielhs dompn'ab si retener,
Quar mais i a poder e senhorīa.

Per ver vos jur, dompna, e.us pliu e.us man,
Qu'ieu non am tan
Ren cum vos, cuy honor;
Per que.n laissi mans bels plazers d'alhor.
Pro.y fas folor,
Mas be.m podetz aitan,
O neis cen tens esmendar, si.us plazīa.
Pero ueymais vos deurīa plazer;
Per que no.us platz, dompna? Qu'ieu fas saber
Qu'atressi.us er a far, coras que sīa.

N'Esclarmunda, vostre noms signifīa
Que vos donatz clardat al mon, per ver;
Et etz monda, que no fes non-dever.
Aitals etz, plan, com al ric nom tanhīa.

Worthiness tells you to act always well, and Love wills that you love, not out of duty, but the most true, even though he should be less powerful; for the less eminent he is, the more grateful to you would he be.

I have selected for you, lady, myself, without guile, and right willing to defend well your honour, just as, without fear, years ago, Frederick selected himself for Emperor; he put himself forward because no one else was as worth it. In like wise, I tell you that no one is as worth this as I, for no living thing, lady, loves you so much, in truth; hence I am worth more to you than any other would be.

A lady can well choose one true lover alone, without unseemliness, her equal or a little superior; and yet she is not at fault if she chooses one more lowly, if she sees in him worthiness, provided there's no bar. For the lesser is always more grateful to her than the greater or the equal, if she does him pleasure. Hence should a lady rather retain him by her, for therein she has more power and dominion.

In truth I swear to you, lady, and pledge and assure you, that I love nothing as much as you, whom I honour; on this account I renounce many fine pleasures from elsewhere. Therein I do great folly, but for that you can well make me amends, and even a hundred times over, if it so pleased you. Indeed it ought to please you from this moment forth; why does it not please you, lady? For I tell you now that thus you will have to do, at some time or another.

Lady Esclarmunda, your name signifies that you give light to the world, in truth; and you are pure, for you do not that which should not be done. You are such, clearly, as befits this splendid name.

V. Ar ab lo coinde pascor,
Quan vei de bella color
Flors per vergiers e per pratz,
E aug chantar daus totz latz
Los auzeletz per doussor,
Vueilh far ab coindïa
Chanso tal que sïa
Plazens als enamoratz,
E a midons majormen,
Qe.m don'en trobar engenh.

Ben devon li amador
De bon cor servir amor,
Qar amors non es peccatz,
Anz es vertutz qe.ls malvatz
Fai bons, e.ll bo.n son meillor,
E met hom'en vïa
De ben far tot dïa;
E d'amor mou castitatz,
Qar qi.n amor ben s'enten
Non pot far qe pueis mal renh.

E pos tant a de valor
Amors, ben fan gran follor
Las domnas on es beutatz,
Qar non amon los prezatz
Pos o connoisson en lor;
Qar pueis lor plairïa
Jois e cortezïa,
E chans e totz bels solatz,
Mas greu faran tan de sen
S'amors no las i empenh.

Amors, de vos fatz lauzor,
Q'amar mi fatz la gensor,
Don mi son tan aut pujatz
Qe.l morirs neis m'es onratz,
Tan es de nobla ricor.
E s'ieu joi n'avïa,
Sai qe non morrïa;
Anz viurïa gen pagatz. *over*

V. Now at graceful Easter-tide, when I see flowers of lovely colour in meadows and fields, and on all sides I hear the young birds sing in delight, I wish to make with grace a song such as may please those enamoured, and above all my mistress, who gives me skill in composing song.

Rightly should lovers with willing heart serve love, for love is no sin, it is, rather, a virtue which renders good the wicked, and the good are better by it, and it encourages one always to act well; and from love is born purity, for he who rightly sets his mind on love, it cannot be that he should then act basely.

And since love has such worth, they indeed do great folly, those ladies in whom beauty dwells, because they love not men of merit once they know them to be so; for then joy and courtliness would please them, and song and all fair pleasure, but they'll hardly act so wisely unless love impels them thereto.

Love, it is your praise I sing, for you cause me to love the most noble—she through whom I'm so exalted that even death is to me honourable, she is of such noble excellence. And if I had joy from her, I know I would not die; rather I'd live, finely rewarded.

Si non l'ai, morrai breumen,
Q'ieu l'am tan qe.l cor m'estenh.

Qi ve la fresca color
De vos, bella, cui ador,
E.ls uelhs vairs e.ls cilhs delgatz
[. . . . . atz]
De natural resplandor;
Totz hom pert feunïa,
Qi.us esgar', amïa.
E ieu, las, a cui mais platz,
Mueir, qan vei vostre cors gen,
D'enveia tan mi destrenh.

Fis pretz deschairïa,
Si no.l sostenïa
Lo reis Castellans onratz,
Qe fai totz sos faitz tan gen
Q'en ren non cal q'om l'ensenh.

VI.   Per lo mon fan li un dels autres rancura,
Li clerc dels laycx e.l laic d'elhs yssamen;
E li poble.s planhon de desmezura
De lor senhors, e.l senhor d'elhs, söen.
Aissi es ples lo mons de mal talen,
Mas ar venon sai deves Orïen
Li Tartari, si Dieus non o defen,
Que.ls faran totz estar d'una mensura.

Per manh forfag e per manhta laidura
Qu'an fag, e fan, clerc e laic malamen,
Venra, si ve, esta dezaventura
A Crestïas, s'a Dieu merces non pren,
Que fassa.l Papa metr'atempramen
En so don an li clerc e.l laic conten;
Quar s'el los fai ben d'un acordamen,
Non lor pot pueys nozer nulh'aventura.   *over*

If I have it not, I'll soon die, for I love her so much that my heart grows faint.

He who sees your fresh complexion, fair one whom I adore, and your bright eyes and their delicate lashes [. . .] of natural splendour; every man loses ill-feeling if he beholds you, beloved. And I, alas, to whom you are most pleasing, I die when I see your fair person, with longing it so torments me.

Fine merit would decline if the honoured king of Castile did not maintain it, for he does so graciously all that he does that he has no need to be taught anything more.

VI. Throughout the world men find fault with one another, the clerics with the laymen and the laymen with them, likewise; and the people complain of their lords' excesses, and the lords often of them. Thus is the world full of ill-will, but now there come from out of the East the Tartars who, unless God forbids it, will reduce them all to a common measure.

Through many a crime and many an ugly deed which clerics and laymen have done, and do, wickedly, will this disaster come, if it comes, to Christendom, unless God takes pity and makes the Pope bring to a settlement that over which the clerics and the laymen quarrel; for if he well makes them of one accord, then nothing can happen to harm them.

A! Per que vol clercx belha vestidura,
Ni per que vol viure tan ricamen,
Ni per que vol belha cavalgadura,
Qu'el sap que Dieus volc viure paubramen?
Ni per que vol tan l'autrui n'i enten,
Qu'el sap que tot quan met ni quan despen,
Part son manjar e son vestir vilmen,
Tolh als paubres, si no men la Scriptura?

E.l gran senhor, per que no prenden cura
Que no fasson tort ni fors'a lur gen?
Qu'ieu non tenc ges per menor desmezura
Qu'om forse.ls sieus cum quan l'autruy dreg pren;
Ans es mager, quar falhis doblamen,
Quar s'om de se ni d'autruy non defen
A son poder los sieus adrechamen,
Falh endreg lor tan que.n pert sa drechura.

Mas totz pobles a de bon sen frachura,
Qu'a son senhor fass'en re falhimen,
Quar totz hom deu amar d'amistat pura
Son bon senhor, e servir leyalmen;
E senher tanh qu'am los sieus bonamen,
Que lïaltatz lor ne fai mandamen
Que l'us ame l'autre tan coralmen
Que no se puesc entr'els metre falsura.

Reys Castellas, l'emperis vos aten,
Mas sai dizon, senher, qu'atendemen
Fai de Breto, per que.s mou grans rancura.

Que d'aut rey tanh, quant un gran fag enpren,
Que.l trag'a cap o.n segua l'aventura.

Ah! Why does the cleric want fine raiments, and why does he want to live so splendidly, and why does he want a fine stable of horses, when he knows that God was willing to live in poverty? And why does he want so much of another's goods, and sets his heart on them, when he knows that all that he disburses and all that he spends, apart from his food and his clothing alone, he takes from the poor, according to the Scriptures?

And the great lords, why do they not take care not to do wrong or violence to their own people? For I hold it by no means a lesser excess to do violence to one's own people than to usurp another's right; rather it's greater, for one is doubly at fault because, if a man protects not from himself or from another his own people, as justly as he is able, then he fails them so much that he loses thereby all his rights.

But any people has a lack of good sense if in anything they fail their lord, for every man should love with pure love his rightful lord and serve him loyally. And it is fitting that a lord love with good heart his people, for loyalty commands them in this to love one another so cordially that falseness could not come between them.

King of Castile, the Empire awaits you, but here they are saying, Sire, that it is a Breton's wait, because of which there arises great blame.

For it behoves a mighty king, when he undertakes a great deed, to see it through or submit to whatever befalls.

Peire Cardenal

LIFE. According to an early biographer writing *c.* 1300, Peire Cardenal belonged to a well-to-do family of Le Puy, studied at the cathedral college of that city in preparation for an ecclesiastical career but, on reaching manhood, beguiled by the world's vanities, became a troubadour; together with his minstrel he visited the courts of kings and barons and, when he died, was nearly 100 years old. Contemporary documents attest the presence at Le Puy of an important Cardenal family, while Peire's own work confirms other details of this account, as well as indicating that the poet was probably married, with children, by the early 1230s. Furthermore, of the few poems which can be dated with any certainty, the earliest seems to belong to the year 1216, the latest to *c.* 1271. Other aspects of the poet's life, however, remain somewhat problematic. A few flattering references to the court of Toulouse, an interest in the local affairs of Le Puy, and the isolated praise of such men as James of Aragon and Edward of England scarcely suffice to make clear which courts the poet actually frequented and when, or which noblemen accorded him their favour and protection. As for his reported longevity, though just possible—in which case he might well be the *Petrus Cardinalis* mentioned as a scribe at the court of Toulouse in 1204—it is so unusual that one would have expected some further contemporary comment. On the contrary, no thirteenth century troubadour seems to have known, or known of, Peire Cardenal, and he himself gives few hints at the material circumstances of his life. Nevertheless, of all the later troubadours, he is one of the few really dominant figures. His life spans the whole of that period during which the culture of the Midi waned, and was finally destroyed, under the pressure of historical events, and his work, which is in essence a vigorous reaction to those events, represents

the last flamboyant flowering of southern French poetry.
WORKS. Some ninety-six compositions are now attributed to Peire Cardenal, and although at least fifteen of these are of doubtful authenticity, he remains one of the most prolific of all the troubadours. In his work one notes, firstly, a relative abundance of *coblas*, terse, epigrammatic pieces of one or two stanzas only which, for the most part, summarize themes treated at length elsewhere; secondly, a rarity of both *cansos* and minor 'communal' forms—of the three songs inspired by love two at least are satirical in intent, while the one *tenso* and the one *partimen* in which Peire Cardenal took part are both of questionable attribution; and, lastly, a scattering of rare, unusual genres such as the *estribot*, the *descort*, two 'sermons' in multi-stanza form, two purely religious, hymn-like, compositions, etc. All these minor or isolated pieces, however, are subsidiary to the major part of his work, consisting of nearly sixty *sirventès*, moral, social, political and personal, which date from all periods of his life. Adopting a standpoint in which the most authentic religious convictions are fused with the highest ideals of courtliness, and varying in tone from light-hearted jocularity to earnest exhortation and, further, to harsh and forceful invective, the poet reviews not only great historical events and processes such as the Albigensian Crusade, the Inquisition and the northern French occupation, but also the crimes, vices, and foibles of individuals, types, and social groups. Sharpness of moral and material perception combines with a vigour and economy of expression to create a total vision of man's social, moral and spiritual condition. Individual, particular and subjective this vision may well be, to a large extent, but, in its scope, in its coherence, and in its artistically convincing formulation it remains unsurpassed by any other mediaeval poet, and comparable only to that of a Marcabrun, a Rutebeuf or a François Villon.

EDITION. R. Lavaud *Poésies complètes du troubadour Peire Cardenal* (Toulouse 1957).

SELECTION. The first piece (Lavaud No. 2) is one of Peire Cardenal's few *cansos*: rejecting the exaggerations of contemporary troubadours and reaffirming the original ideal of mutual devotion and loyalty, it neatly summarizes the poet's concept of courtly love. In much the same way, the second piece (Lavaud No. 60) is, by its formal and thematic structure, eminently representative of a large number of the poet's *sirventès*; the characteristic failings of various social groups are highlighted against a background of earnestly propounded, conventional, christian morality, and a fine balance is achieved between the wide scope of the thematic material and the economical pointedness and simplicity of its formulation. To it, the next poem (Lavaud no. 27), one of a limited number of personal *sirventès*, stands in strong contrast. Here, one individual is the object of the poet's detailed and heavily ironic strictures, although its effect is in no way diminished by the fact that little is now known of that individual apart from what the poet alleges. The facts of the case, doubtless well known to Peire's contemporaries, are here as elsewhere simply grounds on which to construct yet another indictment of the ways of the world. Alongside the decline of courtliness which, for the poet, leads to such crime, the betrayal of religion by a corrupt and hypocritical clergy provides a second dominant theme, of which the next three *sirventès* (Lavaud Nos. 74, 28, 34) are certainly among the most lastingly impressive formulations. In the first, the sharp violence of the opening stanza gradually gives way, through an ever-widening contemplation of society and of man's condition, to the gentle calm of the closing prayer; in the second, the mood of unrelentingly concentrated satire is sustained throughout by an extraordinary tightness and density of expression, while in the third poem, the *estribot*, of which only one other example is known, the attack is launched in massively solid blocks of alexandrines, unsupported by any melody and each ending in the harsh, hammer-like rime in -*atz*. In all three, unity and coherence of inspiration are no less perceptible than the rich variety of the poet's artistic resources. The last two poems, finally (Lavaud Nos. 36, 30), represent more direct and positive expressions of Peire Cardenal's moral-religious concepts, and each, in its distinctive way, is marked by that fusion of the personal, social and spiritual planes which endows his work with its characteristic totality of vision. The jestingly truculent tone of the first gives added point to the serious moral and religious problems which underlie it, while the second, for all its seemingly objective didacticism and its conventional scholastic imagery, still corresponds both in mood and substance to the poet's most personal and essential inspiration.

I. Ben teinh per fol e per muzart
    Cel qu'ab amor se lïa,
    Quar en amor pren peior part
    Aquel que plus s'i fïa;
    Tals se cuida calfar que s'art.
    Los bes d'amor a hom a tart
    E.ls mals a cascun dïa;
    Li fol e.l fellon, e.l moyssart,
    Aquil an sa parïa,
    Per qu'ieu m'en part.

    Ja m'amïa no mi tenra
    Si ieu leis non tenïa;
    Ni ja de me non jauzira
    S'ieu de leis non jauzïa.
    Conseilh n'ai pres, bon e certa:
    Farai li segon que.m fara.
    E s'ella mi galïa
    Galïador mi trobara,
    E si.m vai dreita vïa,
    Ieu l'irai pla.

    Anc non gazanhei tan gran re
    Con quam perdei ma mïa;
    Quar, perden leis, gazanhei me,
    Qu'il gazainhat m'avïa.
    Petit gazainha qui pert se,
    Mas qui pert so que dan li te,
    Ieu cre que gazainhs sïa.
    Qu'ieu m'era donatz, per ma fe,
    A tal que.m destruzïa,
    Non sai per que.

    Donan me, mes en sa merce
    Mi, mon cor, e ma vïa—
    De leis, que.m vir'e.m desmante
    Per autrui, e.m cambïa!
    Qui dona mais que non rete
    Et ama mais autrui que se,
    Chauzis avol partïa,

over

I. I hold him indeed for a fool and timewaster who joins company with love, for in love he has the worst who most trusts in it; such a one thinks to get warm who burns himself. The good things of love one has tardily, and the bad things every day; the fools, the felons and the tricksters, these have its friendship and so I part from it.

Never will my mistress possess me if I possessed her not; nor will she ever have joy of me if I had not joy of her. I've made a decision, good and sure: I'll treat her as she treats me. Then if she deceives me she'll find me a deceiver, and if she goes straight for me, for her I'll go smoothly.

I never won anything so great as when I lost my mistress; for, losing her, I won back myself when she had won me over. He wins little who loses himself, but if one loses that which does one harm, then I think that it's a gain. For I had given myself, in faith, to one such who was destroying me, I know not why.

Giving myself, at her mercy I put myself, my heart, and my life —hers, who casts me aside, and abandons and changes me for another! He who gives more than he keeps and loves another more than himself chooses a bad deal,

Quan de se no.ilh cal ni.l sove,
E per aco s'oblīa
Que pro no.ilh te.

De leis pren comjat per jasse,
Que ja mais sieus non sīa;
Qu'anc jorn no.i trobei lei ni fe,
Mas engan e bauzīa.
Ai! Doussors plena de vere,
Qu'amors eissorba sel que ve
E l'osta de sa vīa,
Quant ama so qu'ilh descove,
E so qu'amar deurīa
Gurp e mescre!

De leial amīa cove
Qu'om leials amics sīa;
Mas de leis estarīa be
Qu'en galīar se fīa,
Qu'om galīes, quan sap de que.
Per qu'a mi plai quan s'esdeve
Qu'eu trob qui la galīa,
E garda sa honor e se
De dan e de folīa,
E.il tira.l fre.

II. Mon chantar vueil retraire al comunal
De totas gens, e si.l deinhon auzir,
Ni l'entendon ni.l sabon devezir,
Cascuns poira traïr lo ben del mal.
Que cobeitatz a tant sazit en brieu
Lo mon que no.i cor dregz, ni temon Dieu,
Ni no.i trob'om merce, ni chauzimen,
Ni vergoinha, ab lo plus de la gen.

Rei e comte, bailho e senescal,
Volo.ls castels e las terras sazir
A lur acort, e paubra gent delir;
E li baro son, li plus, atretal, *over*

since he has no care or thought for himself, and he is self-forgetful for that which profits him not.

Of her I take my leave for ever, so that I may never more be hers; for at no time found I in her fairness or faith, only guile and deceit. Ah! Sweetness, full of venom, how love blinds the seeing man and leads him astray when he loves that which ill behoves him, and that which he ought to love quits and distrusts!

With a loyal mistress it behoves that one be a loyal lover; but with her who relies on deception, it would be well to deceive, when one has good reason. And so I'm pleased when it happens that I find one who deceives her, who guards himself and his honour from harm and folly, and keeps her on tight rein.

11. I want to recite my song to all peoples in common, and if they deign to hear it and understand it and can construe it, each will be able to distinguish good from evil. Now, greed has in short so seized the world that right's writ runs not there, and they fear not God. Nor does one find there pity, indulgence, or modesty, in the majority of people.

Kings and counts, bailiffs and seneschals, seek to seize castles and lands at their pleasure, and to plunder the poor; and the barons are, most of them, just the same,

Que cascuns ditz: ieu penrai d'aco mieu.
E ab tot son plus paure que romieu,
E non tenon vertat ni sagramen,
E nos autre em d'aquel mezeis sen.

Clerzīa vol, trastot l'an per egal,
Ab cobeitat gen caussar e vestir;
E.l gran prelat volo.s tant enantir
Que ses razon alargan lor deptal.
E si tenes del lor un onrat fieu,
Volran l'aver, e no.l cobraretz lieu
Si non lor datz une soma d'argen,
O non lor faitz plus estreg covinen.

Si morgue nier vol Dieus que sīan sal
Per trop manjar, ni per femnas tenir,
Ni monge blanc per bolas a mentir,
Ni per erguelh Temple ni Espital,
Ni canorgue per prestar a renieu,
Ben tenc per fols san Peire e sant Andrieu
Que sufriron per Dieu tan gran turmen,
S'aquist venon aissi a salvamen.

Si capellan per trop beure anöal,
Ni legistas per tort a mantenir,
Ni albergier per lor oste traïr,
Ni logadier per falsar lor jornal,
Ni regidor ni baile ni corrieu
Rauban la gen si salvan, no cre ieu
Que Menudet non reinhon follamen,
E sil qu'estan confes e peneden.

Revendedor, obrier e menestral,
Iran ab Dieu, so lor o vol sufrir,
Ab car vendre e ab menten plevir;
E camjador e home de portal
E renoier atressi com Juzieu,
E noirigier panan so c'om lor plieu,
Läorador terras sensals menten,
Obran festas e faitilhas crezen.   *over*

for each one says 'I'll take some of that for my own'. And with all that they're poorer than pilgrims, and they keep not to truth nor to their oath, and we ourselves are of the selfsame mind.

The clergy want, all through the year the same, in their greed to be well-shod and clad; and the great prelates seek such self-advancement that without reason they put up their dues. If you hold of theirs a fief in honour, they'll want to have it, and you'll not recover it easily unless you give them a deal of money, or make in their favour a more stringent bond.

If God desires that the black monks be saved by over-eating and by keeping women, and the white monks by making boundary-stones lie, the Temple and the Hospital by pride, and canons by lending on interest, then I indeed hold for fools Saint Peter and Saint Andrew who suffered for God such great torment, if all those come thus to salvation.

If chaplains by drinking too much on feast-days, and lawyers by upholding wrong, and innkeepers by cheating their customers, hirelings by fiddling the daybook, and if stewards and bailiffs and emissaries by robbing people are saved, then I believe not that Friars Minors behave not like fools, and those who stand confessed and penitent.

Retailers, labourers, and artisans, they'll go with God, if He permits it them, by selling dear and making false pledges; and money-changers and traffickers and usurers like Jews, and herdsmen stealing from what is entrusted to them, ploughmen lying about taxable lands, working on feast-days and believing sorcerers' spells.

A tota gen darai conseil leial,
Si tot no.l sai a mos ops retenir:
Que cadaüs volgues ben far e dir
A son poder. Car plus de bon captal
Non portarem escrit en nostre brieu,
Can nos n'irem e rendrem comte grieu
De totz los faitz, al jorn del jutjamen,
Al franc senhor que.ns formet de nïen.

Ges qui.m repren mon chantar no m'es grieu,
Car man far ben, si tot n'en fauc pauc ieu;
Ab que la gen renhesson ben e gen,
Pois pogran dir: de fol apren hom sen.

III. Un sirventes ai en cor que comens
    Que cantarai al despieg de trachors,
    En que dirai blasmes e dezonors
    E trassïons, a miliers e a cens.
    Car, si Caïms a del segle semensa,
    Esteves cre que fos de sa naissensa,
    Qu'az Aënac fes tals tres trassïos
    Que non fera Judas, ni Gainelos.

    Quar aquil dui traïron en vendens;
    L'un vendet Crist e l'autr'els ponhedors,
    E.s feron fort descauzitz vendedors.
    Mas Esteves traïs en aucizens,
    Qu'anc sos pairis non i trobet guirensa,
    Ni sos fillols, don fes tal descrezensa
    Qu'a lur disnar los aucis ambedos.
    E pres lur ben quar l'avïan somos!

    Quant Esteves vai vezer sos parens,
    El fa semblans que lur aia amors;
    E ten auzels e cans e cassadors,
    E fai si mot amoros e rizens,
    E vai manjar ab bella captenensa.   *over*

Peire Cardenal

To all people I'll give true advice, though I don't know how to follow it for my own good: that each one be willing to act and speak as well as he is able. For more to our credit shall we not have written down in the record, when we depart and give dire account of all deeds, that day of Judgement, to the noble Lord who made us from naught.

By no means if one blames my song does it bother me, for I commend good to be done, even though I do little myself; provided that people behaved well and rightly, then they could say 'from a fool can a man learn sense'.

III. I have in mind to begin a sirventes which I'll sing in despite of traitors, wherein I'll speak of blames and dishonours and treacheries, by the hundreds and thousands. For, if Cain has offspring in this world, I believe that Stephen was born of his line, since at Eynac he did three deeds of treachery such as Judas would not have done, nor Guanelon.

For these two betrayed in selling out; one sold Christ and the other the warriors, and they made themselves most vile vendors. But Stephen betrayed in killing, and his godfather never had a chance against him, nor his godson, for on them he wrought such betrayal of trust as to kill them both while they were at dinner. Much good it did them to have invited him!

When Stephen goes to see his kinsfolk, he makes a show of having love for them; he brings birds and dogs and hunters, and behaves most lovingly and smilingly, and goes to eat in gracious manner.

E, quant il an en servir entendensa,
El salh en pes com trachers desuptos,
E auci cuecx e portiers e bailos.

Esteves es, a for dels aguilens,
Gros e redons, ples de malas humors,
E es dels fins trachors del mon la flors.
Per que l'agr'ops us fort grans pendemens,
Mas als pendutz serïa viltenensa,
Si el era de lur obedïensa,
Ni sela claustra era rezensïos,
Quar anc no.i ac pendutz que tan fals fos.

Esteves fes, l'autrier, us ignocens,
Quan fazïa martirs e confessors
Az Aënac; e fes enguanadors,
E fes trachors tot ab uns ferramens!
Mas aras fai hueimais tal penedensa:
Qu'el fa ergueilz e las guerras comensa,
E alberga las tozas e.ls lairos,
E embla buous e froment e bacos.

Esteves, cant penras ta penedensa
Al capelan, diguas en passïensa
Dels sirventes que t'ai fach un o dos;
Qu'adoncx poira auzir tas trassïos!

IV.   Tartarassa ni voutor
     No sent tan leu carn puden
     Quom clerc e prezicador
     Senton ont es lo manen.
     Mantenen son sei privat,
     E quant malautïa.l bat,
     Fan li far donassïo
     Tal que.l paren no.i an pro.   *over*

Then, when they are busy serving he leaps to his feet, like the sudden traitor he is, and kills the cooks and the doormen and the stewards.

Stephen is, in the manner of the eglantine, plump and round and full of horrid humours, and of the world's cunning traitors he's the flower. For this a mighty hanging would serve him well, except it would be an insult to all men hanged if he were to be of their number, and if that cloister were to be his redemption, for there was never hanged one who was so false.

Stephen acted, the other day, like an innocent, when he was making martyrs and penitents at Eynac; he behaved like a trickster and a traitor, all with the same set of irons! Yet now such is the penance he does henceforth: he lords it proudly and stirs up trouble, and harbours loose women and robbers, and steals oxen and wheat and pickled pork.

Stephen, when you take your penance of the chaplain, just tell him, in patience, one or two of the poems I've made for you; then he'll be able to hear about your treacheries!

IV. Neither buzzard nor vulture smells stinking flesh so soon as clergy and preaching friars smell out where the rich man is. Straightway they're his friends, and, when sickness strikes him, they have him make a bequest such that his kinsfolk gain from it naught.

Franses e clerc an lauzor
De mal, quar ben lur en pren;
E renovier e trachor
An tot lo segl'eissamen,
C'ab mentir et ab barat
An si tot lo mon torbat
Que no.i a religio
Que no.n sapcha sa leisso.

Saps qu'endeven la ricor
De sels que l'an malamen?
Venra un fort raubador
Que non lur laissara ren;
So es la mortz, que.ls abat,
C'ab catr'aunas de filat
Los tramet en tal maizo
Ont atrobon de mal pro.

Hom, per que fas tal follor
Que passes lo mandamen
De Dieu, quez es ton senhor
E t'a format de nien?
La trueia ten al mercat
Sel que ab Dieu si combat,
Que.l n'aura tal guizardo
Com ac Judas lo fello.

Dieus verais, plens de doussor,
Senher, sias nos guiren!
Gardas d'enfernal dolor
Peccadors, e de turmen;
E solves los del peccat
En que son pres e liat,
E faitz lur veray perdo,
Ab vera confessio!

Frenchmen and clergy are renowned for their evil, because it works well for them; and usurers and traitors possess all the world likewise, for with lying and cheating they've so confused everyone that there's no religious order which learns not its lessons from them.

Know you what becomes of the wealth of those who come by it evilly? There'll come a great robber who'll leave them nothing; that is, death, who strikes them down and in four yards of winding-sheet dispatches them to such a dwelling where they find pain in abundance.

Man, why do you such folly as to transgress the law of God Who is your Lord and Who made you from nothing? He takes his sow to market who contends with God, and from it will have such deserts as had Judas the traitor.

True God, full of sweetness, Lord, be our protector! Preserve from hell's anguish all sinners, and from torment; and free them from the sin in which they are caught and bound, and grant them true pardon, with true confession.

V. Ab votz d'angel, lengu'esperta, non bleza;
    Ab motz sotils, plans plus c'obra d'engles,
    Ben assetatz, ben ditz e sens repreza,
    Miels escoutatz, ses tossir, que apres;
    Ab plans, sanglotz, mostran la vīa
    De Jhesu-Christ que quex deurīa
    Tener, com el per nos la volc tener,
    Van prezican com puescam Dieu vezer.

    Si non, con il, mangem la bona freza;
    E.l mortairol si batut c'o.l begues,
    E.l gras sabrier de galina pageza
    E, d'autra part, jove jusvert ab bles,
    E vin qui millior non poirīa,
    Don Franses plus leu s'enebrīa.
    S'ab bel vieure, vestir, manjar, jazer
    Conquer hom Dieu, be.l poden conquerer . . .

    Aissi con cill que bevon la serveza,
    E manjo.l pan de juel e de regres;
    E.l bro del gras buou lur fai gran fereza,
    Et onchura d'oli non volon ges,
    Ni peis fresc gras de pescarīa,
    Ni brōet ni salsa que frīa.
    Per qu'ieu conseil qui.n Dieu a son esper
    C'ab lurs condutz passe—qui.n pot aver!

    Religīos fon, li premieir', enpreza
    Per gent que treu ni bruida non volgues;
    Mas Jacopin apres manjar n'an queza,
    Ans desputan del vin, cals mieillers es.
    Et an de plaitz cort establīa
    Et es Vaudes qui.ls ne desvīa;
    E los secretz d'ome volon saber,
    Per tal que miels si puescan far temer.

    Esperitals non es la lur paubreza;
    Gardan lo lor, prenon so que mieus es.
    Per mols gonels, tescutz de lan'engleza,
    Laisson selis car trop aspre lur es.

over

Peire Cardenal

V. With angel's voice, with expert tongue not lisping; with subtle words, smoother than English cloth, well placed, well said, without repeat, more listened to, without a cough, than taken to heart; with moans, with sobs, showing the way of Jesus Christ which each should keep to as He was willing to keep to it for us, they go preaching how we might see God.

If we don't, then like them let us eat fine fare; purée so pulped that you could drink it, and the thick soup of a good farm chicken and, added to that, young verjuice with chards, and wine which couldn't be better, such as a Frenchman would get drunk on most quickly. If by fine living, dressing, eating and sleeping, one wins God, then they can as well win Him . . .

. . . as they who drink small beer, and eat bread of wholemeal and bran; who are frightened to ask for fat beef broth and don't even wish for seasoning of oil, for fat fresh fish from the fishpool, for broth or simmering sauce. Wherefore I advise whoever in God has his hope that he should feed on their dishes—if he can get them!

There was a religious order, the first, founded by men who would have neither uproar nor noise; but the Jacobins, after meals, do not keep silent, but rather argue about which is the better wine. And they've established courts of inquiry, and anyone's a Valdensian who deters them therefrom; they want to know a man's secrets, so that they may better make themselves feared.

Their poverty is not the spiritual one; keeping what's theirs, they take that which is mine. For soft tunics, woven in English wool, they quit the haircloth because that's too rough for them.

Ni parton ges lur draparīa
Aissi com sains Martins fazīa;
Mas almornas, de c'om sol sostener
La paura gent, volon totas aver.

Ab prims vestirs, amples, ab capa teza—
D'un camelin d'estiu, d'invern espes;
Ab prims caussatz, solatz a la francesa
Can fai gran freg, de fin cuer marselhes,
Ben ferm līatz per maīstrīa—
Car mal līars es grans follīa—
Van prezicant, ab lur sotil saber,
Qu'en Dieu servir metam cor e aver.

S'ieu fos maritz mot agra gran fereza
C'oms desbraiatz lonc ma moiller segues;
Qu'ellas e il an faudas d'un'ampleza,
E fuoc ab grais fort leumen s'es empres.
De Beguinas re no.us dirīa;
Tals es turgua que fructifīa.
Tals miracles fan, aiso sai per ver:
De sainz paires saint podon esser l'er.

VI. Un estribot farai que er mot maīstratz,
De motz novels e d'al, e de divinitatz.

Qu'ieu ai en Dieu crezensa que fon de maire natz,
D'una santa pieusela, per que.l mons es salvatz.
E es paire e filhs e santa trinitatz,
E es en tres personas e una unitatz.
E cre que.l cels e.l tros ne fos per el traucatz,
E.n trabuquet los angels can los trobet dampnatz.
E crey que sans Jöans lo tenc entre sos bratz
E.l bateget en l'aigua el flum, can fo propchatz;
E conoc be la senha abanchas que fo natz:
El ventre de sa maire que.s volc al destre latz.
E cre Rom'e sant Peire a cuy fon comandatz
Jutge de penedensa, de sen e de foldatz. *over*

Peire Cardenal

Nor do they share at all their cloak like Saint Martin did; and as for alms, by which one used to sustain the poor, they want to have them all.

With fine-spun, ample robes, with spreading capes—of camlet cloth in summer, in winter thick; with fine-made footwear, soled in the French style when it's very cold, of good Marseilles leather, well and truly stitched with a master's craft—for loose stitching's a terrible waste—they go preaching with their subtle science, that we should devote to God's service heart and possessions.

If I were a husband I'd be most frightened that a man without breeks should sit alongside my wife; for the women and they have skirts of the same fulness, and fire with fat most easily bursts into flame. Of the Béguine nuns, I'll tell you naught; such a one's barren who then bears fruit. Such miracles do they work, I know this for certain: of saintly fathers can saints be the sons and heirs!

VI. I'll write an 'estribot' which will be most masterly wrought, of new things to say and of others, and of divinity's lore.

I have in God my belief Who was born of mother, of a holy maiden, and through Whom the world is saved. And He is Father and Son and Holy Trinity, and He is in three persons and in one Unity. And I believe that heaven and its vault were by Him rent asunder, and that He cast down the angels when He found them corrupt. I believe, too, that Saint John held Him in his arms and baptized Him in the river's water, when He had drawn near; he well knew the sign even before he was born, for in his mother's womb he leapt on his right side. And I believe Rome and Saint Peter, to whom was commended the judgement of penitence, of wisdom and of folly.

Mas so non crezon clergue, que fan las falcetatz,
Que son larc d'aver penre et escas de bontatz.
E son bel per la cara et ore de peccatz,
E devedon als autres d'aco que fan lurs atz,
E en loc de matinas an us ordes trobatz
Que jazon ab putanas tro.l solelhs es levatz,
Enans canton baladas e prozels trasgitatz;
Abans conquerran Dieu Caïfas o Pilatz!

Monge solon estar dins los mostiers serratz,
On azoravan Dieu denan las magestatz;
E can son en las vilas on an lurs pöestatz,
Si avetz bela femna o es homs molheratz,
El seran cobertor, si.eus peza o si.eus platz.
E can el son desus e.l cons es sagelatz
Ab las bolas redondas que pendon al matratz,
Con las letras son clausas e lo traucs es serratz,
D'aqui eyson l'iretge e li essabatatz,
Que juron e renegon e jogon a tres datz.
Aiso fan monge negre en loc de caritatz!

Mon estribot fenisc que es tot compassatz,
C'ai trag de gramatica e de divinitatz;
E si mal o ai dig, que.m sïa perdonatz,
Que yeu o dic per Dieu, qu'en sïa pus amatz,
E per mal estribatz
Clergues.

VII. Un sirventes novel vueill comensar
Que retrairai al jor del jujamen
A sel que.m fes e.m formet de nïen.
S'el me cuja de ren arazonar,
E s'el me vol metr'en la diablïa,
Ieu li dirai : 'Seinher, merce, non sïa!
Qu'el mal segle tormentiei totz mos ans;
E guardas mi, si.us plas, dels tormentans.'   *over*

Peire Cardenal

But this the clergy believe not, who do false things, who are open-handed in taking wealth and tight-fisted in bounty. They are fair of face and foul in sins, and forbid others that with which they suit themselves. And in place of matins they've devised a service where they lie abed with whores till the sun is up, and before that they sing ballads and sprightly versets; Caiaphas and Pilate will sooner win God!

Monks used to live confined within the monasteries, where they adored God before the holy images; now, when they're in the towns where they have their strongholds, if you've a fair woman or if you're a married man, they'll be the ones to do the covering, whether you like it or not. And when they're mounted and the cunt is sealed with the round balls which hang from their prick, as a letter is closed and the opening shut, then from that are born the heretics and Valdensians who curse and renegue and play with three dice. This the black monks do instead of charity!

I finish my 'estribot', now fully encompassed, which I have drawn from grammar and divinity; and if I've spoken it ill, be it forgiven me, for I say it for God's sake that He might the more be loved, and for the sake of evil-goaded clergy.

VII. I want to begin a new sirventes which I'll recite on Judgement Day to Him Who made and fashioned me from naught. If He thinks to arraign me for anything and if He wants to send me to devildom, I'll say to Him: 'Lord, mercy, let that not be! For in the wicked world I was tormented all my days; and so preserve me, if it please You, from the tormentors.'

Tota sa cort farai meravillar
Cant auziran lo mieu plaideiamen,
Qu'eu dic qu'el fa ves los sieus faillimen
Si los cuja delir ni enfernar.
Car qui pert so que gazanhar poiria,
Per bon dreg a de viutat carestia,
Qu'el deu esser dous e multiplicans
De retener las armas trespassans.

Los dïables degra dezeretar,
Et agra mais d'armas, e plus soven,
E.l dezeretz plagra a tota gen
Et el mezeis pogra s'o perdonar.
Car per mon grat trastotz los destruiria
Pos tut sabem c'absolver s'en poiria.
Bels seinhers Dieus, sias dezeretans
Dels enemix enuios e pezans!

Vostra porta non degras ja vedar,
Que sans Peires i pren trop d'aunimen
Que n'es portiers; mas que intres rizen
Tota arma que lai volgues intrar,
Car nuilla cortz non er ja ben complia
Que l'uns en plor e que l'autre en rïa.
E sitot ses sobeirans reis poissans,
Si no m'ubres, er vos en fatz demans.

Ieu no me vueill de vos dezesperar,
Anz ai en vos mon bon esperamen
Que me vaillas a mon trespassamen;
Per que deves m'arm'e mon cors salvar.
E farai vos una bella partïa:
Que.m tornetz lai don moc lo premier dia,
O que.m sïatz de mos tortz perdonans,
Qu'ieu no.ls feira si non fos natz enans.

S'ieu ai sai mal et en enfern l'avia,
Segon ma fe tortz e peccatz seria!
Qu'ieu vos puesc ben esser recastenans
Que, per un ben, ai de mal mil aitans.

over

I'll set His whole court agog when they hear my pleading, and I say that He fails His own if He thinks to destroy them or send them to hell. Because he who loses what he could gain has, most rightly, a dearth of what's abundant, He should then be gentle and solicitous to take to Himself the souls of the dead.

He should dispossess the devils, then He would have more souls, and more often; and the dispossession would please all people, and He Himself could permit Himself it. For it would be to my pleasing that He destroyed them all, since we all know that He could absolve Himself for it. Fair Lord God, be You the dispossessor of the hurtful and grievous fiends!

You ought not to bar Your gate, for Saint Peter who is its keeper suffers thereby great shame; but let there enter, smiling, every soul who would therein enter, for no court will ever indeed be complete if one weeps for it while another laughs. And though You are the sovereign, mighty King, if You open not for me, a complaint will be laid against You.

I do not want to despair of You, but rather have in You all my good hope that You may avail me at my death; wherefore You should save my body and my soul. I'll make You a fair deal: either You return me there whence I sprang on my first day, or You forgive me my wrongs, for I would not have done them had I not first been born.

If I have pain here and had it in hell, by my faith that would be a wrong and a sin! For I can indeed charge this against You, that for one good I have a thousand times as much pain.

Per merce.us prec, donna sancta Marīa,
C'al vostre fill mi fassas garentīa,
Si qu'el prenda lo paire e.ls enfans
E.ls meta lay on esta sans Johans.

VIII. Dels quatre caps que a la crotz,
    Ten l'us sus vas lo fermamen,
    L'autre vas abis, selh de jos;
    E l'autre ten vas orīen,
    E l'autre ten vas occiden;
    E per aital entresenha
    Que Cristz o a tot en poder.

    La crotz es lo dreitz gofainos
    Del rey cuy tot cant es apen,
    Qu'om deu seguir totas sazos,
    Las süas volontatz fazen.
    Car qui mais y fay mais y pren,
    E totz homs qu'ab lui se tenha
    Es segurs de bon loc aver.

    Cristz mori en la crotz per nos,
    E destruis nostra mort, moren;
    E en crotz venset l'ergulhos,
    El leinh on vensīa la gen.
    Et en crotz obret salvamen,
    Et en crotz renhet e renha,
    Et en crotz nos volc rezemer.

    Aquest fagz fo meravilhos,
    Qu'el leinh on pres mortz naissemen,
    Nos nasquet vida e perdos,
    E repaus en loc de tormen.
    En crotz pot trobar veramen
    Totz homs, que querre l'i denha,
    Lo frug del albre de saber.

over

Peire Cardenal

For mercy's sake I pray you, my Lady, Holy Mary, that with your son you be my guarantee, that He might take the father and the children and set them there where dwells Saint John.

VIII. Of the four arms which the cross has, one points up towards the firmament, another towards the abyss, the one beneath; one points towards the orient, and the other towards the west; and by such it signifies that Christ has all in His power.

The cross is the rightful banner of the king to Whom all that there is belongs, and Whom one should at all times follow, doing whatever He wills. For he who does more thereof gains therefrom the more, and any man who keeps His company is sure to have a good home.

Christ died on the cross for us and, dying, destroyed our death; and on the cross He vanquished the proud one, on that piece of wood where he used to vanquish men. And on the cross He wrought salvation, on the cross He reigned and does reign, and on the cross He was willing to redeem us.

This fact was miraculous, that on that wood where death had its birth, there was for us born life and forgiveness, and rest in place of torment. On the cross can every man truly find, if he deigns to seek it, the fruit of the tree of knowledge.

Ad aquest frug em tug somos,
Que.l culham amorozamen,
Que.l frugz es tan bels e tan bos
Que qui.l culhira, ben ni gen,
Tostemps aura vida valen.
Per qu'om de culhir no.s fenha,
Mentre qu'en a loc e lezer.

Lo dous frug cuelh qui la crotz pren
E sec Crist vas on que tenha,
Que Cristz es lo frugz de saber.

To that fruit we are all summoned, so that we might lovingly cull it; for the fruit is so fair and fine that he who culls it, well and rightly, will always have everlasting life. Wherefore let no one hold back from culling it, while he has for it time and occasion.

He culls the sweet fruit who takes the cross and follows Christ to wherever He may lead, for Christ is the fruit of knowledge.

Guiraut Riquier

LIFE. As for most of the professional troubadours, our knowledge of Guiraut Riquier's life is limited to those general circumstances of his career which figure in his own poetry. Such is the nature of that poetry however, and the manner of its conservation, that these circumstances can be described with a more than usual measure of accuracy, for not only does one of the base manuscripts claim to reproduce the poet's original holograph in which most of the works are precisely dated, but much of the poet's thematic material derives directly from his personal and professional situation. Of this, the dominant feature is the fact that Guiraut, as he himself grew increasingly aware, was to be the last of the troubadours. Thus, from his earliest poem of 1254 to his latest, of 1292, one can trace his efforts to maintain in the face of growing neglect and indifference the traditions of troubadour lyric poetry, to establish a livelihood on their cultivation, and finally to seek consolation for repeated failures in a form of poetry which itself marks their end. During the first part of his career, from 1254 to 1270, Guiraut worked in Narbonne, seeking the patronage of the local viscount Aimery IV. Whether he did secure the latter's recognition is already somewhat problematical since, although Aimery's name figures frequently in poems of the period, other, minor noblemen of the region, named less often, are yet addressed more warmly, more hopefully, and with greater enthusiasm. Even in the 1250s Guiraut introduces what will become in time a dominant theme, the failure of noble society to appreciate the poet of true courtliness, while in the 1260s he makes increasingly plain his intentions of seeking fairer fortune elsewhere. This he does in 1270, journeying to Spain and coming to settle, for a period of nine years or so, at the court of King Alfonso X. But the court of Castile in the 70's, like that of Narbonne in the preceding decade, had already passed its peak as a centre of a flourishing literary culture, open to all comers and welcoming especially the troubadours. Alfonso himself was increasingly beset with material, dynastic and political difficulties, and in all events his court had by this time developed highly specific, native poetic forms dependent no longer on the once prestigious traditions which Guiraut represented. The themes of disappointment and deception are taken up more frequently, more bitterly, as the decade wore on, and at its end Guiraut returns to the Midi. Here, at the court of Count Henry II of Rodez, one of the last to maintain, albeit on a restricted scale, some vestiges of literary activity, Guiraut's hopes are for a time revived. New projects are conceived, new forms and themes worked on, but to no lasting avail. In a poem of 1286 he laments once more the absence of patronage and protection, and it is impossible to trace his whereabouts thereafter. If, as is likely, he returned to Narbonne, nothing suggests that he found there even the limited favour he had enjoyed some thirty years earlier. In his last dated composition he turns away from the world, finally admitting that he had come too late; too late, that is, to achieve that to which, despite all the changing circumstances, he had devoted his long career. Late in 1292 or soon after, Guiraut Riquier disappears without trace, and the last shadows of a once great and flourishing art fade away.

WORKS. The number of this poet's compositions, just over a hundred in all, their unprecedented generic variety and novelty, with the classic *canso* and *sirventès* accounting for little more than half, and the remainder provided by an assortment of genres such as the *rotroencha*, the *pastorella, tensos, albas* and non-lyric verse epistles, together with the markedly even rate of production, averaging between two and three pieces each year for nearly forty years, all this bears witness to the conscientious dedication with which Guiraut sought to fulfil his self-appointed mission. Equally indicative is the register in which the greater part of his work is written. The moral, religious, and literary advice and exposition to which his long verse epistles are devoted are as unrelievedly earnest and solemn as, in his lyrics, the more conventional laments of unrequited love, the protestations of unconditioned loyalty, the prayers to God and the Virgin Mary, the complaints about the decline of courtliness and about his own failure to secure recognition. Yet it must be admitted that if Guiraut's mission was so constantly and, at the end, so definitively frustrated, the fault lies as much in the nature of his own art as in the changing nature of external circumstances. The variety and the novelty of genres practised and developed throughout his career fail to make good a lack of genuine creativity and, while a certain amount of his verse does rise above the general level of facile prolixity, even his best work is distinguished by little more than adequate resolutions of unambitious technical problems and satisfactorily coherent formulations of long-established themes. If his numerous religious lyrics constitute in fact an authentically personal and individual achievement, they also tend, by their very nature, at first to rival and ultimately to replace the secular ideals on which the troubadour lyric had been founded. Their emergence in his own work as a dominant lyric form, together with the steady development of the long verse composition as a vehicle of moral, religious and literary discourse, is paralleled by the gradual abandonment of the courtly love-song, more than half his compositions of this genre dating from his first period and none at all from his last, post-Castilian period. Both religious lyrics and long verse treatises, finally, while leaving far behind the art and inspiration of Guiraut's predecessors, already announce two distinctive features of later medieval poetry, be it that cultivated by the good burgesses of Toulouse in the *Consistoire del Gay Saber*, or that of the professional writers labouring in the courts of northern France. In his work as in his life, Guiraut Riquier thus figures, in spite of himself no doubt, as the last of the troubadours.

EDITION. S. L. H. Pfaff, in C. A. F. Mahn's *Die Werke der Trobadors*, (5 Vols., Berlin 1846–1886) Vol. 4, 1853.

SELECTION. Beyond stating that even the briefest selection would illustrate the main features of Guiraut Riquier's art and inspiration, there is little occasion for further, detailed comment. Thus the first two pieces (Pfaff, nos. 7 and 23), written in Narbonne, 1259, and Castile, 1275, show well the exclusive consistency with which the poet maintained through much of his career the most characteristic and conventional features of the *canso d'amor*. Similarly in the next piece (Pfaff, no. 45), a *sirventès* dating from 1286, if a note of individuality can be perceived, it is in the very completeness with which the poet identifies himself with all the current topics of moral and social comment, a completeness aptly mirrored in the formal coherence and neat regularity of the composition. The following piece (Pfaff, no. 50, dated 1289) is undoubtedly more innovatory. The sustained and detailed adaptation of the language, style and topics of the courtly love-song to what is, in essence, a hymn of praise to the Virgin Mary contrasts strongly with the traditional pattern of such compositions, closely based hitherto on liturgical and mediaeval Latin models. With the exception of a few minor troubadours of the late thirteenth century the device is unique to Guiraut himself. Its significance, with regard both to the poet's personal situation and to the contemporary literary and cultural context, is to be seen again in the fifth selected piece, a *sirventès* dating from 1292 (Pfaff, no. 53). As the last of his compositions one cannot help but read it as the poet's farewell to the world, a farewell which, in its pathetic simplicity, envisions the whole of Guiraut's experience and endows it with a meaningful unity. To the very last word we see the poet striving to maintain the fundamental traditions of the troubadours; in the profoundly modified sense in which that last word is used we see, too, that those traditions are now at their end.

I. No.m sai, d'amor, si m'es mala o bona,
    O.m val o.m notz, o.m manten o m'azira;
    Ni sai, del mal ni del ben, quals se sobra.
    Ni no conosc si m'aleuja o.m carga,
    Ni entendi si.m dic ver o messonja,
    Ni si vau dreg o tenc vïa traversa.
    Qu'est pessamens me destrenh e.m taborna,
    Don trac trop pieytz que selh qu'om viu escorja.

    Qu'amors me fa chauzir per la pus bona
    Lieys qu'ieu dezir et am, per que m'azira,
    E.m fa sufrir, ses camjar, so que.m sobra;
    E.m fa voler tal re que.m sobrecarga,
    E.m fa semblar vertat de la messonja
    Tant que mo mielhs me trastolh e.m traversa;
    E.m fa tornar al dur colp que.m taborna,
    E.m fa portar lo cotelh que m'escorja.

    Si aissi.m notz amors, en als m'es bona,
    Qu'a luex vils faitz per lieys mon cor azira,
    E.m fa eslir aquelhs don bos pretz sobra.
    E m'a donat tal saber que no.m carga,
    Ans me fa dir mant bon vers ses messonja;
    E.m dona grat dels pros, senes traversa,
    Ab tal engenh que.ls pecx amans taborna,
    Quar mos braus ditz, per semblant, los escorja.

    Pero mai vuelh que.m sïa d'aitant bona
    Que si m'aizis amors lieys que m'azira,
    Senes tot l'als, si tot l'afans me sobra.
    E pur manda.m suffrir, d'als no.m descarga,
    Quar ab suffrir n'aurai joy ses messonja.
    Et on mais am midons, pus m'es traversa;
    Aissi no truep vertat, per que.m taborna,
    Si.m val o.m notz, o.m sana o m'escorja.

    Al vescomte N'Amalric de Narbona
    Vir ma chanso, quar tot vil fag azira,
    E manten pretz, per que valors li sobra
    Tant que.ls vils ricx de mals pessamens carga,
    E manten joy e gab senes messonja,   *over*

Guiraut Riquier

I. I know not, concerning love, whether it's bad or good to me, whether it profits or harms me, or helps or hates me; nor do I know, of the bad and the good, which overwhelms the other. I do not recognize whether it pleases or oppresses me, nor do I understand whether it tells me truth or falsehood, or whether I go straight or keep to a path perverse. And by this state of mind am I tortured and stricken; I suffer far worse from it than one who is flayed alive.

Love has me choose as the most good her whom I love and desire, whereby Love hates me and makes me endure, without alteration, that which overwhelms me; it makes me want such a thing as oppresses me greatly, and it so much makes truth appear to me from falsehood that it robs me of what is best and perverts it for me; it makes me run into the hard knock that's struck against me, and has me bear the knife which flays me.

If Love thus harms me, in other ways it's good; for betimes my heart, for its sake, hates base deeds, and it makes me opt for those whose fine merit is overwhelming. It has given me such knowledge as does not oppress me but, rather, has me say many a fine verse, without falsehood; it earns for me the goodwill of the worthy, pure of perversion, and with such skill as strikes against foolish lovers, for my harsh words, to all appearances, flay them.

For all this I'd rather that Love were so good as to win over for me her who hates me, without all else, though the anguish overwhelms me. But it bids me only to endure—by naught else does it relieve me—for by enduring will I have its joy, without falsehood. Yet the more I love my lady, the more she's perverse towards me, and so I discover not the truth—and thereby she afflicts me—as to whether she profits or harms me, or heals or flays me.

To the Viscount Lord Aimery of Narbonne I address my song, for he hates every base deed and upholds merit, whereby valour so triumphs in him that he oppresses the base rich with their evil thoughts, and upholds joy and jesting without falsehood,

Ab grat dels pros, senes tota traversa;
E sap valer tant que.ls estranhs taborna,
Salvan s'onor, per que ira.ls escorja.

Midons bona sai, qu'azira traversa;
Si be.m sobra, no.s carga ni.s taborna,
Car messonja tem que valor escorja.

11. Fis e verays e pus ferms que no suelh
Suy vas amor endreg mon Belh Deport.
Non que m'aja fag semblan de conort,
Mas que.m soven qui fuy ans que ames,
E que.m cossir qui fora ses amor,
Et aug per qui.m teno.l conoyssedor.
Per qu'ieu am fis, quar d'amar ay l'enans.

L'enans que n'ay m'es mout plazens e grans,
Qu'ieu non saupi penre ni far honor,
Ni negus faitz d'azaut no m'ac sabor,
Tro.m fes plazer amors qu'ieu lieys ames
Qu'ab mi no fon en lunh fag d'un acort,
Sal quar son pretz creysser dezira fort;
Que s'ylh o vol, ieu atretant o vuelh.

D'aquelh voler ni dels autres no.m duelh
Endreg de lieys, ans m'a d'afan estort,
Qu'ieu non dezir qu'autres plazers m'aport.
Mas si.m disses que.l plagues qu'ieu l'ames,
Foran complit mey dezirier maior.
Mas non o vuelh, qu'ilh no.y agues honor,
Quar d'aquella creysser suy dezirans.

Amors fa far totz bos faitz benestans,
E dona.ls ayps qu'a pretz son valedor.
Doncx amors es doctrina de valor,
Que non es hom tan pecx, sol ben ames,
Que no.l menes amors a valent port.
Mas ad enjan es datz sos noms a tort,
Qu'amors enjan ni barat non acuelh. *over*

and with the goodwill of the worthy, pure of all perversion; and he is capable of such valour that he strikes against the foreigners, preserving his honour, wherefore frustration flays them.

I know my lady is good, who hates perversion; though she overwhelms me, she's not oppressed or stricken, for she fears falsehood which flays valour.

II. Noble and true and more constant than is my wont am I towards love for my Fair Delight. Not that she's made me any show of comfort, but because I recall who I was ere I loved, and I consider who I would be without love and hear whom those who know take me to be. For this I love nobly, that by loving I am enhanced.

The enhancement which I have thereby is to me most great and pleasing, for I knew not how to win or how to do honour, and no gracious deed appealed to me, until love made it please me that I should love her who was in no way of one accord with me, except that she greatly desires to increase her merit, for, as she wants it, so I want it just as much.

For such wanting and others I've no regret regarding her; it has, rather, freed me from anguish, and I desire not that it should bring me other pleasures. But if she told me that it pleased her that I loved her, my greatest desires would be fulfilled. But this I want not: that she thereby should not have honour, since I am desirous of increasing that.

Love causes all good, seemly deeds to be done, and bestows those qualities which pertain to merit. Thus love is a school of valour, for no man is so stupid but, provided he love, love guides him to valorous port. But to deceit is its name wrongly given, for love has no dealings with deceit or guile.

Tals ditz 'Ieu am selha que.m fa erguelh'
Que dezira de lieys pieitz de sa mort,
E.l pus, conosc, que son d'aquella sort.
Mas si quascus sa dona fis ames,
Totz sos enans, say, que l'agra sabor;
E.l contraris fera.l mout gran temor,
Quar aital es l'esser dels fis amans.

S'al rey degues dire que ieu l'ames!
Assatz sembla que.l porti fin'amor,
Quar per sos ops dezir mil tans d'onor
Que per lo mieu, si.m sïa Dieus enans.

Reys Castellas, vostre laus m'a sabor,
E si per vos non venh en gran ricor,
Al mens per tot n'er pus grazitz mos chans.

III. Ja mais non er hom en est mon grazitz
    Per ben trobar belhs digz e plazens sos,
    Ni per esser de bon grat enveyos,
    Tant es lo muns avengutz deschauzitz.
    Quar so que sol dar pretz, grat, e lauzor,
    Aug repenre per folhïa major;
    E so qu'om sol repenre e blasmar
    Vey mantener, et aug per tot lauzar.

    De tolre vey los poderos arditz,
    E.ls vey volpilhs de condutz e de dos;
    E de dir ver tardius e vergonhos,
    E de mentir frontiers et yssernitz.
    E lïaltat no servan, ni amor,
    Mas ab enjan s'aziran entre lor;
    Et a merce no.s volon regardar,
    E son cobe d'aizina de peccar.

    Ab tot ditz hom que.l mun es corregitz,
    E pus que mais no fo es valoros!
    E pareys be de conoyssensa blos
    Qui so pessa, e trop pus qui o ditz.

over

Guiraut Riquier

Such a one says 'I love her who is proud towards me' who desires of her worse than her death; and the most, I am aware, are of that sort. But if each loved his lady nobly, I know that all that which enhanced her would appeal to him; and the contrary would inspire in him great dread, because such is the essence of noble lovers.

If only she were to tell the king that I loved her! It's clear enough that I bear her noble love because, for her sake, I desire a thousand times more honour than for my own, so help me God.

King of Castile, I take pleasure in your praise, and if by you I come not to great wealth, at least for it will my song be by all more favoured.

III. Never more will a man be in this world thanked for well composing fair words and pleasant airs, nor for being eager for esteem, so much is the world come to its decline. For that which used to inspire merit, approval, and praise, I hear blamed as the utmost folly; and that which one used to criticize and blame, I see upheld, and hear it praised by all.

I see those in power bold to take, and see them reluctant to welcome and give; tardy and bashful to speak the truth, and shameless and clever in lying. Loyalty they serve not, nor love, but with deceit they contend among themselves; they would have no regard for mercy and are avid of occasion to sin.

Withal it's said that the world is improved, and that it's more valorous than it ever was! And he seems indeed bereft of wit who thinks that, and he far more who says so.

Qu'anc el mon mais tant no foron trachor
Ni falsari sufert, que.l gran senhor
Fan de gran tort, ab elh, bon dreg semblar,
Et es volgutz mais qui.n sap pus obrar.

Perparan dreg, es tortz tant enantitz
Que.l mons es ples de platz e de tensos,
Qu'om sec apelhs assizas volontos,
Meten lo sieu tro n'es empaubrezitz.
E caritatz no troba valedor,
Don vey camjar totz jorns mal per peior;
E pot quascus en si meteys trobar
Que vertatz es, si so sap cossirar.

Ab aquelh mal qu'es dels autres razitz,
Et ab erguelh em tug contrarïos
A tot dever, qu'entre mil non a dos
Que.s conoscan, car bos sens no.ns es guitz.
Ni temem mort, ni pena, ni dolor,
Ni vergonha, et aujatz gran folhor:
Qu'apres la mort mandam so acabar,
Per nos, que viu no sabem comensar!

E tuch avem los mandamens auzitz
Que nos a faitz Dieus, qu'es totz poderos,
E totz savis, drechuriers, e totz bos,
Ples de merces; mas pauc n'es obezitz.
E sol qu'aman, luy honran ab temor,
E l'us l'autre, visquessem ses rancor,
Fazen lo ben que pogram, ses mal far,
Crey certamen qu'elh nos volgra salvar.

Sanctz paires Dieus, sanctz filhs, sanctz esperitz,
Qu'etz caritatz, misericordïos,
E tot quant es, es nïens senes vos,
Senher, tot so de que vos etz servitz
Nos faitz obrar, a la vostra honor;
E de tot l'als, per la vostre doussor,
Faitz nos partir, e.ns o faitz azirar,
E.ns datz guida que.ns sapcha dreg guidar.   *over*

Guiraut Riquier

For never in the world were knaves and cheats so suffered as now, when the great lords make great wrong, with their help, seem natural right, and when he is most sought after who best knows how to work it.

Right being up for sale, wrong has so prospered that the world is full of quarrels and disputes, and men take their pleas to court most readily, spending whatever they have until they're impoverished. Charity finds no champion, whence I see bad changed every day for worse; and each can discover in himself that that's the truth, if he's able to think on it.

By that evil which is the root of all others, and by pride are we all against all duty, so that in a thousand there are not two who are in accord, for good sense guides us not. Nor fear we death, pain, suffering, or shame, and just listen to this folly: we expect, after death, that to be done for us which we, in this life, know not even how to begin!

Yet we all have heard the commandments which God gave us, He Who is almighty and all-knowing, just and wholly good and merciful; but for all that He is not much obeyed. If only, in loving, honouring Him in awe, and one another, we lived without ill-will, doing the good that we could, without doing evil, I surely believe that He would be willing to save us.

God, Holy Father, Holy Son, Holy Spirit, You who are charity itself, and merciful, and all that is, is nothing without You, cause us to do all that by which You are served, and to labour in Your honour; and all else, through Your sweetness, have us shun, have us hate it, and give us that guidance by which we might rightly be guided.

De far l'obra son trop li dictator
De drechura, e pauc li fazedor;
L'un trop escur e li autre pro clar;
Mas tant sofre Dieus que.ns deu temor far.

Anc pus perdei l'onrat rey plen d'amor
De Castella, N'Anfos, non ayc senhor
Que.m conogues, ni.m saubes tant honrar
Que m'en pogues de vergonha cessar.

Greu me sera si.m coven ablasmar
Un senhor mieu que solia lauzar.

IV. Ieu cujava soven d'amor chantar
El temps passat, e non la conoyssia,
Qu'ieu nomnava per amor ma folia.
Mas era.m fai amors tal don'amar
Que non la puesc honrar pro, ni temer,
Ni tener car endreg del sieu dever;
Ans ai dezir que s'amors me destrenha
Tant que l'esper, qu'ieu ai en lieys, n'atenha.

Quar per s'amor esper en pretz montar,
Et en honor et en gran manentia,
Et en gran gauch, doncx en als non deuria
Mos pessamens ni mos dezirs estar;
Que pus per lieys puesc tot quant vuelh aver,
Al sieu servir dey far tot mon poder.
Quar amatz suy per lieys, sol que.m captenha
Vas lieys aissi co fin'amors essenha.

E per aisso dey m'en miels esforssar,
Pus ylh me vol si.m vuelh, qu'ieu no poiria
Entendr'en lieys, si de lieys no.m venia.
Doncx per s'amor dey ben la mia dar;
Quar ieu no puesc ses ella re valer,
Ni puesc a lieys, sal d'onrar, pro tener;
E fassa.m Dieus, que pot, tener la senha
Endreg midons dels fis, on amors renha.

over

To do that work the teachers of righteousness are many, and few the doers; these hard to find, the others manifest enough; but God endures so much that it must strike us with fear.

Since I lost the honoured, loving king of Castile, Lord Alfonso, I never had a lord who acknowledged me, or who could so honour me that I might cease feeling shame.

It will be hard for me if I'm to blame a lord of mine whom I used to praise.

IV. I often thought to sing of love in times gone by, and I knew nothing of it for I named by love's name my folly. But now love has me love a lady such that I cannot honour her enough, hold her in awe or cherish her as she ought to be; I rather desire her love so to constrain me that I might thereby attain the hope which I have in her.

Since through her love I hope to rise to merit, to honour, to great wealth and to great joy, I should not therefore set elsewhere my thoughts or my desires; and since through her I can have all I desire, I must in her service do all that is in my power. For I am loved by her, if only I act so towards her as noble love commends.

And for this I should better strive, that she wants me if I so want, and I could not aspire to her unless, of herself, she came to me. Hence for her love I must indeed give mine, for I cannot, without her, be worth anything, nor can I to her, save by honouring, be of avail. Then may God, who is able to, have me bear on behalf of my lady the banner of the noble over whom love reigns.

Saber non ay ni sen per lieys lauzar;
Tant a d'onor que pus non y cabrïa,
E tant de ben que res no.l creysserïa.
Doncx ma lauzors de que la pot honrar?
Ieu prenc l'onor, quar no.n puesc dir mas ver.
Per que m'en dey esforsar jorn e ser;
Quar, a lunh for, en ren qu'a mi covenha
No puesc pecar, que midons mi sovenha.

Tan gran beutat a que no pot mermar,
Ni res no.y falh, ans resplan nuech e dïa;
Et a poder tal qu'en ren no.s fadïa,
Et gracïa en tot quan que vol far,
Humilitat, caritat, sen, saber,
E pïetat e merce, per qu'esper
Ay en s'amor, pus ylh amar me denha,
Que.m tenra gay, sol qu'ieu dreg a lieys venha.

Ma dona puesc nomnar ben per dever
Mon Belh Deport, pus ay mon bon esper
Qu'ilh me fassa selh que razos m'essenha,
Per que la prec, per merce, que.m revenha.

Gilos non suy, qui s'amor vol aver,
De lieys qu'ieu am, ans n'ay mot gran plazer,
E.m desplay fort, qui amar non la denha.
Quar per s'amor crey cert que totz bes venha.

Sos amadors prec midons que mantenha,
Si que quasqus son dezirier n'atenha.

Guiraut Riquier

Knowledge I have not, nor sense enough to praise her; so much honour she has that there'd be no place for more, and so much good that nothing would increase it. Then in what way could my praise honour her? Mine is the honour, for I cannot speak of her but the truth. Wherefore I must strive morn and evening, for, on no account, can I sin in whatever it behoves me to do, provided my lady helps me.

She has such great beauty that it cannot wane, it lacks in nothing but is resplendent night and day; and she has such power that in nothing does it abate, and grace in all that she is pleased to do, humility, charity, sense and knowledge, and pity and mercy; wherefore I have hope in her love, since she deigns to love me, that it will keep me joyful, if only I come to her straightway.

I can indeed by rights name my lady My Fair Delight, since I have good hope that she will make me such that reason guides me; wherefore I pray her, through mercy, to restore me.

I am not jealous if one would have the love of her whom I love; I rather take great pleasure in it and am most displeased with whoever deigns not to love her. For through love of her I firmly believe that all good comes.

I pray that my lady so maintain her lovers that each one may thereby attain his desire.

V. Be.m degra de chantar tener,
    Quar a chan coven alegriers,
    E mi destrenh tant cossiriers
    Que.m fa de totas partz doler;
    Remembran mon greu temps passat,
    Esgardan lo prezent forsat,
    E cossiran l'avenidor,
    Que per totz ai razon que plor.

    Per que no.m deu aver sabor
    Mos chans, qu'es ses alegretat;
    Mas Dieus m'a tal saber donat
    Qu'en chantan retrac ma folhor,
    Mo sen, mon gauch, mon desplazer,
    E mon dan et mon pro, per ver;
    Qu'a penas dic ren ben estiers,
    Mas trop suy vengutz als derriers.

    Qu'er non es grazitz lunhs mestiers
    Menhs en cort que de belh saber
    De trobar; qu'auzir e vezer
    Hi vol hom mais captenhs leugiers
    E critz mesclatz ab dezonor;
    Quar tot quan sol donar lauzor,
    Es, al pus del tot, oblidat,
    Que.l mons es, quays, totz en barat.

    Per erguelh e per malvestat
    Dels Christīas ditz, luenh d'amor
    E dels mans de Nostre Senhor,
    Em del sieu Sant Loc discipat,
    Ab massa d'autres encombriers;
    Don par qu'elh nos es aversiers
    Per desadordenat voler
    E per outracujat poder.

over

V. I should indeed refrain from singing because for song there's need of gaiety, and care constrains me so much that from all sides it causes me pain; remembering my hard times past, considering the difficult present, and thinking on the future, so that for all times I have cause to weep.

Wherefore my song should have no pleasure for me, for it is without any gayness; but God has given me such art that in singing I recount my folly, my sense, my joy, my displeasure, and my losses and my gains, in truth; I scarcely say anything worthwhile otherwise, but I have come too late, among the last.

For now no craft is less well-received in courts than the fair art of writing poetry; one there prefers to see and hear frivolous pastimes and shameful chatter. Because all that which used to give rise to praise is, most of all, forgotten, the world is, so to speak, all up for sale.

Through the pride and wickedness of so-called Christians, far from the love and the biddings of Our Lord, we are now driven from His holy Sepulchre, not to speak of the mass of other setbacks; whence it seems that He is hostile to us, on account of unruly desire and overweening power.

Lo greu perilh devem temer
De dobla mort qu'es prezentiers:
Que.ns sentam Sarrazis sobriers,
E Dieus que.ns giet a non-chaler.
Et entre nos, qu'em azirat,
Tost serem del tot aterrat;
E no.s cossiran la part lor,
Segon que.m par, nostre rector.

Selh que crezem en unitat,
Poder, savieza, bontat,
Done a sas obras lugor
Don sïan mundat peccador.

Dona, maires de caritat,
Acapta nos, per pïetat,
De ton filh nostre redemptor,
Gracia, perdon, et amor.

Guiraut Riquier

We should fear the grievous peril of twofold death which now is present: of our feeling the Saracens victors, and of God forsaking us. We who are in mutual strife will swiftly be struck down, and they think not on their rôle, so it appears to me, these our leaders.

May He in Whose oneness we believe, as in His power, wisdom and goodness, cast light on His works by which sinners might be made pure.

Lady, Mother of Charity, secure for us in pity from your son Our Redeemer, grace, forgiveness, and love.